1100 HOSTELS: SPAIN, ALPS & SOUTH EUROPE HYPER-GUIDE

Backpackers & Flashpackers

Hardie Karges

ISBN: 0988490552

ISBN 13: 9780988490550

Library of Congress Control Number: 2013954745

Hypertravel Books,
Los Angeles, California

Table of Contents

Preface:
That's a Wrap, 2013

North Europe may be the birthplace and historic heartland of hostelling, but South Europe has greater numbers nowadays, and the quality is as good, if not better. The northern concept of *jugendherberge, wandrarhem*, and 'hostel' has simply been transferred down south and exists as *auberge, albergue, hostal, ostello, gite (d'etape)*, and of course just plain 'hostel' borrowed from the English. South Europe may just have the greatest number of hostels in the world, in fact, but the distribution of them might surprise you.

For while France may be the Number One tourist destination in the world, it's not at the top of the hostel list, far from it in fact, almost in spooky symmetry with its Lafayette-inspired US cousin across the drink. With this book I hope to help change all that, yep. You're on notice, *mon ami!* Tourist-inundated Italy is better, but the quality is uneven, the midday lockouts are long and the reception hours are weird. No, the greatest number of hostels in the world is in the Iberian Peninsula, in modern-day Spain and Portugal. "But what about Australia and New Zealand," you ask. "Didn't you say the same thing about them? Okay so let's clarify terms. As a percentage of population, the proportions in Oz and NZ are higher. For density within a given area, it'd have to be Spain and Portugal. Okay? Bottom line: they're both full of 'em, so that's good.

The quality in Spain and Portugal is very good, in fact, exactly the paradigm of what a modern 'flashpacker' hostel should be. There are almost 500 of them here in this book, complete with specs and details. But that's not all. The expensive Alpine countries of Austria and Switzerland are here, too, now affordable with the sudden wide spread of hostels. And Greece is here, of course, with its fabulous sun-soaked islands, timeless culture, and... self-contained party compounds.

The smart money is on East Europe, though, with (almost) everything you can find in the West, and all at half the price. The Cold War is but a memory, too, with borders little more than formalities, if even that. In none of the countries listed in this book is a visa required of a Westerner. You can simply hop on the plane, or train, or bus… and go.

If it seems strange to be dividing Europe along the fiftieth degree north parallel of latitude, more or less, then just think of it as the USA and Canada, more or less. Thank God for the Gulf Stream and Mediterranean Sea that keep the temps mild. At the latitude where you find polar bears in Canada, you'd be surfing in Europe. The population numbers of Europeans that live on each side of this line are more or less equal in number, though each have their quirks, anomalies, and peculiarities.

And so it is with hostels, with the greatest area of disagreement apparently in the availability of kitchens. Something so natural as kitchens to us Anglo-hyphenated cultures apparently seems bizarre to our squeaky-clean northern neighbors and some traditionalist southerners, though widely embraced by highly competitive (and lower labor-cost) Iberians and Easterners. Some southerners apparently don't seem to think any man belongs in a kitchen anywhere, except maybe in a restaurant. If you can find a way into an Italian's kitchen, then marry her.

So this book wraps up 2013 and the first phase of the 'Backpackers & Flashpackers' publishing project. Six books in one year is a decent output, I figure. If I do half that number next year, then we'll be good. That should include Asia, Latin America, and hopefully even Africa and the Middle East. Yes, they're full of hostels. That's the whole world, mate, and something like 5000 hostels; real ones, too! Now you're getting the picture that I've been trying to paint for you. The best antidote to an increasingly hostile world is an increasingly hostel world; don't ya' think?

As with the last 'hyper-guide' on North Europe, I'll assume you are all experienced travelers, but maybe not experienced hostelers, so maybe a few pages of explanation are in order. If you've read this all before, then please bear with me. It's only a few pages.

Introduction

What is a hostel? Originally they were places, mostly in Europe, where students could sleep for cheap on extended country outings, frequently established at appropriate intervals over and about the landscape and which corresponded more or less to the amount of distance a student might hike or bike in the course of a day. Since those outings usually occurred in the summer when schools were otherwise uncommitted, the schools themselves became the logical place for seasonal conversion. That still happens sometimes, but not so much nowadays.

The concept has expanded dramatically over the last decade, for a variety of reasons, no doubt; among them: rising hotel prices, rising restaurant prices, and—drum roll here, please—Internet. For the rise of Internet has not only made advance booking widely accessible for both hostel and traveler, but it also became a reasonably-priced accommodation where a traveler would almost certainly have access to that same Internet. This fueled an explosion which is still happening to this day, and has barely scratched the surface yet in many places.

What any good hostel should have, by my own current standards, are: 1) cheap dorm beds, 2) English language, 3) a kitchen, 4) storage lockers, and 5) easy access to Internet. Of course within each of those categories there exists significant margin for deviation, but a place of lodging should make the effort to at least offer something in each of these five basic requirements in my humble opinion (IMHO for short: critics please note that my use of common 21st Century text-talk shorthand is the result of a conscious stylistic decision, not bad editing, thank you).

Other things you can expect that probably wouldn't be considered "amenities" include DIY bedding (you know how to make a bed, right?) and the likely absence of a towel (though many have it, but some charge a fee). For purposes of this guide I had to decide what ultimately defines a hostel, and for me that's the shared rooms. It's nice if they have private rooms also, but if they don't have dorms, then they won't be in this book. Nowhere else has the term been defined so concisely and precisely, to my knowledge. Just because a place calls itself a hostel is not enough for me.

This book is intended to be comprehensive, but I have to maintain some standards and criteria for inclusion, so there are a few issues to consider. The presence of dorms is not an issue; that's a definition. The main issues for me are age limits and websites. Most backpackers' hostels simply have no age limit, and that's the way it should be, I feel. Any problems can be dealt with on an individual basis. Another related problem is that in some cities hostel beds rank as decent long-term accommodations for some individuals and even families, who attempt to live there. Most hostels rightfully attempt to discourage this, as they should. Hostels are not transient hotels, after all.

I try to weed those places out of this guide and include only "real" hostels. With this guide you can contact hostels directly before committing any money, which is good. That way you can do some weeding, too, even at the last minute. You can't do that with most hostel-booking sites, which for some hostels is their only connection to potential customers. To do it right, then, a hostel must have a website with contact information. If they don't, then they won't be in this book (okay, on rare occasions I let one in that has a FaceBook page instead of a website, but not often). That tends to weed out shoddy operators, too. In general I also shy away from places that are only seasonal, but there's a sliding scale there, so many places with winter-only closure ARE included.

For better or worse, consolidation is setting in to the hostel scene rapidly, and the days of the "hippie hostel" may be numbered. The most obvious manifestation of this trend is the appearance of hostel chains, not only within a city or country, but in multiple cities across a region. I think that this in general is not a bad thing, as it establishes standards of services and expectations. The downside, that quirky little mom-and-pop operations may get squeezed out, is probably misplaced, since many of those places wouldn't rate very highly on my hostel-meter anyway, and the current "Air BnB" trend is probably more suitable to their offerings.

A word should be mentioned about HI, Hostelling International, which is often affiliated with YHA and such. This is the original hostel chain, and largely responsible for the existence of hostels, or at least their smooth transition from those early schoolboy barracks into modern backpackers' party hostels. They are a membership organization and you will need to pay an extra charge to stay there if you're not a member. When you've done this a half-dozen times or so, you'll be a member (current blurbs suggest you join in advance in your own country for best results).

But this guide is not about HI, though some are listed, particularly the ones that offer beds on the major hostel-booking sites and in the major cities. For better or worse, they tend to represent the old school of "youth hostels" more than the modern era of "backpackers." Check them out here and at *hihostels.com*. If you're looking for something out in the countryside, they may indeed be best, but many are only open seasonally.

This book is intended as an introduction and complement to the vast online resources and hopefully a broader view. Still, hostel-booking sites are invaluable for feedback, specific information and special promotions, and I urge everyone to consult them. Two of the bigger ones that I know best are *hostelbookers.com* and *hostelworld.com*, though there are many others, and *hostelz.com* acts as something of a "kayak" for them all, so that's good. So what makes this book better than a website for booking hostels? That's like comparing apples and oranges.

For one thing, we give you the hostel's own website and/or e-mail address and phone number for direct communication. So, not only can we be more objective than a booking site that receives a commission, but a booking site may show a hostel to be full when a call or e-mail to the hostel itself will get you a bed immediately. For another, as mentioned before, we try to include only the "real" hostels, hopefully with good reviews.

Best Westerns and Ibises won't be listed here—unless they offer shared rooms. Don't laugh. It's happening. And DO NOT USE A HOSTEL-BOOKING SITE LESS THAN THREE DAYS BEFORE YOUR STAY! It's too late. You'll be standing in line there at midnight out by the Bangkok airport with a number, but no room. Contact the hostel directly. That's what this book is for, Internet optional.

By the way in some quarters a hostel itself is known as a "backpackers," short for "backpackers' hostel," I assume. Make a note. What's a "flashpacker?" That's me, I think, a backpacker who's grown up and has a little extra time to kill and a few extra bucks to spend on comfort, maybe increasingly oriented to the cultural offerings of cities rather than the raw wilds of the outback. I will try to give you at least a glimpse of those offerings here. Room and bed rates can be elaborate and confusing, and frequently changing, so are included here for comparison purposes only.

Some issues of previous concern have become less so recently. Thus, unless otherwise stated, and unlike previous versions, it can be assumed that the hostel provides Internet service of some kind, hopefully free WiFi, and if I know definitely that they do NOT provide that, then I will indicate so, most likely in rural hostels. Likewise it can be assumed that there is no curfew; if I know otherwise, then I will indicate it.

Ditto for seasonality, per our previous discussion... and smoking, not an issue limited to hostels, but definitely an issue. If they permit smoking, I'll try to let you know. Did you know that once upon a time, hostels expected you to pitch in with chores? Don't laugh; it's been partially revived in some Scandinavian hostels who want you to clean up your mess or hire someone to do it. I'll discuss it more when we get there.

Hostels and their websites have some of their own vocabulary, and so do I:

Key to Symbols: Here are some symbols, shorthand and abbreviations used here:

–$bed = lowest price for a dorm bed that we can find for a typical day, for comparison only (they change with seasons, promotions, and currency fluctuations). Pvt. = private room, yes or no, multiply $bed by 2-3 for price, the number of people expected to share.

–B'fast = Breakfast (free or not or for purchase only); don't expect too much.

–c.c. = credit card, OK meaning they're accepted, +/% indicating a surcharge for use;

–cash (only) = even if you reserved with plastic, they want cash for the balance

–Recep = times when there should be someone to check you in. Don't press your luck.

–24/7 = they never close, supposedly. I suggest advising and confirming late arrival.

–HI, YHA, etc. are clubs that require a small fee; current recommendations are to join in advance in your home country, if you plan to use their services often.

–Y.H. = Youth Hostel (term I usually reserve only for organizations like HI/YHA, etc.)

–central, center, ctr = hostel is centrally located in the city, generally a good thing...

–luggage room/bag hold = you can stash your luggage to pick up later, very handy

-(used with Reception times) ltd = limited, / = midday break, // = long naps, /// = lazy

-party = they get down; partyy = they stay down; partyyy = they don't get up

-T/F = number for both phone and fax

-TF = Toll free number (usually only within the country; or Skype)

-lift = that's a bloody elevator, mate

-ETA = estimated time of arrival

-resto = restaurant

-CBD = Central Business District = city center = 'downtown'

-min/max = the minimum and maximum number of nights' stay allowed

-*Jack1Free@ hypertravel.biz/* (for example) = my way of contracting e-mail addresses contained within domains. The second half is the website address (add 'www' if necessary). All listings contain websites; some have forms inside for contacting, instead of e-mail addresses.

Note on telephone numbers: they are given here in several different ways, hopefully to show you how they work. Numbers that begin with a '+' should be ready for international use. Hold the '0' button down on a cell phone and the '+' appears, eliminating the need to know a country's international dialing code. The 2-3 digit country code then follows. For local use, drop that and **usually** add a zero, then the 9-10 digit local number. Where the local number is given, reverse that procedure. Add a '0' to the front if necessary. Some add no '0'; Russia and related systems add '8'. A picture is worth a thousand words.

Note on other related websites: you will also see a mini-UK flag on websites to indicate English language. That's the Union Jack, Jack.

Beware mid-day lockouts. That is the practice of some establishments of closing entirely for a specified period of time during the day, during which you will be forced to leave. This is much more common than seems reasonable and cheapens the whole movement.

Final note on hostel room and bed rates: in reality they are all over the place, depending on the booking site, the day of the week, the month of the year, current exchange rate, and general market conditions (prices in general seem to follow real estate values, I've noticed). Prices seem to be lower than the same period last year, so that likely reflects a maturing of the market. Numbers given here are for general reference and tend toward the lower range, though neither lowest nor highest.

Shop booking sites and the hostel's own website, especially if you plan an extended stay. Weekly rates might be negotiable. Prices are most erratic in the largest most developed markets, like Barcelona and Belgrade. Off-season rates there of less than twenty bucks a bed are truly incredible, but not illogical, since cheap private digs have long been available for no more than forty. But do they have WiFi? The cheapest places don't always have the most satisfied customers. Now go travel. That's the fun part.

Part I: France & The Iberian Peninsula

1) France

The area now occupied by France was a Celtic region during the days of the Roman Empire, when a Gallic-Roman Latin-speaking culture was forged. After the fall of Rome and the invasion by Germanic tribes, the victorious Franks gradually absorbed that culture as their own and successfully parlayed that stable population base into Europe's first great post-Roman empire, the Carolingian one of Charlemagne which ruled the area from 800 AD until almost 1000 in a proto-Holy Roman Empire. Around that time the Holy Roman Empire shifted eastward into German lands, while a united French kingdom gradually began to emerge in the decentralized feudal countryside. Viking invasions were a major problem and the Crusades were a major diversion at this time. Monarchs ruled until the end of the 18th century, when the French revolution set a course of events into motion the effects of which are still being felt to this day.

France became a major colonial power, and arguably the only one to successfully integrate those colonies as overseas departments into a modern state. France is one of the greenest of modern developed countries and one of the more equitable and socially balanced. At the same time it maintains a large military defense and space industry. Spanning both north and south Europe, in many ways it IS the symbol of Europe, and a European Union without France at the center of it is unthinkable.

France is the most visited country in the world, for its mountains, its beaches, and Paris. Travel here is mostly by train, some of them very fast (TGV). Buses are mostly for very local and Eurolines international service. Hostels are relatively few, unfortunately, boo hoo, just like America. Euro is the currency. Telephone country code is +33. French is the language.

1

ALBI is a city of 50,000 in southern France, 50mi/85km northeast of Toulouse. With origins in the pre-historic Bronze Age and roots as a *provence* in the Roman era, Albi gained fame in the Middle Ages as the home of the Albigensian crusade against the heretic Cathars. Today the *Palais de la Berbie* is one of France's oldest and most prominent castles. The *pont vieux* ('old bridge') is still in use, and the entire Episcopal city is a UNESCO world heritage site.

Le Clos de Morphée, 9 place de l'église, Tanus, Albi; T:0563541608, *le-clos-de-morphee.fr/*; $25Bed, Kitchen:N, B'fast:N, Pvt.room:N, Locker:N, Recep:ltd; Note: laundry, parking, terrace, remote/need car

ANNECY is a commune of 50,000 in the far east of France 22mi/35km south of Geneva in Switzerland. The *Palais de l'Ile* from the 12th Century is the most prominent landmark. Others are the Annecy Castle, rue St. Claire, and the Cathedral of St. Pierre. There is an international animated film festival.

Annecy Hostel, 32 Av. de Loverchy, Annecy; *annecyhostel.fr/en/*, T:+33/953120290; $31Bed, Kitchen:Y, B'fast:$, Pvt.room:Y, Locker:Y, Recep:ltd; Note: bikes, café, laundry, bag hold, parking, tea/cof, lake, hard find, not center

2 Hostels) ARLES is another city of 50,000, on the Mediterranean coast, and with roots in the Ligurian, Celtic, Phoenician, and Roman eras there. It was a frequent rival of Marseilles/Massalia for prominence. Its Roman architecture has earned it UNESCO world heritage status. Van Gogh produced over 300 works during his time here. There is a photography festival, a running of the bulls, and an open-air street market.

HI Arles YH, 20 Av. Foch, Arles; *hihostels.com/*, T:+33/490961825, *arles@ fuaj.org/*; $27Bed, Kitchen:N, B'fast:Y, Pvt.room:N, Locker:Y, Recep:7a//11p; Note: cafe/bar, bikes, luggage room, meals, central

Auberge du Voyageur, 26 Place Pomme, Arles; *arles-aubergepelerins.com/*, T:+33/699711189, *aubergepelerins@gmail.com;* $35Bed, Kitchen:Y, B'fast:Y, Pvt. room:N, Locker:N, Recep:ltd; Note: cash only, historic center

2 Hostels) AVIGNON is a city of 95,000 in the far south of France, and famous as the only city to have ever served as the Holy See of the Catholic Church besides Rome, from 1309 to 1423. The historic center is a UNESCO world heritage site. In the 8th Century it sided with the Arabs against the northern Franks; bad career move. During the 13th Century they declared independence and refused admittance to Louis VIII; oops. Sounds like a good place to move the Vatican to me. The Black Death wiped it out in 1348. It finally became French in 1791. There is an annual theatre festival. It's on my list.

Pop' Hostel, 17 rue de la République, Avignon; *contact@ pophostel.fr/*, T:0432405060; $21Bed, Kitchen:N, B'fast:$, Pvt.room:Y, Locker:Y, Recep:6a>11p; Note: bar, café, billiards, lift, bag hold, tea/coffee, tours

Auberge Bagatelle, 25 allées Antoine Pinay, Ile Barthelasse; *campingbagatelle. com/*, T:0490863039, *camping.bagatelle@wannadoo.fr*; $17Bed, Kitchen:N, B'fast:$, Pvt.room:Y, Locker:N, Recep:7:30a>9p; Note: cafe/bar, WiFi $

2 Hostels) BOURG-SAINT-MAURICE is a town of almost 8000 in the heart of the French Alps. The skiing is good, and summertime is nice, too. LES ARCS is one of France's premier ski resorts, a "mega-resort," with 171 lifts and 470 snow-making machines. Ski that. There's a school, too.

Maison des Quatre Balcons, Nancroix T9, Peisey-Nancroix, Les Arcs; T:+33(0)479042815, *maison-des-quatre-balcons.hostel.com/*; $26Bed, Kitchen:N, B'fast:N, Pvt.room:Y, Locker:N, Recep:24/7; Note: Ski Hostel, cash only, parking, TV

Loft Mountain Hostel, 440 Av Maréchal Leclerc, Bourg-Saint-Maurice, *loftbourg.com/*, T:0646217161; *hello@loftmountainhostel.com/*; $31Bed, Kitchen:Y, B'fast:N, Pvt.room:N, Locker:N, Recep:24/7; Note: arpt trans, billiards, pool, bag hold

BREST is a city of over 140,000 in France's (and Europe's) westernmost Brittany (Bretagne) province. There is a castle and a festival of the sea.

Ethic Etapes Brest, 5 Rue de Kerbriant, Brest; *ethic-etapes.com/*, T:+33/298419041; $27Bed, Kitchen:Y, B'fast:Y, Pvt.room:Y, Locker:N, Recep:ltd; Note: mem fee, wh/chair ok, laundry, bag hold, 5p check-in

CALAIS is a city of 125,000 on the English Channel's Strait of Dover, its narrowest passage. This is where you catch the ferry or enter the Chunnel. It used to be a Dutch-speaking area. There is an ancient cathedral, towers, and fort.

Ethic Etapes Calais, Av. du Maréchal De Lattre de Tassigny, Calais; T:+33/321347020, *auberge-jeunesse-calais.com/*; $31Bed, Kitchen:N, B'fast:Y, Pvt. room:Y, Locker:N, Recep:24/7; Note: resto/bar, wh/chair ok, bag hold, parking

2 Hostels) CARCASONNE is a small city of almost 50,000 in the southernmost Languedoc region, divided into the historic upper fortified city, and the lower much-expanded modern city. With roots stretching in prehistory and fortifications started by the Romans, it was officially founded by the Visigoths in 462, and when fully constructed, was virtually impregnable. It was a stronghold of Cathars in the Albigensian Crusades, and a center of the wool industry when finally ceded to France in the 13th century. The reconstructed city is a UNESCO world heritage site, not totally authentic, but seldom matched in splendor.

Castel Chambres, Av du château de Malves, Malves en Minervois, Carcassonne; *castelchambres.com/*, T:0468722896; $22Bed, Kitchen:Y, B'fast:$, Pvt.room:Y, Locker:N, Recep:11a>8p; Note: bikes, nature, not central, free pick-up, in castle

Sidsmums Travellers Retreat, 11 Chemin de la Croix d'Achille, Preixan, Carcassonne, T:+33/468269449, *bookings@ sidsmums.com/*; $32Bed, Kitchen:Y, B'fast:$, Pvt.room:Y, Locker:N, Recep:ltd; Note: arpt trans, bikes, bag hold, prkng

CASSIS is a commune of almost 8000, on the south coast of France, east of Marseilles, and famous for its cliffs and coastline and… wines, both white and rose'.

Cassis Hostel, Les Heures Claires 4 Ave. du Picouveau, Cassis; T:+ 33/954379982, *Info@ cassishostel.com/*; $28Bed, Kitchen:Y, B'fast:Y, Pvt. room:Y, Locker:Y, Recep:ltd; Note: cash, laundry, bag hold, parking, pool, tea/cof, tours

2 Hostels) CHAMONIX was the site of the first winter Olympics in 1924. Situated at only a little over 1000 meters (3400 feet), the surrounding peaks rise to almost 5000 meters, including Mont Blanc at 4807 (15,771 feet). The highest cable-car system in the world is located here. In summer it is a mecca for mountain bikers.

Hostel Le Chamoniard Volant, 45 Route de la Frasse, Chamonix; T:0450531409, *mail@ chamoniard.com/*; $20bed, Kitchen:Y, B'fast:$, Pvt.room:N, Locker:Y, Recep:10a>10p; Note: near train/center, café, parking, c.c. ok, 7-day cancel

Mountain Highs, 92 Chemin de la Ch'na, Chamonix; T:+33/608042500, *Info@ mountain-highs.com/*; $24Bed, Kitchen:Y, B'fast:$, Pvt.room:Y, Locker:Y, Recep:4>7p; Note: billiards, hot tub, bag hold, parking, tea/coffee, tours

CLERMONT FERRAND is a city of 140,000 (metro area 400K) in the center of France, and one of its oldest cities. This was the starting point of the First Crusade in 1095. It hosts a short film festival, and many other cultural events. There are two distinct CBD's.

Home Dome, 12, place de Regensburg, Clermont Ferrand; *homedome.fr/*; T:0473294070; $30Bed, Kitchen:N, B'fast:Y, Pvt.room:Y, Locker:N, Recep:24/7; Note: resto, lift, luggage room, parking, tours

CONCARNEAU is a town of 20,000 on the far western Brittany coast. There is a modern town and the ancient *Ville Close*, spiffed up for tourism these days. The *Fete de Filets Bleus* celebrates Celtic/Bretonic culture, including traditional dress.

Auberge de Jeunesse-Éthic Étapes , Quai de la Croix, Concarneau; *ajconcarneau.com/*, T:+33/298970347; $24Bed, Kitchen:Y, B'fast:Y, Pvt.room:Y, Locker:N, Recep:9a>8p; Note: resto, billiards, laundry, central

DIJON is a city of over 150,000 in northeast central France. It's famous for its mustard, of course. It lies 190mi/300km southeast of Paris. Landmarks include the Notre Dame and Dijon cathedrals, the Ducal Palace, the Musee des Beaux Arts, and much more.

Ethic Etapes Dijon, 1 bd de Champollion, Dijon; *cri-dijon.com/*, T:+33/380729520; $29Bed, Kitchen:N, B'fast:Y, Pvt.room:Y, Locker:N, Recep:24/7; Note: pool, resto, wh/chair ok, lift, luggage room, parking, not central

HOSSEGOR is a town of a few thou on the southwest coast of France, and renowned for its surfing. Long ago settled by Viking invaders, it was a whaling center for many years.

Hossegor Surf Hostel, 1888 Avenue du Golf, Hossegor; *Rob@ hossegorsurfhostel.com/*; T:0558737259; $49Bed, Kitchen:Y, B'fast:$, Pvt. room:Y, Locker:Y, Recep:24/7; Note: arpt trans, wh/chair ok, parking, tea/ coffee, cash only

LILLE is a city of a 250,000 in an urban area of a cool Mil (and 2x that if you count Belgium) in the far northern Flanders region of France. Gauls were here before Germanic peoples. The name comes from its status of "L'Isle" in a marshy area. Landmarks are the cathedral, citadel, Palais des Beaux Arts, *et beaucoups des jardins.*

Hostel Gastama, 109/115 rue de Saint Andre, Lille; T:+33/320060680, *gastama.com/*, $28Bed, Kitchen:Y, B'fast:$, Pvt.room:Y, Locker:Y, Recep:24/7; Note: bar, wh/chair ok, lift, luggage room, meals, central

LYON is a city of two million in the east-central part of the country, largest outside Paris and halfway between there and Marseille. It is a UNESCO world heritage site for its architecture, including the Roman and Renaissance districts. The Festival of Lights is in December. The local Lumiere brothers have a cinema museum dedicated to them. There is an African museum, and many other churches, museums, and parks.

Cool & Bed, 32 Quai Arloing, Lyon; *coolandbed.com/*, T:0426180528; $28Bed, Kitchen:Y, B'fast:Y, Pvt.room:N, Locker:Y, Recep:24/7; Note: wh/ chair ok, lift, laundry, tea, tours, luggage room, resto/bar

5 Hostels) MARSEILLES is France's third-largest city and largest on the Mediterranean coast. It is also France's oldest city, founded by the Greeks as Massalia before it became Roman as Massilia. After the fall of Rome, the Visigoths took over briefly before the Franks and Charlemagne came in, then the counts of Provence. It was reincorporated into France in the 15th century and served as naval base for the Franco-Ottoman alliance. As a major port it suffered badly during the various plagues and was always at odds with authority. It strongly supported the French revolution and more recent socialist and communist political movements. They say Mary Magdalene and Lazarus preached the Gospel here.

Fort St. Jean overlooks the harbor and was a 13th C. outpost of the Knights Hospitaller. Fort Saint-Nicholas occupies the other side. The Place de la Major holds the city's cathedral and dates from the 11th century. So does the square-towered basilica of Saint-Victor. Notre-Dame-de-la-Garde stands high on the hill over the south side of the port. Marseilles couldn't be more different from Paris. If Paris is up and stuffy, then Marseilles is down and dirty. This is where Europe meets the Middle East, and where Europe meets Africa. Maybe 25% of the population is Muslim. Maybe 10% is Jewish. Algerian *rai* musicians do here what they can't do back home; so do the Guineans. Cheap rooms are a tradition, with or without baths. You can try the local *hammam* for that. But hostels are better.

Hotel Vertigo Vieux Port, 38 rue Fort Notre Dame, Marseille; T:0491544295, *contact-vieuxport@ hotelvertigo.fr/*; $34bed, Kitchen:Y, B'fast:Y, Pvt.room:N, Locker:Y, Recep:24/7; Note: bag hold, tours, a/c, c.c. ok, port area

Vertigo Hostel Center, 42 Rue des Petites Maries, Marseille; T:0491910711, *contact@ hotelvertigo.fr/*; $34bed, Kitchen:N, B'fast:$, Pvt.room:N, Locker:N, Recep:24/7; Note: bar, tours, bag hold, laundry, no lift, near train

Hostel Sylvabelle Marseille, 63 Rue Sylvabelle, Marseille; T:0491377583, *hotel-sylvabelle-marseille.com/*; $28bed, Kitchen:N, B'fast:N, Pvt.room:Y, Locker:N, Recep:24/7; Note: c.c. ok, no lift, curfew, hotel & hostel

Hello Marseille, 12 rue de Breteuil, Marseille; *hellomarseille.com/*, T:0954807505, *hellomarseille@gmail.com*; $35bed, Kitchen:Y, B'fast:Y, Pvt. room:N, Locker:Y, Recep:24/7; Note: luggage room, laundry, c.c. ok, stairs, central, bikes

YesWeCamp, Quai de la Lave, Marseille; *reservation@ yeswecamp. org/*; T:+33/781147844; $22Bed, Kitchen:N, B'fast:Y, Pvt.room:N, Locker:N, Recep:ltd; Note: resto/bar, bag hold, meals, parking, tea/coffee, seaside eco-camp

NARBONNE is a small city of 50,000 only 9mi/15km from the sea in Languedoc. Its history began as a crossroads on the Roman Via Domitia connecting Italy and Spain and the Via Aquitania, which led to the Atlantic. Keeping the Aude River channel silt-free to the sea has always been crucial to its success. It was once an important Jewish center of learning. The never-finished Narbonne Cathedral is a major landmark.

Ethic Etape-CIS-Narbonne, Place Roger Salengro, Narbonne; T:0468320100, *cis-narbonne.com/*; $25Bed, Kitchen:N, B'fast:Y, Pvt.room:N, Locker:N, Recep:24/7; Note: bar, café, wh/chair ok, lift, bag hold, tours, parking, central, hard find

12 Hostels) NICE is the heart of the French Riviera. The beach is the big deal here, but Monaco is nearby, and Italy not much farther. In fact much of Nice's history lies with Italy, not France. Founded by Greeks before the Common Era it was in league with Genoa and/or Pisa after the Fall of Rome and in constant struggle against the Arabs and later Barbary pirates. It was ceded to France in 1860, though Italy returned in WWII.

Things are calmer now, and tourism is king. Blessed with coastal beaches, nearby mountains and mild winters, Nice attracts visitors and immigrants from all over the world. There is an old town with narrow winding streets and a harbor with regular boat service to the island of Corsica. The Musee' des Beaux Arts and the Musee' Massena specialize in paintings. Northeast of the center is the ancient Episcopal town of Cimiez, with Roman ruins. Hostel quality is uneven in the French style, but quite passable.

Hostel Paradis, Rue Paradis, Nice; *paradishotel.com/*, T:0493877123, *hotelparadisnice@gmail.com*; $20bed, Kitchen:N, B'fast:$, Pvt.room:Y, Locker:N, Recep:>8p; Note: lift, bag hold, tea/coffee, tours, c.c. ok, no bunks, on beach

Hostel Meyerbeer Beach, 15 Rue Meyerbeer, Nice; *hotel-meyerbeer-beach-nice.cote.azur.fr/*, T:0493889565; $28bed, Kitchen:Y, B'fast:Y, Pvt.room:Y, Locker:N, Recep:>12m; Note: bikes, café, bag hold, tea/cof, tours, a/c, c.c. ok, nr beach, cheap wine

Altea Hostel, 3 Boulevard Raimbaldi, Nice; T:0493851522, *Info@ Hostel-Nice.com*; $20bed, Kitchen:N, B'fast:N, Pvt.room:Y, Locker:N, Recep:8a>10:30p; Note: lift, bag hold, safe dep, fridge/microwave, near train, walk to beach

Villa St Exupery Gardens, 22 Avenue Gravier, Nice; T:0493844283, *gardens@*

Villa St. Exupery Beach, 6 Rue Sacha Guitry, Nice; T:0493161345, *beach@ villahostels.com/*; $21bed, Kitchen:Y, B'fast:Y, Pvt.room:Y, Locker:N, Recep:24/7; Note: bikes, gym, c.c. ok, forex, resto/bar, tours, laundry, prkng, bag hold

Antares Hostel, 5 Av Thiers, Nice; T:+33/493882287, *antaresnice.hostel.com/*; $24Bed, Kitchen:Y, B'fast:$, Pvt.room:Y, Locker:N, Recep:11a>9p; Note: lift, luggage room, a/c, hotel-like, central, near supermkt/station/beach

Victoria Meublé Hostel, 6 Rue Docteur Jacques Guidoni, Nice; *hostelnice@ gmail.com*, T:+33/603621050, (see FB page); $39Bed, Kitchen:Y, B'fast:$, Pvt.room:Y, Locker:Y, Recep:2>10p; Note: lift, bag hold, maps, books

Backpackers Chez Patrick, 32 Rue Pertinax, Nice; T:+33/493803072, *booking@ chezpatrick.com/*; $22Bed, Kitchen:N, B'fast:N, Pvt.room:Y, Locker:N, Recep:ltd; Note: lockout 11>14, café, lift, laundry, tea/coffee, tours, maps, central

Hostel Smith, 20 Rue Droite, Nice; *hostelsmith.com/*, T:+33/609145347; $24Bed, Kitchen:Y, B'fast:Y, Pvt.room:Y, Locker:Y, Recep:ltd; Note: café, club, bikes, luggage room, tea/coffee, central, old town, basic

Lou Souleou B&B, 26 Rue des Ponchettes, Nice, *lelousouleou.nice.free.fr/*, T:0649957625, *lou.souleou.nice@gmail.com*; $49Bed, Kitchen:N, B'fast:Y, Pvt.room:Y, Locker:N, Recep:ltd; Note: cash only, bag hold, near old town/market/beach

Hostel Belle Meuniere, 21 Av Durante, Nice; *bellemeuniere.com/*, T:0493886615, *hotel.belle.meuniere@cegetel.com*; $28Bed, Kitchen:N, B'fast:$, Pvt.

room:Y, Locker:N, Recep:ltd; Note: arpt trans, café, laundry, bag hold, parking, tours

Nice Art Hotel, 35 Rue d'Angleterre, Nice; *nice-art-hotel.com/*, T:+33(0)493887507, *nice_art_hotel@orange.fr*; $22Bed, Kitchen:N, B'fast:$, Pvt. room:Y, Locker:N, Recep:>7p; Note: nr train, bag hold, maps, tea/coffee, basic

22 Hostels) PARIS is the largest city, capital, and heart of the French republic, of course, and got its start as capital of the Frankish Merovingian dynasty in the year 508. After losing that role, it returned as capital of the first Capetian kindon in 987, a role it held for most of the next thousand years with France. After much political uncertainty with the French Revolution and Napoleon, Paris finally entered the Industrial Revolution with the 1852 Second Republic, and in a way that differed greatly from the misery of it elsewhere.

Paris was rapidly gaining a reputation as a city with a difference, a view only heightened by the Commune established after defeat in the Franco-Prussian War. If that was ultimately a disaster, the Expositions of 1889 and 1900 were anything but. The Eiffel Tower was a raging success, the Paris Metro was built, electric lights were installed, and the "city of lights" with a reputation as the most romantic city in the world was born. I don't know about all that, but it certainly has plenty to offer a tourist.

Much of Paris has been declared a UN World Heritage site, to mention but a few of the main sights: the Eiffel Tower, the Louvre Museum, Notre Dame Cathedral, the Arc d' Triomphe, the Pont Neuf, the Place Dauphine, the Palace of Justice, the Grand Chambre, the Sainte-Chapelle, the Tuileries Garden, the Musee Orsay, the Champs-Elysees, the Hotel des Invalides, the Quartier Latin, the Pantheon, the Hotel de Ville, the Paris Opera House, les Places des Concorde et Pyramides, dozens of museums and much more.

Better develop an espresso habit in order to see it all. They're cheap, as long as you don't sit down. Unfortunately, it doesn't have the number of hostels that many of the other largest cities in Europe have, and what they have are not as high quality. Many of them are clustered in Montmartre.

Le Village Hostel, 20 Rue d'Orsel, Paris, Île-de-France; T:+33/142642202, *bonjour@ villagehostel.fr/*; $35bed, Kitchen:Y, B'fast:Y, Pvt.room:Y, Locker:Y,

Recep:24/7; Note: arpt trans. bar, café, bikes, lift, bag hold, parking, tours, nr metro/Gare

Caulaincourt Hostel, 2 Square Caulaincourt, Paris; T:0146064606; *bienvenue@ caulaincourt.com/*; $35bed, Kitchen:Y, B'fast:Y, Pvt.room:Y, Locker:N, Recep:ltd; Note: bar, bag hold, maps, books, 2am curfew, free calls, Montmartre, midday lock-out

Oops Hostel, 50 Ave. des Gobelins, Paris; *bonjour@ oops-paris.com*, T:0147074700; $34bed, Kitchen:N, B'fast:Y, Pvt.room:N, Locker:N, Recep:24/7; Note: wh/chair ok, lockout 11a>4p, left luggage, lift, a/c, tours, maps, cash only

Le Regent Montmartre, 37 Blvd. de Rochechouart, Paris; T:0148782400, *bonjour@ leregent.com/*; $28bed, Kitchen:Y, B'fast:Y, Pvt.room:Y, Locker:N, Recep:24/7; Note: arpt trans, lift, bag hold, laundry, tours, near Metro, WiFi$, maps

The Plug-Inn Hostel, 7 Rue Aristide Bruant, Paris; T:0142584258, *bonjour@ plug-inn.fr/*; $36bed, Kitchen:Y, B'fast:Y, Pvt.room:Y, Locker:N, Recep:24/7; Note: arpt trans, like, tours, midday lockout, c.c. ok, luggage room, Montmartre

Vintage Hostel, 73 Rue Dunkerque, Paris; *contact@ vintage-hostel.com/*, T:0140161640; $28bed, Kitchen:N, B'fast:Y, Pvt.room:N, Locker:Y, Recep:24/7; Note: a/c, c.c. ok, tours, near Gare du Nord, bag hold, tea/coffee, map

Absolute Hostel, 1 Rue Fontaine au Roi, Paris; *bonjour@absolute-paris.com*, T:147004700; $40bed, Kitchen:N, B'fast:Y, Pvt.room:N, Locker:N, Recep:24/7; Note: café, bag hold, max.15N, c.c. ok, cozy, lift, bike & city tours, forex, maps

Le Montclaire Montmartre, 62 Rue Ramey, Paris; *montclair-hostel.com/*, T:0146064607, *bonjour@lemontclair.com*; $25bed, Kitchen:Y, B'fast:Y, Pvt.room:Y, Locker:N, Recep:24/7; Note: 6 Fl no lift, books, maps, bag hold, tours, foosball

Woodstock Hostel, 48 Rue Rodier, Paris; T:0148788776, *flowers@ woodstock. fr/*; $27bed, Kitchen:Y, B'fast:Y, Pvt.room:Y, Locker:N, Recep:24/7; Note: 2am curfew, bag hold, bar, linen fee, cash only, midday lockout, tours

Aloha Hostel, 1 Rue Borromée, Paris, France; T:0142730303, *friends@ aloha. fr/*; $39bed, Kitchen:Y, B'fast:Y, Pvt.room:N, Locker:N, Recep:24/7; Note: linen fee, tour, few sockets, 4p check-in, beer machine

Sabine House, 58 Rue Du Garde Chasse, Les Lilas, Paris; *sabinehouse.net/*, T:0141832200, *sabinehouse1@naver.com*; $42Bed, Kitchen:Y, B'fast:Y, Pvt.room:Y, Locker:N, Recep:24/7; Note: café, laundry, bag hold, parking, tea/cof, meals, Korean, far

St Christopher's Gare du Nord, 5 Rue Dunkerque; *gdnreception@*,0170085222

St Christopher's Canal, 159 rue de Crimée, Paris; *st-christophers.co.uk/*, T:+33(0)140343440, *paris@st-christophers.co.uk*; $28Bed, Kitchen:N, B'fast:Y, Pvt.room:Y, Locker:Y, Recep:24/7; Note: café/bar/club, lift, laundry, bag hold, not cntr

Arty Paris, Rue des Morillons, Paris; T:+33/145339906, *Info@ artyparis. fr/*; $25Bed, Kitchen:Y, B'fast:Y, Pvt.room:Y, Locker:Y, Recep:24/7; Note: lift, luggage room, foosball, maps, not central

Smart Place Paris, 28 Rue de Dunkerque. Paris; T:+33/148782515, *bookings@ smartplaceparis.com/*; $28Bed, Kitchen:Y, B'fast:$, Pvt.room:Y, Locker:Y, Recep:24/7; Note: lift, bag hold, parking, shuttle, tours, central, north train station

FIAP Jean Monnet, 30 Rue Cabanis, Paris; T:+33/143131700, *fiap.asso.fr/*; $31Bed, Kitchen:Y, B'fast:Y, Pvt.room:Y, Locker:Y, Recep:24/7; Note: bar, café, billiards, wh/chair ok, lift, laundry, meals, near metro, hotel-like

Young & Happy Hostel, 80 Rue Mouffetard, Paris; T+33/147074707, *smile@ youngandhappy.fr*; $28Bed, Kitchen:Y, B'fast:Y, Pvt.room:Y, Locker:Y, Recep:24/7; Note: bar, laundry, luggage room, maps, books, central/Latin Quarter, basic

Aloha Hostel, 1 Rue Borromée, Paris; T:+33/142730303; *friends@ aloha.fr/*; $32Bed, Kitchen:Y, B'fast:Y, Pvt.room:N, Locker:N, Recep:24/7; Note: tours, books, maps, central, basic

Peace & Love Hostel, 245 Rue la Fayette, Paris; *pl@ paris-hostels.com/*, T:+33/146076511; $Bed, Kitchen:Y, B'fast:$, Pvt.room:N, Locker:Y, Recep:24/7; Note: ages 18-35, café/bar/club, luggage room, parking, tours, stairs no lift, basic, near metro

The Loft Paris, 70 Rue Julien Lacroix, Paris; T:0142024202, *bonjour@ theloft-paris.com/*; $28Bed, Kitchen:Y, B'fast:Y, Pvt.room:N, Locker:N, Recep:24/7;

Note: bar, wh/chair ok, bag hold, tea/coffee, books, maps, colorful 'hood, near metro

BVJ Hotel (2 Empereurs), 20 Rue Jean-Jacques Rousseau, Paris; *bvjhotel. com/*, T:0153009090, *bvj@wanadoo.fr*; $46Bed, Kitchen:N, B'fast:Y, Pvt.room:Y, Locker:Y, Recep:ltd; Note: 15-35y.o, cash only, bag hold, 5 fl no lift, maps, central, basic

Perfect Hostel, 39 Rue Rodier, Paris; *welcome@ paris-hostel.biz/*, T:+33/142811886, $31Bed, Kitchen:N, B'fast:Y, Pvt.room:Y, Locker:Y, Recep:24/7; Note: lift, bag hold, tour desk, near Gare du Nord

REIMS is a city of 185,000 in the north of France, famous for its cathedral, which is a UNESCO world heritage site. Founded by the Roman-era Celtic Remi, there are a few prominent landmarks, including the Place Royale, Port de Mars, *Salle de Tau*, Saint Remi Basilica, and more. This is a center of champagne production.

CIS de Champagne, 21 Chaussée Bocquaine, Reims, *cis-reims.com/*, T:+33/326405260; $21Bed, Kitchen:N, B'fast:N, Pvt.room:Y, Locker:N, Recep:24/7; Note: resto, wh/chair ok, lift, bag hold, free parking, central

SAINT MALO is a small city of about 47,000 on the north Breton coast. Always with a fierce independent streak, it was also known for piracy. Today it is known for the walled city on a tidal island that appears to rise and fall from the sea.

Centre Patrick Varangot, 37 Av du Rév Père Umbricht, Saint-Malo; T:0299402980, *info@ centrevarangot.com/*; $34Bed, Kitchen:Y, B'fast:Y, Pvt. room:Y, Locker:Y, Recep:24/7; Note: resto/bar, bikes, gym, lift, bag hold, parking, tours, HI %

2 Hostels) STRASBOURG is a city of 275,000 on the Franco-German border, originally a Celtic village, and later a Roman one, then Frank. It is a UNESCO world heritage site for its 'big island' and particularly, the cathedral. There is also the Chateau des Rohan, the La Petite District, and several museums.

Ciarus, 7 rue Finkmatt, Strasbourg; T:+33(0)388152788, *ciarus@ ciarus. com/*; $28Bed, Kitchen:N, B'fast:N, Pvt.room:Y, Locker:Y, Recep:24/7; Note: resto/bar, wh/chair, lift, parking, tours, bag hold, bikes, forex, maps, central

Chicag' Hostel Toulon, 3 rue des Bonnetieres, Toulon; *bonjour@ chicaghosteltoulon.com/*, T:0489665266; $35Bed, Kitchen:Y, B'fast:Y, Pvt.room:N, Locker:Y, Recep:ltd; Note: café, laundry, tours, tea/cof, central, cash only, new

2 Hostels) TOULOUSE is France's fourth-largest city, a major university town and center of Europe's aerospace industry, including Airbus. It lies in the mid-Pyrenees region of southern France, so something of a capital for the Languedoc region. Its history goes back to the Roman and Merovingian eras and it withstood the northern advance of Muslim conquerors. Its medieval buildings include the Gothic cathedral of Saint-Étienne, the Romanesque basilica of Saint-Sernin, and the Gothic Église des Jacobins.

La Petite Auberge de Compostelle (St-Sernin), 17 rue d'Embarthe, Toulouse; *gite-compostelle-toulouse.com/*, T:0760881717; $31bed, Kitchen:Y, B'fast:N, Pvtroom:N, Locker:Y, Recep:10a>9p; Note: lift, noon lockout, laundry, central, books

In Toulouse Hostel, 1 Impasse du Prof. Nougayrol, Toulouse; T:0561166625, *contact@ hostel-toulouse.com/*; $25Bed, Kitchen:Y, B'fast:$, Pvt. room:Y, Locker:N, Recep: advise ETA; Note: cash only, bag hold, tea/cof, forex, maps, TV, not central

2) Portugal

Portugal once had an influence far beyond its narrow borders and established the paradigm for the European Age of Discovery, founding colonies on every continent, and at one point collaborating with Spain and the Pope in dividing the world between them. The two countries had similar historical beginnings, but the Portuguese managed to extricate themselves from Moorish oversight more quickly, and was able to proclaim independence in 1139, Europe's first modern nation-state. Somewhere along the way (thank the Moors) they learned how to sail, and were the first Europeans to sail the open seas, first rounding Africa, and then moving on to Asia and Brazil, in the process creating the world's first global empire, all from a nation of only a scarce few million people.

Their empire lasted even into the 1970's, though by then Portugal was the poorest country in Western Europe. Its fortunes have improved since shedding itself of its outliers, though still it is no wealthier than you would expect from such a small and largely rural country. So its prices are more like Eastern Europe than the West, and that's good for us tourists. Tourism in fact has exploded in the last decade, major destinations being the sunny southern Algarve coast, the island of Madeira, and the capital Lisbon. Euro is the currency and the telephone country code is +351. Portuguese is the language.

3 Hostels) ALBUFEIRA is a town of 22,000 located on the southern Algarve coast, between Lagos and Faro. Previously Roman and Arab before the re-conquest, it is now mostly tourist, focused on the 'strip.' The old town preserves its original flavor. BOLIQUEIME is a nearby small village of almost 4500, and "well-preserved."

Hostel Boliqueime, Rua Dr João Batista Ramos Faísca 51, Boliqueime; T:289363610, *geral@ hostelboliqueime.com/*; $14Bed, Kitchen:Y, B'fast:$, Pvt.room:Y, Locker:Y, Recep:24/7; Note: arpt trans, pool, bikes, wh/chair ok, laundry

Orange Terrace Hostel, Rua Padre Semedo Azevedo 24, Albufeira; *info@ orange-terrace.com/*, T:351/289047895; $14Bed, Kitchen:Y, B'fast:$, Pvt.room:Y, Locker:Y, Recep:1>10p; Note: laundry, tea/coffee, pay cash, old town

AleHop Albufeira Hostel, Rua 5 de Outubro, 23, Albufeira; T:910783699, *alehopalbufeirahostel@gmail.com*, (see FB page); $28Bed, Kitchen:Y, B'fast:$, Pvt. room:N, Locker:Y, Recep:3>11p; Note: hot tub, café, lift, laundry, bag hold

ALFEIZERAO is a small town of less than 4000 halfway up Portugal's Atlantic coast.

HI Alfeizerão - São Martinho do Porto YH, Estrada Nacional 8, Alfeizerão; *hihostels.com/,* T:262990392, *alfeizerao@movijovem.pt*; $14Bed, Kitchen:N, B'fast:Y, Pvt.room:Y, Locker:Y, Recep:24/7; Note:bar, café, wh/chair ok, prkng, need car

2 Hostels) ALJEZUR is a town of over 5000 on Portugal's far southwest coast.

HI Arrifana YH, Urbanização Arrifamar -Praia da Arrifana, Aljezur; *hihostels.com/,* T:282997455, *arrifana@movijovem.pt*; $16Bed, Kitchen:Y, B'fast:Y, Pvt.room:Y, Locker:Y, Recep:24/7; Note:café, bar, laundry, prkg, surf, need car

Amazig Design Hostel, Rua da Ladeira 5, Aljezur; *amazighostel.net/,* T:282997502, *booking@amazighostel.com*; $17Bed, Kitchen:N, B'fast:$, Pvt. room:Y, Locker:Y, Recep:ltd; Note: arpt trans, pool, bar, bike, bag hold, tours

3 Hostels) AVEIRO is a city of 80,000 on the north coast of Portugal. There are canals, cathedrals, and… beaches of course. It is known for its sweets and its university.

Aveiro Rossio Hostel, R. João Afonso de Aveiro #1, Largo do Rossio, Aveiro, *aveirorossiohostel.com/,* T:+351/234041538, *aveirorossiohostel@gmail.com*; $22Bed, Kitchen:Y, B'fast:Y, Pvt.room:Y, Locker:Y, Recep:24/7; Note: central, café, bikes, cash

HI Aveiro YH, Rua das Pombas, Apartado 182, Aveiro; *hihostels.com/,* T:+351/234482233, *aveiro@movijovem.pt*; $14Bed, Kitchen:N, B'fast:Y, Pvt. room:N, Locker:N, Recep:24/7; Note: wh/chair ok, parking, hard find, remote

Aveiro Binibag GH, Cais dos Santos Martires (Rua João Domingos dos R); *binibag.com/,* T:234041230, *binibaghostel@gmail.com*; $28Bed, Kitchen:Y, B'fast:Y, Pvt.room:Y, Locker:N, Recep:8a>12m; Note: laundry, c.c. ok, noon dep, bikes

BRAGA is a city of 175,000 in northernmost Portugal, the country's third-largest, with over four times that many in the metro area. Its architecture dates back to the Roman era and before. Highlights include Roman Thermae of Maximinus, Fountain of the Idol, Fountain of the Iron Waters, countless churches, chapel, monasteries, and more.

Braga Pop Hostel, Rua do Carmo 61, Braga; *bragapophostel.blogspot.com/*, T:+351/253058806, *bragapophostel@gmail.com*; $21Bed, Kitchen:Y, B'fast:Y, Pvt. room:Y, Locker:Y, Recep:2>8p; Note: cafe, bikes, bag hold, tours, parking

5 Hostels) COIMBRA is Portugal's third city and a university town. From 1139 to 1260 it was capital of Portugal and base for re-conquest from the Moors. The chapel at Universidade de Coimbra has a library with over a million books. There is also a Romanesque old cathedral, a new cathedral, the church of Sao Salvador, the Machado de Castro Museum, the Santa Cruz church, the Aqueduct of Sao Sebastiao, and the Monastery of Celas. The Rolling Stones played here in 2003 during my visit to Portugal, so I ended up avoiding the place entirely, since there were no rooms available.

Serenata Hostel, Largo Sé Velha n° 21/23, Coimbra; T:+351/239853130, *Info@ serenatahostel.com/*; $21Bed, Kitchen:Y, B'fast:Y, Pvt.room:Y, Locker:Y, Recep:24/7; Note: bar, laundry, bag hold, tea/coffee, maps, TV, old city, historic bldg

NS Hostel & Suites, Rua Lourenço Almeida de Azevedo n.s 3 e 4, Coimbra; T:+351/239821343, *welcome@ ns-hostel.com/*; $21Bed, Kitchen:Y, B'fast:Y, Pvt. room:Y, Locker:Y, Recep:24/7; Note: bar, café, bikes, laundry, bag hold, tea/cof

Grande Hostel Coimbra, Rua Antero de Quental 196, Coimbra; T:239108212, *grandehostelcoimbra.com/*, $20Bed, *grandehostelcoimbra@gmail.com*; Kitchen:N, B'fast:Y, Pvt.room:Y, Locker:Y, Recep:2>10p; Note: café, bag hold, tours, prkng

Dream On Coimbra Hostel, Avenida D. Afonso Henriques, n° 31, Coimbra; *dreamoncoimbrahostel.com/*, T:239715702, *dreamoncoimbrahostel@ gmail.com*; $21Bed, Kitchen:Y, B'fast:Y, Pvt.room:Y, Locker:Y, Recep:2>9p; Note: laundry, maps

Coimbra YH, Rua Henrique Seco 14, Coimbra; *hihostels.com/*, T:239822955, *coimbra@movijovem.pt/*; $15Bed, Kitchen:Y, B'fast:Y, Pvt.room:Y, Locker:N, Recep:8a>12m: Note: c.c. ok, central, afternoon lockout

5 Hostels) ERICEIRA is a surfing town of about 6600 people 22mi/35km west of Lisbon. There are forty f*cking beaches.

Blue Buddha Hostel, Moinhos do Mar, Casa 1, Ericeira, T:939549130

Blue Buddha New Hostel, R. Florêncio Granate #19, Ericeira; T:910658849 *bluebuddhahostel.com/*, $28Bed, *bluebuddhahostel@gmail.com*; Kitchen:Y, B'fast:$, Pvt.room:Y, Locker:N, Recep:3>7p; Note: luggage rm, surfboard rent, cobblestone

Amar Hostel & Suites, Rua Prudencio Franco da Trindade n 1, Ericeira; *Info@ amarhostel.com/*, T:261867182; $22Bed, Kitchen:Y, B'fast:$, Pvt.room:Y, Locker:Y, Recep:4p>; Note: hot tub, café, bikes, laundry, bag hold, tours, tea/cof

The 70s Hostel, Rua de Sao Felix, n° 1, Ericeira; *70hostel@gmail.com*, T:+351/911706972, *facebook.com/70sHostel/*; $22Bed, Kitchen:Y, B'fast:$, Pvt. room:Y, Locker:Y, Recep:24/7; Note:cash, arpt trans, bar, café, bikes, laundry

Ericeira Sea Sound GH, Moinhos do Mar, 3, Ericeira; T:351/965100883; *jorge.dias@ericeiraecosound.com*, (see FaceBook page); $25Bed, Kitchen:Y, B'fast:$, Pvt.room:Y, Locker:N, Recep:ltd; Note: pool, bikes, boards, wet suits, beach

ESMORIZ is a small city of about 11,000 on the north coast, and urban in character.

Oporto Surf Camp, Rua Gil Eanes 172, Esmoriz; T:+351/933404957, *contact@ oportosurfcamp.com/*; $28Bed, Kitchen:Y, B'fast:Y, Pvt.room:Y, Locker:N, Recep:24/7; Note: arpt trans, bikes, gym, bar, bag hold, laundry, tours, parking

4 Hostels) EVORA is a city of 57,000 in south central Portugal, and is a UNESCO world heritage site as one of Europe's 'Most Ancient Towns.' It also ranks high for livability. During the Age of Discovery, it was reputed to have a large African population. Sites include the *Água de Prata* Aqueduct, the Roman temple of Evora, and many churches.

Hostel Santantao, Praça de Giraldo 83, Evora, *hostelsantantao.com/*, T:963789142, *hostelsantantao@gmail.com*; $21Bed, Kitchen:Y, B'fast:Y, Pvt. room:Y, Locker:Y, Recep:2>11p; Note: bikes, bag hold, tours, parking

Old Evora Hostel, Travessa do Barão 4, Evora; *oldevorahostel.blogspot.com/*, T:934734493, *oldevorahostel@gmail.com*; $21Bed, Kitchen:Y, B'fast:Y, Pvt.room:Y, Locker:Y, Recep:9a>12m; Note: café, bikes, bag hold, tours, tea/cof

Pensao Policarpo, Rua da Freiria de Baixo 16, Evora; T:+351/266702424, *mail@ pensaopolicarpo.com/*; $22Bed, Kitchen:N, B'fast:Y, Pvt.room:Y, Locker:N, Recep:ltd; Note: cash, bar, bikes, bag hold, parking

Hostel Namaste Evora, Largo Doutor Manuel Alves Branco 12, Évora; *welcome@ hostelnamasteevora.pt/*, T:+351/266743014; $24Bed, Kitchen:N, B'fast:$, Pvt.room:Y, Locker:Y, Recep:24/7; Note: bikes, laundry, tours, tea/cof, parking

7 Hostels) FARO has had a rough life. It was the last Moorish stronghold in Portugal and was sacked in 1596 by the Earl of Essex, who pillaged the former bishop's palace library. It was then almost destroyed by the earthquakes of 1722 and 1755. The cathedral was restored and the Convent of Nossa Senhora da Anunciacao is in ruins. Lagos may be ground zero for the Algarve's fun 'n sun, but Faro is the administrative center. This is where your budget airline will land.

Faro Youth Hostel, R. da PSP, Edifício do IPJ, Faro, Portugal; *hihostels. com/*, T:+351/289878090, *faro@movijovem.pt*; $16bed, Kitchen:Y, B'fast:Y, Pvt. room:N, Locker:Y, Recep:24/7; Note: tours, c.c. ok, TV, store, forex, member discount, center

Casa d'Alagoa/Faro Hostel, Praça Alexandre Herculano 27, Faro; T:289813252, *booking@ farohostel.com/*; $14Bed, Kitchen:Y, B'fast:Y, Pvt.room:Y, Locker:N, Recep:24/7; Note: arpt trans, café, bikes, laundry, tea/cof, bag hold, c.c. ok

Hostel 33, Rua Miguel Bombarda N° 33, Faro; T:+351/969721360, *Info@ hostelfaro.pt,*; $17Bed, Kitchen:Y, B'fast:Y, Pvt.room:Y, Locker:N, Recep:24/7; Note: café, bikes, bag hold $, tea/coffee, nr marina/arpt bus/marina/old town

Blablabla' Faro, rua M Bombarda 12, Faro; *blablabla.rooms@gmail.com*, T:+351/915591888, (see FB page); $23Bed, Kitchen:Y, B'fast:N, Pvt.room:Y, Locker:N, Recep:5p>12m; Note: laundry, bag hold $, tea/coffee, maps

Pension Bicuar, Rua Vasco da Gama 5, Olhão, Faro; *pensionbicuar.com/*, T:+351/289714816, *pensionbicuar.olhao@gmail.com*; $24Bed, Kitchen:Y, B'fast:$, Pvt.room:Y, Locker:N, Recep:12n>11p; Note: bag hold, tea/cof, roof terrace, village

Hospedaria São Filipe, R. Infante Dom Henrique 55-1st Faro; T/F:289824182, *geral@ guesthouse-saofilipe.com/*, $20Bed, Kitchen:N, B'fast:$,

Pvt.room:N, Locker:N, Recep:12n>12m; Note: cash, bag hold, laundry, tea/coffee, center, a/c, hotel-like

Baixa Portugal Terrace Hostel, Rua de Portugal, n°36, Faro; T:289820075, *baixaportugal@gmail.com*, (see FB page); $24Bed, Kitchen:N, B'fast:Y, Pvt. room:Y, Locker:Y, Recep:24/7; Note: center, bar, bikes, laundry, bag hold, tours, c.c. ok

3 Hostels) FIGUEIRA DA FOZ is a city of about 47,000 situated slightly north of center on the Atlantic coast, and 24mi/40km west of Coimbra. Tourism is focused on gambling. Landmarks include the Sotto Mayor Palace, the fishing village of Buarcos, the Serra da Boa Viagem mountain, a promenade, several Churches, a Municipal Museum, the Santa Catarina Fort, the old Buarcos Fortress, the *Relógio Tower*, archaeological vestiges, several palaces and... oh yeah, several beaches.

Paintshop Hostel, Rua Clemência 9, Figueira da Foz; T:233436633; *Info@ paintshophostel.com/*, $28Bed, Kitchen:Y, B'fast:Y, Pvt.room:Y, Locker:Y, Recep:24/7; Note:arpt trans, pool, bar, billiards, bikes, bag hold, laundry, tours, prkng

Puzzle Hostel, Rua Alto do Viso 36, Figueira da Foz; *geral@ puzzlehostel. pt/*, T:916140138; $28Bed, Kitchen:Y, B'fast:Y, Pvt.room:Y, Locker:Y, Recep:ltd; Note: arpt trans, cafre, bikes, luggage room, cash only, surf, puzzle theme

Hospedaria Areia da Foz, Rua Bombeiros Voluntários 9, S. Julião, Figueira; T:233046116, *reservas@ areiadafoz.com/*; $16Bed, Kitchen:Y, B'fast:Y, Pvt.room:N, Locker:Y, Recep:3>7p; Note: café, wh/chair ok, lift, laundry, maps, cash

6 Hostels) GUIMARAES is a town of 52,000 in far northern Portugal, and a UNESCO World Heritage site for its historic center. It is known as the birthplace of Portuguese culture, for events that took place there in 1128 in creating the country. There are major festivals in July, August, and November... and museums, cultural and arts centers.

Hostel Prime Guimaraes, Rua da Liberdade 42–44, São Sebastião, Guimarães; T:967058786, *Info@ hostelprimeguimaraes.com/*; $20Bed, Kitchen:Y, B'fast:$, Pvt.room:Y, Locker:Y, Recep:3p>; Note: arpt trans, café, bag hold, tours, tea/cof

Hostel Santiago 31, Praça de São Tiago 31, Guimarães; T:+351/963368948, *geral@ santiago31hostel.pt/*; $17Bed, Kitchen:N, B'fast:Y, Pvt.room:Y, Locker:Y, Recep:3>7p; Note: bag hold, tea/cof, c.c. ok, club downstairs

My Hostel Guimaraes, Rua Francisco Agra, 135, Guimaraes; *myhostel-guimaraes.webnode.pt/,* T:967075755, *myhostel-guimaraes@gmail.com*; $21Bed, Kitchen:Y, B'fast:Y, Pvt.room:Y, Locker:N, Recep:2>5p; Note:arpt trans, café/ bar, maps

TM Hostel 2, Rua da Rainha D. Maria II 144, Guimarães, T: 968558870

TM Hostel 1, Rua Val de Donas 11, Guimarães; *hostels@ tmhostels. com/*, T:+351/253433504; $24Bed, Kitchen:Y, B'fast:Y, Pvt.room:Y, Locker:Y, Recep:2>8p; Note: new, terrace

Guimarães YH, Complexo Multifuncional De Couros, Largo do Cidade 8; *hihostels.com/*, T:+351/253421380, *guimaraes@movijovem.pt*; $15Bed, Kitchen:N, B'fast:Y, Pvt.room:N, Locker:Y, Recep:24/7; Note: bar, wh/chair, lift, bag hold

LAGOA is a town of almost 15,000 on San Miguel Island in the Azores. It has been settled since the 15th Century. It has much history and culture, in addition to beaches and favorable climate. It has much notable civic architecture, both civic and parochial.

Pousada Juventude Lagoa, Av Vulcanológica, Atalhada, Lagoa; *reservas@ pousadajuventudelagoa.com/*, T:296960610, $19Bed, Kitchen:Y, B'fast:Y, Pvt. room:Y, Locker:Y, Recep:6p>; Note:arpt trans, pool, gym, resto, bikes, lift, wh/ chair ok

19 Hostels) LAGOS was once an historical shipyard and center of the European slave trade, but today it is ground zero for the fun'n sun scene on the Portuguese Algarve, Europe's southernmost strand. Don't forget to wear protection. An SPF rating of at least 15 is usually recommended.

Stumble Inn, Rua Soeiro da Costa 10, Lagos; *stumbleinnlagos.com/*, T:282607081, *stumbleinnlagos@gmail.com*; $21bed, Kitchen:Y, B'fast:N, Pvt. room:Y, Locker:N, Recep:24/7; Note: arpt trans, bar, tours, parties, tea/coffee, central

Casa Sousa, Rua do Jogo da Bola n° 17, Lagos; *casa-sousa.com/*, T:282089461, *casa.sousa@hotmail.com;* $31bed, Kitchen:Y, B'fast:N, Pvt.room:Y, Locker:N, Recep:24/7; Note: cash only, 2N min. stay, central, near beach, a/c, TV, laundry

Rising Cock Hostel, Travessa do Forno 14, Lagos; T:968758785, *info@ risingcock.com/;* $31bed, Kitchen:Y, B'fast:Y, Pvt.room:N, Locker:Y, Recep:24/7; Note: bag hold, tours, prkng, party, Mama's crepes, booze cruise, resto, party anyone?

Cloud 9 Hostel, Rua Soeiro da Costa 9, Lagos; *cloud9hostel.com/*, T:282183355, *cloud9hostel@gmail.com;* $16bed, Kitchen:Y, B'fast:N, Pvt.room:Y, Locker:Y, Recep:24/7; Note: bar, laundry, city tour, bikes, central, tea/coffee, bag hold

Old Town Lagos Hostel, Rua da Barroca 70, 1°, Lagos; T:282087221, *oldtownlagoshostel@gmail.com*, (see FB page); $14Bed, Kitchen:Y, B'fast:Y, Pvt. room:Y, Locker:Y, Recep:24/7; Note: arpt trans, cafe, bikes, bag hold, laundry, prkng

Gold Coast Lagos Hostel, Rua Gil Vicente 48, Lagos, T:916594225, *goldcoast. lagoshostels.com/*, $20Bed, *goldcoast_hostel@yahoo.com;* Kitchen:Y, B'fast:Y, Pvt. room:Y, Locker:Y, Recep:12n>12m; Note: café, laundry, bag hold, tours

Shangri-Lagos Hostel, Travessa Gil Vicente 15, Lagos; T:282185845 *Info@ shangri-lagos.com/*; $32Bed, Kitchen:Y, B'fast:Y, Pvt.room:Y, Locker:Y, Recep:24/7; Note: bar, bikes, laundry, bag hold, tour, tea/coffee, parking, beach

Bura Surfhouse, Rua da Pedra Alcada, Lote 15, Lagos; T:282782030, *Info@ burasurfhouse.com/*, $16Bed, Kitchen:Y, B'fast:Y, Pvt.room:Y, Locker:Y, Recep:24/7; Note: arpt trans, bar, pool, billiards, laundry, bag hold, tours, tea/ cof, prkng, not center

Hostel Caza de Sao Goncalo, Rua Cândido dos Reis 73, Lagos; T:919841622, *hostelsaogoncalo.lagos@gmail.com*, (see Facebook page); $21Bed, Kitchen:Y, B'fast:Y, Pvt.room:Y, Locker:Y, Recep:24/7; Note: hot tub, bikes, laundry, bag hold, tours

Big Chill Hostel, Rua da Ponta da Piedade, Lt23, Lagos; *bigchillhostel.com/*, T:918974820, *bigchillhostel@gmail.com;* $14Bed, Kitchen:Y, B'fast:$, Pvt. room:Y, Locker:Y, Recep:9a>12m; Note: bikes, min 2N, tours, tea/cof, parking

Algarve Surf Hostel, Urb Cerro das Mos lote 55, Lagos; T:927988171, *info@ algarvesurfschool.com/*; $25Bed, Kitchen:Y, B'fast:Y, Pvt.room:Y, Locker:Y, Recep:1>10p; Note: pool, billiards, bikes, tours, tea/coffee, parking

HI Lagos YH, Rue Lançarote de Feitas 50, Lagos; *hihostels.com*, T:+351/282761970, *lagos@movijovem.pt*; $14Bed, Kitchen:Y, B'fast:Y, Pvt.room:Y, Locker:Y, Recep:24/7; Note: billiards, wh/chair ok, laundry, tours, beach

Blue Moon Hostel, Rua 25 de Abril , #34, Lagos; *bluemoonlagos@gmail. com/*, T:+351/282085642, *bluemoonlagos.wix.com/*; $21Bed, Kitchen:Y, B'fast:$, Pvt. room:Y, Locker:Y, Recep:3p>12m; Note: café, laundry, bag hold, tea/ coffee, central

Tag Hostel, Rua Portas de Portugal 63, Lagos; *booking@ taghostel. com/*, T:+351/918780198; $21Bed, Kitchen:Y, B'fast:Y, Pvt.room:Y, Locker:Y, Recep:24/7; Note: 1-2p checkout!, cash only, arpt trans, bar, bikes, tours, tea/ coffee

Residencial Sol a Sol, Rua Lançarote de Freitas 22, Lagos; T:282761290, *residencialsolasol.com/*, $18Bed, *residencialsolasol@gmail.com/*; Kitchen:N, B'fast:Y, Pvt.room:Y, Locker:N, Recep:24/7; Note: café, bar, lift, bag hold, tea/ coffee

The Shelter Lagos, Urbanização Torraltinha, Rua Eça de Queiroz n° 7, Lagos; *theshelterlagos.com/*, T:913718486, *theshelterlagos@gmail.com*; $25Bed, Kitchen:Y, B'fast:Y, Pvt.room:N, Locker:N, Recep:ltd; Note: laundry, bag hold, tea/cof

JJs Yard, Travessa do Forno 10, Lagos; T:+351/961189950, *jjsyardlagosportugal@hotmail.com,* (see FB page); $16Bed, Kitchen:Y, B'fast:Y, Pvt.room:Y, Locker:N, Recep:ltd; Note: cash only, bag hold, laundry

Jah Shaka Surf, Pria de Luz, Algarve, Lagos; *jahshakasurf.com/*, T:912773147 $35Bed, Kitchen:Y, B'fast:Y, Pvt.room:Y, Locker:N, Recep:24/7; Note: arpt trans, bar, bikes, wh/chair ok, tea/coffee, parking, books, meals, cash only

Ocean View Lagos, Rua das Armações de Pesca 21, Lagos; T:282040204, *reservas@ oceanviewlagos.com/*; $16Bed, Kitchen:Y, B'fast:Y, Pvt.room:Y, Locker:Y, Recep:ltd; Note: arpt trans, pool, bar, billiards, bikes, parking, laundry, min 2N

62 Hostels) LISBON (Lisboa) is the capital and largest city of Portugal and shares its history from the beginning. As such it was one of the most important cities in the world in the 16th century. Unfortunately it was also earthquake-prone and had many. The worst was in 1755, which resulted in a tsunami that killed some ten percent of the population and devastated coastal areas from Britain to Morocco. The city was rebuilt in a more modern style, much of which remains today. Today the city has much entertainment and many festivals, especially in summer.

And for those of us who like our nostalgia in dimly-lit clubs, listening to some *fado* in the old Alfama district can be quite worthwhile. Portuguese bullfighting can be witnessed at the old red-brick *Campo Pequeno*. The Tower of Belem, located on the riverbank, is a UN World Heritage site. No place exemplifies the current European hostel explosion better than Lisbon. Quality is very high. Many of these places qualify as "best ever" for many travelers. So many score straight A's on my 5-question report card that it could almost make a proud uncle cry. CASCAIS is a surf village 7mi/12km west of Libon. CARCAVELOS is another.

Carcavelos Surf Hostel, Rua da Beira n°8, Carcavelos; T:+351/911928003, *carcavelossurfhostel.com/*, $19Bed, *carcavelos.surf.hostel@gmail.com*; Kitchen:Y, B'fast:Y, Pvt.room:Y, Locker:Y, Recep:ltd; Note: resto, laundry, bag hold, tours

Carcavelos Beach Hostel, Rua Lourenço Marques 5, Carcavelos; (see FB page), T:+351/214582418, *info@carcavelosbeachhostel.com*; $21Bed, Kitchen:Y, B'fast:Y, Pvt.room:Y, Locker:Y, Recep:ltd; Note: pool, café, bikes, bag hold, parking

Lisbon Surf House, Rua Direita #38 Caxias, Cascais; T:917326613, *Info@ lisbonsurfhouse.com/*; $31Bed, Kitchen:N, B'fast:Y, Pvt.room:Y, Locker:Y, Recep:4:30p>; Note: café, bikes, laundry, bag hold, tea/coffee, parking

Guincho Surf Beachostel, R. do Passo Mau 33, Charneca do Guincho, Cascais; T:962537755, *guinchosurfbeachostel@gmail.com*, (see FB page) $29Bed, Kitchen:Y, B'fast:$, Pvt.room:Y, Locker:Y, Recep:ltd; Note: bikes, books, meals

Cascais Bay Hostel, Largo Luís de Camões 38, Cascais; T:218022629, *Info@ cascaisbayhostel.com/*; $21Bed, Kitchen:Y, B'fast:Y, Pvt.room:Y, Locker:Y, Recep:8a>11p; Note: historic center, sea, beach, terrace, TV, yoga

Agarre O Momento, R. Joaquim Ereira 458, Cascais; T:+351/214064532, *Info@ agarreomomento.com/*; $35Bed, Kitchen:Y, B'fast:Y, Pvt.room:Y, Locker:N, Recep:ltd; Note: café, laundry, tea, maps

Ljmonade, R. Manuel Joaquim Gama Machado #6, Cascais; T:966895616 *hostel@ljmonade.com,* (see FB page); $35Bed, Kitchen:Y, B'fast:Y, Pvt.room:Y, Locker:Y, Recep:ltd; Note: cash only, laundry, bag hold, tea/coffee, parking

Lisbon Surf Camp, Alto de Murches, Rua Principal, s/n, Casa J, Cascais; *Info@ lisbonsurfcamp.com/*, T:+351/918142230; $35Bed, Kitchen:N, B'fast:Y, Pvt. room:Y, Locker:N, Recep:ltd; Note: arpt trans, bag hold, parking, TV

The Spot Portugal, Rua dos Ulmeiros, Casa 18, Cascais; T:929034353, *wannasurf@ thespotportugal.com/*; $28Bed, Kitchen:N, B'fast:Y, Pvt.room:Y, Locker:Y, Recep:ltd; Note: cash only, pool, parking, tea/coffee, a/c

Traveller's House, R. Augusta 89, Lisbon; *info@ travellershouse.com/*, T:210115922; $23bed, Kitchen:Y, B'fast:Y, Pvt.room:N, Locker:Y, Recep:24/7; Note: arpt trans, café, bar, coffee/tea, bag hold, tours, books, TV, happy hour, wine

Lisboa Central Hostel, R. Rodrigues Sampaio 160, Lisbon; T:309881038, *global@ lisboacentralhostel.com/*; $20bed, Kitchen:Y, B'fast:Y, Pvt.room:Y, Locker:Y, Recep:24/7; Note: bag hold, coffee/tea, bar, laundry, games, cafe, tours, pancakes!

This is Lisbon Hostel, Rua da Costa do Castelo 63, Lisbon; T:218014549, *info@ thisislisbonhostel.com/*; $20bed, Kitchen:Y, B'fast:Y, Pvt.room:Y, Locker:Y, Recep:24/7; Note: coffee/tea, cafe, great views, laundry, bar, tours, bag hold

Living Lounge Hostel, Rua do Crucifixo 116, Lisbon; T:213461078, *info@ livingloungehostel.com/*; $25bed, Kitchen:Y, B'fast:Y, Pvt.room:N, Locker:Y, Recep:24/7; Note: bar, laundry, tours, meals, stairs, bag hold, free tour

Lisbon Poets' Hostel, Rua Nova da Trindade 2, Lisbon; *lisbonpoetshostel. com/*, T:213461241, *lisbonpoetshostel@gmail.com*; $21bed, Kitchen:Y, B'fast:Y, Pvt.room:Y, Locker:Y, Recep:24/7; Note:wh/chair ok, lift, min. 4N, bag hold, tours, laundry

Alfama Patio Hostel, Escolas Gerais 3, Lisbon; T:218883127, *contact@ alfamapatio.com/*; $16bed, Kitchen:Y, B'fast:Y, Pvt.room:Y, Locker:Y, Recep:24/7; Note: bar, free tour/info, laundry, activities, bag hold, bikes, tea/coffee

Lisbon Chillout Hostel, Rua Nogueira e Sousa #8, Lisbon; T:212468450; *lisbonchh@gmail.com*, $17bed, *lisbonchillouthostel.com/*; Kitchen:Y, B'fast:Y, Pvt. room:Y, Locker:Y, Recep:24/7; Note: café, bar, bikes, bag hold, tours, laundry, tea/cof

Equity Point Lisboa, Travessa do Fala-Só 9, Lisbon; T:218018211, *infolisboa@ equity-point.com/*; $17bed, Kitchen:Y, B'fast:Y, Pvt.room:Y, Locker:Y, Recep:24/7; Note: café, bar, bikes, books, tours, bag hold, c.c. ok, top of hill, central, no-party

Lisbon Lounge Hostel, R. de São Nicolau 41, Lisbon; T:213462061, *info@ lisbonloungehostel.com/*; $23bed, Kitchen:Y, B'fast:Y, Pvt.room:N, Locker:Y, Recep:24/7; Note: bar, bikes, bag hold, resto, laundry, tours, maps, eggs

Lisbon Old Town Hostel, R. do Ataíde 26A, Lisbon; *lisbonoldtownhostel. com/*, T:213465248, *lisbonoldtownhostel@gmail.com*; $18bed, Kitchen:Y, B'fast:Y, Pvt.room:Y, Locker:Y, Recep:24/7; Note: wh/chair ok, laundry, tours, tea/coffee

People Hostel, R. dos Jerónimos 16, Lisboa; T:218289567, *geral@ peoplehostel. com/*; $12bed, Kitchen:Y, B'fast:Y, Pvt.room:Y, Locker:N, Recep:24/7; Note: bag hold, laundry, bar, minimart, c.c. ok, tours, parking, books

Go Hostel Lisbon, Rua Maria da Fonte 55, Lisbon; *gohostellisbon.com/*, T:218229816, *gohostellisbon@gmail.com*; $16bed, Kitchen:Y, B'fast:Y, Pvt.room:Y, Locker:Y, Recep:24/7; Note: arpt trans, bar, café, bag hold, tea/coffee, laundry

Smile Hostel, Travesa do Almada #12 3DRT, Lisbon; *smilehostel.com/*, T:963736683, *smilehostel@hotmail.com*; $20bed, Kitchen:Y, B'fast:Y, Pvt.room:Y, Locker:Y, Recep:24/7; Note: a/c, c.c. ok, tours, no sign, stairs, central, laundry, min. 2N

Oasis Backpackers' Mansion, R. de Santa Catarina 24, Lisbon; T:213478044, *lisboa@ hostelsoasis.com/*; $14bed, Kitchen:Y, B'fast:Y, Pvt. room:Y, Locker:Y, Recep:24/7; Note: bar, café, lift, tours, bag hold, welcome drink, c.c. ok

Lisbon Shiado Hostel, Rua Anchieta 5, Lisbon; *shiadohostel.com/*, T:213429227, *shiado.hostel@gmail.com*; $18bed, Kitchen:Y, B'fast:Y, Pvt.room:Y, Locker:Y, Recep:24/7; Note: lift, tea/coffee, luggage rm, a/c, TV, central

Unreal Hostel, Rua Pedro Nunes 10, Lisbon; *wix.com/unrealhostel/*, T:213153101, *info@unrealhostel.com*; $17bed, Kitchen:N, B'fast:Y, Pvt.room:Y,

Locker:Y, Recep:24/7; Note: bar/café, lift, bag hold, laundry, tours, parking, res 'hood

Next Hostel, Avenida Almirante Reis 4, Lisbon; *nexthostel.com/*, T:211927746; $19bed, Kitchen:N, B'fast:Y, Pvt.room:Y, Locker:Y, Recep:24/7; Note: c.c. ok, central, lift, luggage room, hard to find, late-night 'hood

Jardim de Santos, Largo Vitorino Damásio 4, Lisbon; T:213974666, *jardimdesantoshostel.com*; $16bed, Kitchen:N, B'fast:Y, Pvt.room:N, Locker:Y, Recep:24/7; Note: bag hold, laundry, c.c. ok, tea/coffee

LxCorner Hostel, Avda da Liberdade, 85, Lisbon; *lxcornerhostel.weebly. com/*, T:+351/218209115, *lxcornerhostel@gmailcom*; $14Bed, Kitchen:Y, B'fast:Y, Pvt.room:N, Locker:Y, Recep:>12m; Note: center, cash, bar, laundry, stairs, tea/coffee

Yes! Lisbon Hostel, Rua de São Julião 148, Lisbon; T:+351/213427171, *infolisbon@ yeshostels.com/*; $18Bed, Kitchen:Y, B'fast:Y, Pvt.room:Y, Locker:Y, Recep:24/7; Note: resto/bar, lift, laundry, bag hold, tea/coffee, tours, central

Sunset Destination, Cais Sodré Trn Stn, Lgo Duque de 3ra, 210997735, *beach@*

Lisbon Destination Hostel, Largo Duque de Cadaval 17, Lisbon; T:213466457, *lisbon@ destinationhostels.com/*; $23Bed, Kitchen:y, B'fast:Y, Pvt. room:Y, Locker:Y, Recep:24/7; Note:resto/bar, billiards, lift, laundry, tea/cof, tours, crepes, @train stn

The Gspot Hostel, Rua Camilo Castelo Branco n 2C, Lisbon; *Info@ gspothostels.com/*, T:211933211, $24Bed, Kitchen:Y, B'fast:Y, Pvt.room:Y, Locker:Y, Recep:24/7; Note:12n checkout, laundry, bag hold, tours, tea/cof, partyyy

Home Hostel, Rua São Nicolau 13, Lisbon; T:+351/218885312; *Info@ mylisbonhome.com/*; $14Bed, Kitchen:Y, B'fast:Y, Pvt.room:N, Locker:Y, Recep:24/7 Note: resto/bar, bikes, lift, laundry, bag hold, tea/coffee, books, meals

Goodnight Hostel, Rua dos Correeiros 113-2nd, Lisbon; *goodnighthostel. com/*, T:+351/213430139; $20Bed, Kitchen:Y, B'fast:Y, Pvt.room:Y, Locker:Y, Recep:24/7; Note: bag hold, tours, books, maps, stairs no lift, pancakes, central

Good Morning Hostel, Praça Restauradores, #65, 2nd fl, Lisbon; T:213421128, *goodmorninghostel.com/*, $20Bed, *goodmorningbookings@gmail.com*;

Kitchen:Y, B'fast:Y, Pvt.room:Y, Locker:Y, Recep:24/7; Note: café, laundry, cash only, hard find

Rossio Hostel, Calçada Carmo 6, Lisbon, *rossiohostel.com/*, T:+351/213426004, *rossiohostel@hotmail.com*; $20Bed, Kitchen:Y, B'fast:Y, Pvt. room:Y, Locker:Y, Recep:24/7; Note: café, bar, bag hold, tours, tea/coffee, books, forex, central

Lisb'on Hostel, Rua Ataíde 7A, Lisbon; *Info@ lisb-onhostel.com*, T:213467413; $17Bed, Kitchen:Y, B'fast:Y, Pvt.room:Y, Locker:Y, Recep:24/7; Note: bar, bikes, center, billiards, lift, bag hold, tours, tea/cof, wh/chair ok, laundry, mart, arpt trans

Stay Inn Lisbon Hostel, Rua Luz Soriano #19-1st andar, Lisbon; *Info@ stayinnlisbonhostel.com/*, T:213425149; $20Bed, Kitchen:Y, B'fast:Y, Pvt.room:Y, Locker:Y, Recep:24/7; Note: laundry, bag hold, tea/coffee, safe deposit, uptown

Lisbon Soul Hostel, Rua de S. Tomé, #23, Lisboa; T:211994226, *geral@ lisbonsoul.com*; $14Bed, Kitchen:Y, B'fast:Y, Pvt.room:Y, Locker:Y, Recep:24/7; Note: café, laundry, bag hold, tea/coffee, maps, games, historic dist, hard find, c.c. ok

BA Hostel, Travessa da Cara, 6, Bairro Alto, Lisbon; T:+351/213421079, *book@ hostelba-bairroalto.com/*; $20Bed, Kitchen:Y, B'fast:Y, Pvt.room:Y, Locker:Y, Recep:24/7; Note: café, laundry, tours, tea/coffee, maps, a/c, entertainment dist

Golden Tram242, Rua Áurea 242; Lisboa; *goldentram242lisbonnehostel. com*, T:213229100, *goldentram242.lisbonnehostel@gmail.com*; $17Bed, Kitchen:Y, B'fast:Y, Pvt.room:Y, Locker:Y, Recep:24/7; Note: bar, lift, laundry, bag hold, meals, maps

Alface Bairro Alto Hostel, Rua do Norte 98, Lisbon; T:+351/213433293 *booking@ alfacehostel.com/*; $21Bed, Kitchen:Y, B'fast:Y, Pvt.room:Y, Locker:Y, Recep:ltd; Note: café, bar, bag hold, tours, tea/coffee, pub party district

The Independente Hostel, R. São Pedro de Alcântara 81, Lisbon; T:213461381, *reservations@ theindependente.pt/*; $16Bed, Kitchen:N, B'fast:Y, Pvt.room:Y, Locker:Y, Recep:advise ETA; Note: resto/bar, bikes, lift, laundry, bag hold, tours, tea/cof, central

We Love F* Tourists, Rua dos Fanqueiros 267, Lisbon; T:218871327, *Info@ weloveftourists.com/*; $20Bed, Kitchen:Y, B'fast:Y, Pvt.room:Y, Locker:Y, Recep:24/7; Note:arpt trans, bar, café, laundry, bag hold, tours, tea/coffee, prkng, center

PH Lisbon Hostel, Calçada do Marquês de Abrantes 40, Lisboa; T:218013771, *info@ phlisbonhostel.com*; $21Bed, Kitchen:Y, B'fast:Y, Pvt.room:Y, Locker:Y, Recep:24/7; Note: central, café, luggage room, tea/coffee

Amazing Hostels Bairro Alto, Rua do Norte, #83–1st, Lisboa; T:213426186

Amazing Hostel Se-Alfama, Beco do Arco Escuro, Lisbon, T:964453972, *lisbonamazinghostels.net/*, $14Bed, *lisbonamazinghostels@gmail.com*; Kitchen:N, B'fast:Y, Pvt.room:Y, Locker:Y, Recep:24/7; Note: billiards, TV, hard find

Fusions Hostel, Campo Pequeno, nr.50-5th Fl/right, Lisboa; *fusionshostel. com/*, T:218078065, *fusionshostel@gmail.com*, $17Bed, Kitchen:Y, B'fast:Y, Pvt. room:Y, Locker:Y, Recep:24/7; Note: car, bar, lift, laundry, bag hold, tours, central

Salitre Hostel, Rua do Salitre 134, Lisbon, *hostelsalitre.com/*, T:+351/218201433, *salitrehostel@gmail.com*; $14Bed, Kitchen:Y, B'fast:Y, Pvt. room:Y, Locker:Y, Recep:24/7; Note: bag hold, near Rossio@Rato stn

Lisbon Calling, Rua de Sao Paulo 126, Fl 3D, Lisbon; T:213432381, *Info@ lisboncalling.net/*; $23Bed, Kitchen:Y, B'fast:Y, Pvt.room:Y, Locker:Y, Recep:24/7; Note: lift, laundry, bag hold, tea/coffee, c.c. ok, maps, books

Johnies Place, Calçada Graça 18F, Lisbon, *johniesplace.com/*, T:216095765, *johniesplace@gmail.com*; $14Bed, Kitchen:Y, B'fast:Y, Pvt.room:Y, Locker:Y, Recep:call; Note: café, laundry, bag hold, tea/coffee, cash only, up Graca hill, quiet

Downtown Design Hostel, Rua dos Sapateiros 231, Lisbon; T:+351/968255312, *info@ downtowndesignhostel.com/*; $35Bed, Kitchen:Y, B'fast:$, Pvt.room:Y, Locker:Y, Recep:24/7; Note: minimart, laundry, bag hold, tea/coffee, 4th Fl no lift

Baluarte Citadino Stay Cool Hostel, Rua Castilho 57, 1st Dto, Lisboa, *staycoolhostel.com/*, T:967480331, *bc.staycoolhostel@hotmail.com*; $14Bed, Kitchen:Y, B'fast:Y, Pvt.room:Y, Locker:N , Recep:ltd; Note: café, lift, laundry, bag hold, tea/cof

Baluarte Citadino Feel Good Hostel, Rua de Santa Marta #45, 4th Dto, Lisbon; *feelgoodhostel.net/*, T:967480331, *bc.feelgoodhostel@hotmail.com*; $14Bed, Kitchen:Y, B'fast:N, Pvt.room:Y, Locker:N, Recep:ltd; Note: lift, laundry, bag hold, c.c. ok

HI Lisbon Centre YH, Rua Andrade Corvo 46, Lisboa; *hihostels.com/*, T;+351/213532696, *lisboa@movijovem.pt*; $19Bed, Kitchen:Y, B'fast:Y, Pvt. room:Y, Locker:Y, Recep:24/7; Note: café, wh/chair ok, lift, bag hold, tea/cof, parking

Hostel Graça 28, Rua da Graça 140, Lisbon; *hostelgraca28.wix.com,* T:918301020, *hostel.graca.28@gmail.com*; $16Bed, Kitchen:Y, B'fast:Y, Pvt.room:Y, Locker:Y, Recep:24/7; Note: bar, laundry, tea/cof, meals, cash, un-central, B&B upscale

Vistas de Lisboa, Rua Douradores 178   Lisbon; T:+351/218867256, *Info@ vistasdelisboa.com/*; $16Bed, Kitchen:Y, B'fast:Y, Pvt.room:Y, Locker:Y, Recep:24/7; Note: arpt trans, café, lift, laundry, bag hold, TV, Fax, central

Famous Crows Hostel, Rua de Belém, #70-1st, Lisboa; T:+351/939890903, geral@ *famous-crows.pt*;$18Bed, Kitchen:Y, B'fast:Y, Pvt.room:N, Locker:Y, Recep:24/7; Note: cash only, bar, laundry, tea/coffee

Lisbon - Parque das Nações, Rua de Moscavide, 47, Lisboa; *hihostels. com*, T:218920890, *lisboaparque@movijovem.pt*; $19Bed, Kitchen:Y, B'fast:Y, Pvt. room:N, Locker:Y, Recep:24/7; Note: resto/bar, wh/chair ok, lift, bag hold, parking, out of town

Residencial Lar do Areeiro, Praça Francisco Sá Carneiro 4, Lisbon; T:+351/218493150, *Info@ residencialardoareeiro.com/*; $27Bed, Kitchen:M, B'fast:Y, Pvt.room:Y, Locker:N, Recep:24/7; Note: cash only, a/c, TV

Passport Lisbon, Praça Luís de Camões 36, Lisbon, T:+351/213427346, *Info@ passporthostel.com/*; $14Bed, Kitchen:Y, B'fast:Y, Pvt.room:Y, Locker:Y, Recep:24/7; Note: arpt trans, minimart, café, lift, laundry, bag hold, tours, parking

Hostel Inn ba Lisbon, trav das Mêrces n 52, Lisbon; *hostelinnba.com/*, T:925164332, *hostelinnba@gmail.com*; $20Bed, Kitchen:N, B'fast:Y, Pvt.room:Y, Locker:N, Recep:24/7; Note: arpt trans, resto/bar, wh/chair, bag hold, tours, tea/cof

3 Hostels) LOURINHA is a town of almost 9000 in a municipality of the same name and almost 25,000 inhabitants. There are scenic beaches and Jurassic-era fossilized remains. PRAIA DE AREIA BRANCA is the main beach, known for its white sand.

Beach Break Portugal, Rua Miramar 9D, Seixal; *beachbreakportugal.com/*, T:914932506, *beachbreakportugal@gmail.com*; $21Bed, Kitchen:Y, B'fast:Y, Pvt. room:Y, Locker:N, Recep:4>11p; Note: arpt tran, café, laundry, bag hold, parking, cash

Areia Branca Beach Hostel, Rua da Foz 5, Lourinhã, *abbhostel@gmail. com*, T:915493034, *areiabrancabeachhostel.com/*: $25Bed, Kitchen:Y, B'fast:Y, Pvt.room:Y, Locker:N, Recep:24/7; Note: arpt trans, bag hold, tours, parking, cash

The Maverick Surfhostel & Guesthouse, Praia da Areia Branca, Lourinha; *bookings@ mysurfhostel.com*, T:262787115, $25Bed, Kitchen:Y, B'fast:$, Pvt. room:Y, Locker:Y, Recep:ltd; Note: parking, safe deposit

MAIA is a city of over 35,000 in northern Portugal.

AirPorto Hostel, Rua da Estrada 244, Moreira – Maia; *airportohostel.com/*, T:+351/229427397, *airportohostel@gmail.com*; $17Bed, Kitchen:Y, B'fast:Y, Pvt. room:Y, Locker:Y, Recep:2p>2a; Note: bikes, bag hold, tours, tea/cof, cash

15 Hostels) PENICHE is a city of 10,000 and municipality of about 28,000 along the central Portuguese coast, and known for its *supertubo* surfing waves. In summer there is a ferry to the Berlingas Islands 6mi/10km offshore, known for their nature reserve.

GeekCo Hostel Atouguia, Rua Porta do Sol 5, Atouguia Da Baleia, T:262759775

GeekCo Hostel, R.Arq. Paulino Montez 25, Peniche; *home@ geekcohostel. com/*, T:262282313; $25Bed, Kitchen:Y, B'fast:Y, Pvt.room:Y, Locker:N, Recep:24/7; Note:cash only, bikes, arpt trans, resto/bar, minimart, laundry, tours, prkng, bag hold

Peniche Surf Lodge, Rua Casal do Viola #6, Papoa, Peniche; T:262759322, *penichesurflodge.co.uk/*, $25Bed, *surfpeniche@gmail.com*; Kitchen:Y, B'fast:Y, Pvt. room:Y, Locker:Y, Recep:ltd; Note: bikes, arpt trans, wh/chair ok, laundry, bag hold

Peniche Hostel, Rua Arquitecto Paulino Montês 6, Peniche; T:+351/969008689, *Bookings@ penichehostel.com/*; $21Bed, Kitchen:Y, B'fast:Y, Pvt.room:Y, Locker:Y, Recep:24/7; Note: arpt trans, café, bikes, tour desk

Peniche Welcome Hostel, Rua dos Hermínios 16, Peniche; T:262784128, *penichewelcomehostel.wix.com/*, $10Bed, *penichewelcomehostel@gmail.com*; Kitchen:Y, B'fast:Y, Pvt.room:Y, Locker:N, Recep:3p>12m; Note: shuttle, hot tub, bikes

Tribo da Praia Eco Hostel, Rua Nossa Senhora da Guia 3, Ferrel, T:968498682

Tribo da Praia, Rua do Catalo 65, Ferrel; T:+351/262381829, *bookings@ tribodapraia.com/*; $25Bed, Kitchen:Y, B'fast:$, Pvt.room:Y, Locker:Y, Recep:24/7; Note: shuttle, café, bikes, laundry, tours, prkng, resto/bar, minimart, bag hold, tea/cof

Martin's lodge, Rua Cidade de Seia, Edifício Berlenga #7-10th D, Peniche; *penichesurfhostel.wix.com/*, T:911141806; $21Bed, Kitchen:Y, B'fast:$, Pvt. room:Y, Locker:Y, Recep:2>10p; Note: shuttle, café, bikes, lift, laundry, tours, parking

Supertubos Beach Hostel, Av do Mar 58d, Consolação, Casal do Butado, *supertubosbeachhostel.com/*, T:939303396, *supertubosbeachhostel@gmail.com*; $17Bed, Kitchen:N, B'fast:Y, Pvt.room:Y, Locker:N, Recep:ltd; Note: arpt trans, pool

Captain's Log House, Av do Mar, 142, Casais do Baleal, Peniche; T:914602183, *captainloghouse.com/*, $20Bed, *captainloghouse@gmail.com*; Kitchen:Y, B'fast:$, Pvt.room:Y, Locker:Y, Recep:ltd; Note: café, laundry, parking, tea/coffee, cash, beach

Surfing Baleal, Rua Ferreira de Castro 14A, Baleal, Peniche; T:+351/918520532, *Info@ surfingbaleal.com/*; $14Bed, Kitchen:Y, B'fast:N, Pvt. room:Y, Locker:N, Recep:9a>10p; Note: cash only, arpt trans, bikes, laundry, bag hold, parking, forex

Surfer's Bay, Rua do Salgado Lote d1, Peniche; *penichesurfersbay.com/*, T:913775077, *penichesurfersbay@gmail.com*; $39Bed, Kitchen:N, B'fast:Y, Pvt. room:Y, Locker:N, Recep:ltd; Note:bikes, hot tub, pool, resto/bar, wh/chair ok, arpt trans

Villa Berlenga, R. José Júlio #12, Casais do Mestre Mendo, Atouguia da Baleia; T:924110033, *reservas@ villaberlenga.com.pt/*; $26Bed, Kitchen:N, B'fast:Y, Pvt.room:Y, Locker:N, Recep:ltd; Note: bar, café, laundry, remote/need car

Bsurf Hostel, Rua Joaquim Barardo 49, Baleal – Peniche; T:965782140, *Info@ bsurfhostel.com*; $27Bed, Kitchen:N, B'fast:N, Pvt.room:Y, Locker:Y, Recep:2>8p; Note: arpt trans, pool, café, bikes, bag hold, tea, parking, cash only

Surfing Inn Peniche, Trav. Cruz das Almas 24, Ferrel; T:+351/924116914, *Info@ surfinginnpeniche.com/*; $25Bed, Kitchen:Y, B'fastY, Pvt.room:Y, Locker:N, Recep:ltd; Note: bikes, laundry, tea/coffee, parking

PONTA DELGADA is a city of 20,000 and the largest city and capital of the Portuguese Azores. Its location on southern San Miguel Island makes it an ideal all-year tourist destination. Its Holy Christ of the Miracles church is a pilgrimage destination.

HI Ponta Delgada YH, Rua S.Francisco Xavier, Ponta Delgada; *hihostels. com/*, T:296629431, *pdelgada@pousadasjuvacores.com/*; $20Bed, Kitchen:Y, B'fast:Y, Pvt.room:Y, Locker:Y, Recep:24/7; Note: arpt trans, billiards, bag hold, parking

PONTE DA BARCA is a municipality of 13,000 in the far north of Portugal and the birthplace of Ferdinand Magellan.

Magalhaes Hostel, Rua Doutor Joaquim Moreira de Barros 14, Ponte da Barca; T:+351/965492032, *Info@ magalhaeshostel.com/*; $21Bed, Kitchen:Y, B'fast:Y, Pvt.room:Y, Locker:Y, Recep:5:30>8:30p; Note:cash only, bikes, tours, tea/cof

2 Hostels) PORTIMAO is yet another town on Portugal's southern Algarve coast, and one of the largest with 55,000 inhabitants, yet one of the least

hosteled. I wonder why. It's famous for sailing and power-boating. Oh, I see.

HI Portimão YH, Lugar do Coca Maravilhas, Portimão; *hihostels.com/*, T:282491804, *portimao@movijovem.pt*; $14Bed, Kitchen:Y, B'fast:Y, Pvt.room:Y, Locker:Y, Recep:8a>12m; Note: resto/bar, pool, billiards, wh/chair ok, bag hold, far

Villa Joaninha Algarve, Rua Bartolomeu Dias, Praia da Rocha, Portimao; *reservas@ villajoaninha.com/*; $28Bed, Kitchen:Y, B'fast:$, Pvt.room:Y, Locker:Y, Recep:4>6p; Note: min 3N, cash only, arpt trans, bikes, bag hold, tours, tea/ coffee

33 Hostels) PORTO (Oporto) is Portugal's second city, far to the north on the Atlantic coast, and its old name *Portus Cale* gives Portugal its name. This is where Prince Henry the navigator initiated his exploration of the world. Its entire traditional center is a UNESCO world heritage site. Its major export is port wine (burp), *yeah*. The Maria Pia Bridge was designed by Gustave Eiffel. Notable buildings are Porto's cathedral, built on the Visigothic citadel, the church of Sao Martinho de Cedofeita, the Torre dos Clerigos, the Basilica of Sao Francisco, and the stock exchange. This would be a good stopover on a trip between Lisbon and the Basque country. As with all of Portugal, many of the hostels are new and the quality is very high. ESPINHO is a beach resort and casino town 9mi/15km from Porto.

Maceda Surf Hostel, R. da Charneca 647, Maceda, Sta Maria da Feira, Espinho; *Info@ portosurf.com/*, T:917127445; $25Bed, Kitchen:Y, B'fast:Y, Pvt. room:Y, Locker:N, Recep:ltd; Note: arpt trans, bikes, bag hold, parking, meals, surfffff

Porto Spot Hostel, Rua de Gonçalo Cristóvão 12, Oporto; T:224085205, *bookings@ spothostel.pt*; $17bed, Kitchen:Y, B'fast:Y, Pvt.room:Y, Locker:Y, Recep:24/7; Note: bar, café, laundry, tours, parking, activities, tea/coffee, maps

Rivoli Cinema Hostel, R. Dr. Magalhães Lemos 83, Oporto; T:220174634, *rivolicinemahostel.com/*, $18bed, *rivolicinemahostel@gmail.com*; Kitchen:Y, B'fast:Y, Pvt.room:Y, Locker:Y, Recep:24/7; Note: bar, laundry, tours, roof, pool, gym, hard find

Oporto Poets Hostel Privates, Travessa do ferraz, 13, Porto

Oporto Poets Hostel, Rua dos Caldeireiros 261, Oporto; *oportopoetshostel. com/*, T:223324209, *oportopoetshostel@gmail.com*; $20bed, Kitchen:Y, B'fast:Y, Pvt.room:N, Locker:Y, Recep:24/7; Note: laundry, parking, tours, dinners, activities, bag hold

Oporto Sky Hostel, Rua da Lapa 33, Oporto; *info@ oportosky.com/*, T:222017069; $18bed, Kitchen:Y, B'fast:Y, Pvt.room:Y, Locker:Y, Recep:24/7; Note: bar, café, market, laundry, tours, activities, central, bag hold, tea/coffee, parking

Steps House, Escadas do Monte dos Judeus 5, Oporto; *stepshouse.hostel. com/*, T:224054051, *facebook.com/stepshouse.hostel*; $20bed, Kitchen:Y, B'fast:Y, Pvt.room:Y, Locker:Y, Recep:ltd; Note: tours, bikes, bag hold, hard find, many steps

Yellow House, Rua de João das Regras 96, Oporto; *yellowhouse.hostel.com/*, T:222014229, *yellowhousehostel@gmail.com*; $18bed, Kitchen:Y, B'fast:Y, Pvt. room:N, Locker:Y, Recep:ltd; Note: luggage room, c.c. ok, parking, bikes

Porto Riad Guesthouse, Rua D. Joao IV 990, Porto, Portugal; T:225107643, *info@ portoriad.com/*; $15bed, Kitchen:Y, B'fast:Y, Pvt.room:Y, Locker:N, Recep:24/7; Note: Moroccan theme, hard find, a/c, laundry, wh/chair ok, bikes, bar, parking

Tattva Design Hostel, Rua do Cativo 26-28, Porto; *tattvadesignhostel.com/*, T:220944622, *tattvadesignhostel@gmail.com*; $17bed, Kitchen:Y, B'fast:Y, Pvt. room:Y, Locker:Y, Recep:24/7; Note: bikes, lift, bag hold, laundry, resto/bar, lift, wh/chair ok, a/c

Garden House Hostel, R. de Santa Catarina 501 Porto; T:222081426, *gardenhousehostelporto.com,* $20bed, *gardenhouse501@gmail.com*; Kitchen:Y, B'fast:Y, Pvt.room:Y, Locker:Y, Recep:24/7; Note: café, bag hold, bar, laundry, tours

Porto Downtown Hostel, Praça de Guilherme Fernandes 66 Oporto; *portodowntownhostel.com/*, T:222018094; $20bed, Kitchen:Y, B'fast:Y, Pvt. room:N, Locker:Y, Recep:24/7; Note: laundry, bag hold, tea/cof, ATM, café, tours, central

Yes Hostels, Rua Arquitecto Nicolau Nazoni 31, Porto; *yeshostels.com/*, T:+351/222082391, *infoporto@yeshostels.com*; $18Bed, Kitchen:Y, B'fast:Y, Pvt. room:N, Locker:Y, Recep:24/7; Note: bar, café, laundry, bag hold, tea/coffee

Dixo's Oporto Hostel, Rua Mouzinho da Silveira 72, Porto; T:222444278, *Info@ dixosoportohostel.com/*; $23Bed, Kitchen:Y, B'fast:Y, Pvt.room:Y, Locker:Y, Recep:24/7; Note: bar, café, laundry, bag hold, tours, tea/coffee, central

Pilot Hostel, Largo Alberto Pimentel 11, Porto; *pilot@ pilothostel.com/*, T:222084362; $14Bed, Kitchen:Y, B'fast:$, Pvt.room:N, Locker:Y, Recep:24/7; Note: central, arpt trans, bar, bikes, laundry, bag hold, tea/coffee, tours

Porto Lounge Hostel, Rua do Almada 317, Porto; T:+351/222085196, *Info@ portoloungehostel.com/*; $18Bed, Kitchen:Y, B'fast:Y, Pvt.room:Y, Locker:Y, Recep:24/7; Note: bar, bag hold, tours, tea/coffee, cash only, central

Oporto Invictus Hostel, Rua Oliveiras 73, Porto; T:222024371, *Info@ oportoinvictushostel.com/*, $20Bed, Kitchen:Y, B'fast:Y, Pvt.room:Y, Locker:Y, Recep:24/7; Note: central, shuttle, café, bar, bikes, laundry, bag hold, tours, tea/cof

Gallery-Hostel, Rua de Miguel Bombarda 222, Porto; T:224964313, *Info@ gallery-hostel.com/*, $21Bed, Kitchen:Y, B'fast:Y, Pvt.room:Y, Locker:Y, Recep:24/7; Note: café, bar, bikes, laundry, bag hold, tours

Wine Hostel, Campo Mártires da Pátria, Porto; T:+351/222013167, *Info@ winehostel.pt/*; $17Bed, Kitchen:Y, B'fast:$, Pvt.room:Y, Locker:Y, Recep:24/7; Note: arpt trans, bikes, laundry, bag hold, tours, maps, TV, partyy

Myosotis Oporto Hostel, Rua de Costa Cabral 690, Porto; T:965119979, *myosotisoportohostel.com/*, *myosotisoportohostel@gmail.com*, Kitchen:Y, B'fast:$, Pvt.room:Y, Locker:Y, Recep:2>10p; Note: laundry, bag hold, not cntr

Magnolia Hostel, Avenida Rodrigues de Freitas 387, Porto; T:222014150, *mail@ magnoliahostel.com /*; $14Bed, Kitchen:Y, B'fast:Y, Pvt.room:Y, Locker:Y, Recep:24/7; Note: arpt trans, bar, laundry, bag hold, parking, tour desk, central

Oporto City Hostel, Rua Guedes de Azevedo 219, Porto; *oportocityhostel. com/*, T:222084452, *oportocityhostel@gmail.com*; $13Bed, Kitchen:Y, B'fast:$, Pvt. room:Y, Locker:N, Recep:ltd; Note: cash only, arpt trans, bag hold, tea/coffee

Porto Alive Hostel, Rua das Flores 138, Porto; *portoalivehostel.com/*, T:220937693, *portoalivehostel@gmail.com*; $14Bed, Kitchen:Y, B'fast:Y, Pvt. room:Y, Locker:Y, Recep:24/7; Note: arpt trans, café, bar, bikes, laundry, bag hold, tours, central

Eden House-Porto Hostel, Rua dos Bragas 95, Porto; T:914167886, *Info@ edenhouse-portohostel.com/*, $14Bed, Kitchen:N, B'fast:Y, Pvt.room:Y, Locker:N, Recep:ltd; Note: arpt trans, café, minibar, laundry, bag hold, tea/coffee, cash, center

Nasoni Guest Hostel, Galeria de Paris 82, Porto; *nasoniguesthostel.org/*, T:222083807, *nasoniguesthostel@gmail.com*; $23Bed, Kitchen:Y, B'fast:Y, Pvt. room:Y, Locker:N, Recep:3>11p; Note: bikes, bag hold, tea/coffee, parking $

Andarilho Oporto Hostel, Rua da Firmeza n° 364, Porto; *andarilhohostel. com/*, T:222012073, *andarilhohostel@gmail.com*; $17Bed, Kitchen:Y, B'fast:Y, Pvt. room:N, Locker:Y, Recep:24/7; Note: arpt trans, café, bar, bikes, laundry, bag hold, tea/cof, tours

Hostel Gaia Porto, Rua Cândido dos Reis, #374-376, Vila Nova de Gaia T:224968282, *info@ hostelgaiaporto.pt/*; $20Bed, Kitchen:Y, B'fast:Y, Pvt.room:Y, Locker:Y, Recep:7;30a>12m; Note: arpt trans, bar, café, tea/cof, parking, bikes, laundry

Peste Surf Camp, Avenida Vasco da Gama 720, Arcozelo; T:+351/916493826, *Info@ pestesurfcamp.com/*; $31Bed, Kitchen:Y, B'fast:Y, Pvt.room:Y, Locker:N, Recep:ltd; Note: arpt trans, bar, parking

Antas Ville, Rua da Vigorosa, 736, Porto; *antasville@gmail.com*, T:225020414, (see FB page); $18Bed, Kitchen:Y, B'fast:Y, Pvt.room:Y, Locker:Y, Recep:24/7; Note: arpt trans, bar, bikes, laundry, bag hold, tea/coffee, parking, not central

HI Porto YH, Rua Paulo da Gama 551, Porto; *hihostels.com/*, T:226177257, *porto@movijovem.pt*; $17Bed, Kitchen:Y, B'fast:Y, Pvt.room:Y, Locker:N, Recep:ltd; Note: close 12n>5p, bar, café, billiards, wh/chair ok, lift, laundry, bag hold, tours, beach

Oporto Fado Hostel, Rua Álvares Cabral 213, Porto, *oportofadohostel.com/*, T:910635555, *oportofadohostel@gmail.com*; $18Bed, Kitchen:Y, B'fast:Y, Pvt. room:N, Locker:N, Recep:2>10p; Note: arpt trans, bag hold, tea/coffee, maps

Duas Nacoes, Praça de Guilherme Gomes Fernandes 59, Oporto; *duasnacoes.com.pt/*, T:+351/222081616, *duasnacoes@sapo.pt*; $27Bed, Kitchen:Y, B'fast:$, Pvt.room:Y, Locker:N, Recep:call 5p>; Note: bikes, bag hold, parking $, cash

Into the Blue Hostel, Rua Godinho 612, Matosinhos, *anubys.wix.com/ hostel/*, T:+351/219376043, *intothebluehostel@gmail.com*; $21Bed, Kitchen:Y, B'fast:Y, Pvt.room:Y, Locker:Y, Recep:4>8:30p; Note: café, TV, cash only, surf camp

POVOA DE VARZIM is a city of 64,000 on the far north coast of Portugal, with an ancient history going back thousands of years. It is also one of Portugal's foremost beach resorts. Carnaval is big, as is the festival to St. Peter in late June and Anjo at Easter. Fishermen there have a unique culture with possible Nordic roots.

Sardines and Friends, R. Ponte 4, Povoa de Varzim; T:913048648, *hostel@ sardinesandfriends.com/*; $21Bed, Kitchen:Y, B'fast:$, Pvt.room:Y, Locker:Y, Recep: advise ETA; Note: arpt trans, café, bag hold, tea/coffee, cash only

3 Hostels) SAGRES is a town of almost 2000 on Portugal's southwesternmost tip. Prince Henry the navigator lived here, the better to discover a whole new world.

Good Feeling, Sitio Eiras de Cima - Raposeira, Sagres; T:914658807, *Info@ thegoodfeeling.com/*; $21Bed, Kitchen:Y, B'fast:$, Pvt.room:Y, Locker:Y, Recep:24/7; Note: resto/bar/club, laundry, bag hold, tea/cof, tours, shuttle, bikes, parking

Algarve Surf Hostel Sagres, rua Mestre Antonio Galhardo, Sagres; *Info@ algarvesurfschool.com/*, T:962846771; $25Bed, Kitchen:Y, B'fast:Y, Pvt.room:Y, Locker:Y, Recep:>10p; Note: min 2N, minimart, laundry, parking, tea/coffee

Sagres Natura Surf Camp, R. Mestre António Galhardo, Sagres; T:282624134, *sagresnatura.com/*, $21Bed, *sagresnatura@hotmail.com*;, Kitchen:Y, B'fast:$, Pvt. room:Y, Locker:Y, Recep:12n>9p; Note: café, bikes, hot tub, laundry, prkng, tea/cof

2 Hostels) SETUBAL is a city of 90,000 on the Atlantic coast some 25mi/40km south of Lisbon. There is a dolphin colony in the river and many beaches.

Blue Coast Hostel, Avenida 5 de Outubro, Setúbal; *bluecoasthostel@gmail. com,* T:966363438, *facebook.com/BlueCoastHostel;* $17Bed, Kitchen:N, B'fast:Y, Pvt.room:Y, Locker:N, Recep:24/7; Note: bag hold, tea/coffee, tours, central

Cool Hostel Setubal, Largo do Poço do Concelho n°3, 4°Esq., Setubal; *cool-hostel.pt/,* T:919526111, *cool.hostel.setubal@gmail.com;* $23Bed, Kitchen:Y, B'fast:Y, Pvt.room:N, Locker:Y, Recep: 10a>6p; Note: lift, tea/coffee, hard to find, quiet

2 Hostels) SINTRA is a town of 33,000 within the greater Lisbon metro area. It once was the Moorish stronghold. The castle and environs are now a UNESCO world heritage site. There are also mountains and a nature park.

Sintra Palace, Rua Sotto Mayor, 22, Sintra; *Info@ sintrapalace.com/,* T:219249800; $21Bed, Kitchen:Y, B'fast:Y, Pvt.room:Y, Locker:Y, Recep:24/7; Note: bikes, luggage room, parking, tour desk, central

Almaa Sintra Hostel, Caminho dos Frades 1, Sintra; T:219240008, *Info@ almaasintrahostel.com/;* $25Bed, Kitchen:Y, B'fast:Y, Pvt.room:Y, Locker:Y, Recep:2p>12m; Note: bikes, luggage room, parking, not central

TAVIRA is a city of 26,000 18mi/30km east of Faro. It has roots in ancient Rome and medieval al-Andalus. The Moorish architecture is the main attraction today.

HI Tavira YH, Rua Miguel Bombarda, 36-38, Tavira; *hihostels.com/,* T+351/281326731, *tavira@movijovem.pt;* $16Bed, Kitchen:Y, B'fast:Y, Pvt. room:N, Locker:N, Recep:24/7; Note: billiards, laundry

TOMAR is a city of some 20,000 in central Portugal, and one of its historical jewels. It was originally built by the Knights Templar and was a centre of overseas expansion under Prince Henry. There are many prominent churches and synagogues.

Hostel 2300 Thomar, Rua Serpa Pinto, 43 1º, Tomar; *2300thomar@gmail. com*, T:+351/249324256, (see FB page); $22Bed, Kitchen:Y, B'fast:$, Pvt. room:N, Locker:Y, Recep:9a>11p; Note: bikes, laundry, luggage room, tea/ coffee

TORRES VEDRAS is a city of 75,000 people 30mi/50km north of Lisbon. It is famous for a line of forts built by the British during the Peninsular War in 1810 to defend Lisbon.

Fisica Beach Hostel, Rua da Colonia Balnear, Santa Cruz, Torres Vedras; T:261937220, *geral@ fisicabeachhostel.com* /; $18Bed, Kitchen:Y, B'fast:$, Pvt. room:Y, Locker:Y, Recep:24/7; Note: arpt trans, bar/club, bag hold, parking

5 Hostels) VILA NOVA DE MILFONTES was originally a fishing village, though tourism is now more important, as part of the Nature Park of the Southwest Alentejo and Vicentine Coast. In addition to birds and marine life, there are beaches and ecological tourism, paragliding, a safari park and waterfalls.

Greenway Hostel, Rua Brejo da Estrada 14-A, V.N. Milfontes; T:283997254, *greenwayhostel.com/*, $20Bed, *greenwayhostel@gmail.com*; Kitchen:Y, B'fast:$, Pvt.room:Y, Locker:Y, Recep:ltd; Note: cash only, bikes, café, laundry, tours

Alentejo Surf Camp, Zambujeira do Mar, V.N. de Milfontes; *Info@ alentejosurfcamp.com/*, T: 962349417; $22Bed, Kitchen:N, B'fast:Y, Pvt.room:N, Locker:N, Recep:24/7; Note: arpt trans, resto/bar, bikes, minimart, tours

HI Almograve YH, R. Do Chafariz, Vila Nova de Milfontes; *hihostels. com/*, T:283640000, *almograve@movijovem.pt/*; $14Bed, Kitchen:Y, B'fast:Y, Pvt.room:Y, Locker:Y, Recep:24/7; Note: bar, billiards, café, wh/chair ok, lift, laundry

Ecosurfcamp, Pousadas Velhas apartado 577, Vila Nova de Milfontes; *ecosurfcamp.blogspot.com/*, T:914732652, *surfmilfontes@gmail.com*; $21Bed, Kitchen:Y, B'fast:$, Pvt.room:Y, Locker:Y, Recep:ltd; Note: cash only, bikes, maps

Hakuna Matata Hostel, Rua Dr. Jaures nº3, Zambujeira do Mar; T:918470038, *hostel.hakunamatata@gmail.com*, (see FB page); $21Bed, Kitchen:Y, B'fast:$, Pvt. room:Y, Locker:Y, Recep:ltd; Note: cash only, laundry, tea/coffee

3) Spain

Last bastion of Neanderthals and place of high culture for Cro-Magnons, Spain entered the historical age populated by Celts, Iberians, and Basques. Phoenicians and Greeks founded trading colonies, until the Romans finally conquered and assimilated it totally, calling it Hispania. All Hell broke loose in the 5th century AD with the weakening and eventual fall of Rome, of course, but the country was reunited under the Visigoths.

Muslim Moors arrived in 711 to conquer the country and ruled an ever-diminshing colony there until 1492, the same year that Columbus's discovery of America heralded Spain's arrival on the world stage with the Age of Discovery. That lasted over three hundred years before a decline set in that saw Spain lose almost all of its overseas colonies and then the establishment of a fascist government under Francisco Franco from 1939-1975. With Franco's death, Spain rejoined the European community of which it is now a full member.

For us travelers back in the old days (the 1970's) Spain was almost as much different from the rich countries of Europe as were its Latin American cousins. All that changed with the demise of Generalissimo Franco and Spain's modernization and subsequent inclusion into the Eurozone. It's still a long fall from the glory days of the colonial Golden Age, but many countries have been and will go through that. So it's not as cheap as it was a few generations ago, but still cheaper than the northern European big boys, and indeed one of the liveliest of European countries these days. The nightlife only ends with daylight. Euro is the currency. Spanish is the language. Phone code is +34.

3 Hostels) ALICANTE is a city of over 300,000 in a metro area of almost half a million along the central Valencia coast. The area has been inhabited for over 7000 years, including Greeks and Phoenicians, Carthage and Rome, and finally the Arab Moors until the *Reconquista* in 1246. More recently, it was at the center of the Costa Blanca construction boom... until 2008. Sights include Santa Bárbara castle on Mount Benacantil, the waterfront promenade, Barrio de la Santa Cruz, and L'Areta and El Palmeral Parks. The Bonfires of St. John occur on the summer solstice.

X Hostel, Calle del Tucuman 28, Alicante, *xhostel.com/*, T:+34/654220317; $26Bed, Kitchen:Y, B'fast:$, Pvt.room:Y, Locker:Y, Recep:9a>12m; Note: wh/ chair ok, lift, laundry, tours, tea/coffee, books, c.c. ok, central, roof terrace

Old Centre Hostel, Plaza del Ayuntamiento, 3–1st Fl, Alicante, Valencia, T:965141118, *oldcentrehostel.es/*; $21Bed, Kitchen:Y, B'fast:Y, Pvt.room:Y, Locker:Y, Recep:8a>11p; Note: cash only, maps, beach, marina, central

Hostal de Sal, Carrer del Carmen 9, Alicante; T:+34/965211720, *Info@ hostaldesal.com*; $22Bed, Kitchen:N, B'fast:Y, Pvt.room:Y, Locker:Y, Recep:8:30a>0:30a Note: café/bar, bikes, laundry, luggage room, c.c. ok, maps, central

ALMERIA is a city of almost 200,000 in the southernmost Andalusian region, and capital of the province of the same name. Established by the Moors, its castle Alcazaba is second-largest after the Alhambra. It only fell to the *Reconquista* in 1489.

Albergue Inturjoven Almeria, c/Isla de Fuerteventura, Almeria; *hihostels. com/*, T:902510000, *almeria.itj@juntadeandalucia.es*; $25Bed, Kitchen:N, B'fast:Y, Pvt.room:Y, Locker:Y, Recep:24/7; Note: luggage rm, wh/chair, laundry, nr beach/not ctr

ARCOS de la FRONTERA is a city of 30,000 in southernmost Spain, once on the 'frontier' of the Reconquest, and famous for its ten bells, which tolled throughout the Moorish war. It has a castle, a convent, and numerous historic churches.

CasaBlues, Callejas 19, Arcos de la Frontera, Andalucia, T:34/956700615, *Info@ CasaBlues.com/*; $24Bed, Kitchen:N, B'fast:$, Pvt.room:Y, Locker:N, Recep: call B4; Note: tea/coffee, cat, laundry, luggage room, cliff view, B&B-like

88 Hostels) BARCELONA has a history that goes back to the Romans and the Carthaginians before them, the name possibly deriving from Hamilcar Barca, Hannibal's father. It was a camp for the Romans and gradually grew into a city, briefly the capital of Visigothic Spain, and then a victim of Arab conquest for some years before being liberated by Charlemagne's son Louis. It reached its peak of importance as part of the Crown of Aragon until union with Castile initiated a decline as second city to Madrid. Nowadays it may not be the country's capital of government, but it's definitely the capital of fun. It used to be the capital of industry.

Barcelona is well-connected to the rest of Europe by budget airlines, trains and Eurolines buses. This is the jumping-off point to Andorra, also, both of them members of the Catalonia club. The Gothic Quarter and Gaudi's Sagrada Familia church are top destinations in the city. Then there's Luis Doménechi Montaner's Music Palace, a UNESCO World Heritage site. Museums range from the maritime museum to the waxworks museum, the National Museum of Art of Catalonia, the Federico Marés Museum, the Museum of Modern Art and the Casa de Cervantes. There are also excellent beaches. Las Ramblas is ground zero for hostels, partying, and fun. Barcelona has one of the largest numbers of hostels in the world and quality is good.

Alberg de Centre Esplai, C/ Rlu Anoia 42-54, El Prat de Llobregat, Barcelona; *alberguesplaibarcelona.com/*, T:934747474, *acces@esplai.org*; $31Bed, Kitchen:N, B'fast:N, Pvt.room:Y, Locker:Y, Recep:24/7; Note:resto, bikes, wh/chair ok, lift, laundry

Estrella de Mar Hostel, C/ del Turisme 60, Calella, Barcelona; *estrella@estrellademarhostel.com/*, T:+34/937662604; $19Bed, Kitchen:Y, B'fast:$, Pvt.room:Y, Locker:N, Recep:24/7; Note: lift, tour desk, beach, laundry, 1 hr>Barcelona

Barcelona Central Garden Hostel, C/ Roger de Llúria 41, Barcelona; *barcelonacentralgarden.com/*, T:935006999, *barcelonagarden@gmail.com*; $18bed,

Kitchen:Y, B'fast:N, Pvt.room:Y, Locker:Y, Recep:9a>12m; Note: laundry, no party

Casa Gracia Barcelona Hostel, Passeig Gràcia 116, Barcelona; T:931874497, *info@ casagraciabcn.com/*; $21bed, Kitchen:Y, B'fast:Y, Pvt.room:Y, Locker:Y, Recep:24/7; Note: c.c. surcharge, laundry, lift, no party

Alberguinn Y. H., Melcior de Palau 70-74, Entresuelo, Barcelona; T:934905965, *alberguinn@ alberguinn.com/*; $18bed, Kitchen:Y, B'fast:Y, Pvt. room:N, Locker:Y, Recep:24/7; Note: a/c, c.c. ok, close to Sants station, not central

Barcelona Pere Tarres Hostel, C/ de Numància, 149 Barcelona; T:934301606, *alberg@ peretarres.org/*; $14bed, Kitchen:Y, B'fast:Y, Pvt.room:Y, Locker:Y, Recep:24/7; Note: a/c, terrace, laundry, bar, restaurant, metro close, not central

Alternative Creative YH, Ronda de la Universitat 17, Barcelona; *alternative-barcelona.com/*, T:635669021, *alvand@alberguest.com*; $23bed, Kitchen:Y, B'fast:N, Pvt.room:N, Locker:Y, Recep:24/7; Note:ages 17-40, café, bikes, a/c, c.c. ok, non-party

Hello BCN Hostel, C/ de Lafont 8, Barcelona; T:934428392, *info@ hellobcnhostel.com*; $23bed, Kitchen:Y, B'fast:Y, Pvt.room:Y, Locker:Y, Recep:24/7; Note: bar, wheelchair ok, luggage room, laundry, tour desk, a/c, c.c. ok

Downtown Paraiso Hostal, C/ de la Junta de Comerç, 13, Barcelona; *hostaldowntownbarcelona.com/*, T:933026134; $33bed, Kitchen:Y, B'fast:N, Pvt. room:Y, Locker:Y, Recep:>10p; Note: luggage room, c.c. ok, TV/DVD, some noise

Albareda Youth Hostel, Carrer d'Albareda 12, Barcelona; T: 934439466, *albareda-youthhostel.com/*; $12bed, Kitchen:Y, B'fast:Y, Pvt.room:Y, Locker:Y, Recep:24/7; Note: min. stay 2N, tour desk, a/c, c.c. ok, central, left luggage fee

Hostel Duo, C/ del Rosselló 220, principal, Barcelona; T:+34(0)932720977, *info@ hostelduo.com/*; $24bed, Kitchen:N, B'fast:$, Pvt.room:Y, Locker:Y, Recep:24/7; Note: lift, luggage room, c.c. ok

Buba House, C/ d'Aragó 239, Barcelona; T:935008318, *info@ bubahouse. com/*; $24bed, Kitchen:Y, B'fast:Y, Pvt.room:Y, Locker:Y, Recep:24/7; Note: lift, luggge room, free tour, travel desk, central

The Kabul Hostel, Plaça Reial 17, Barcelona; T:933185190, *info@ kabul. es/*; $18bed, Kitchen:N, B'fast:Y, Pvt.room:N, Locker:N, Recep:24/7; Note: wheelchair ok, bar/club, free tour, travel desk, laundry, a/c

Lullaby Plaza Catalunya, Rambla Catalunya 12 Ppal; T:933019610, $30bed

Lullaby Gardens Hostel, C/ Provença 318, E 1°, Barcelona; T:934961874, *provenca@ lullabyhostels.com/*; $18bed, Kitchen:Y, B'fast:Y, Pvt.room:N, Locker:Y, Recep:24/7; Note: café, lift, luggage room, laundry, a/c, c.c. ok, parties

Ona Barcelona, C/ del Consell de Cent 413, Barcelona; T:931858317, *info@ onabarcelona.com/*; $21bed, Kitchen:N, B'fast:N, Pvt.room:Y, Locker:Y, Recep:24/7; Note: laundry, a/c, c.c. ok, non-tourist area

Mediterranean YH, C/ de la Diputació 335, Barcelona; T:932440278, *info@ mediterraneanhostel.com/*; $15bed, Kitchen:Y, B'fast:N, Pvt.room:Y, Locker:Y, Recep:24/7; Note:wh/chair ok, luggage room, laundry, a/c, c.c. ok

Hip Karma Hostel, Ronda de Sant Pere 39, Barcelona; *hipkarmahostel. com/*, T:933021159, *hipkarmahostel@gmail.com*; $22bed, Kitchen:Y, B'fast:N, Pvt. room:N, Locker:Y, Recep:24/7; Note: lift, bikes, free tour, a/c, c.c. ok, hard find, bunk curtains

A&A Arco YH, C/ de l'Arc de Santa Eulàlia, 1 Barcelona; *hostalarco.com/*, T:934125468; $24bed, Kitchen:Y, B'fast:Y, Pvt. room:N, Locker:Y, Recep:24/7; Note: wheelchairs OK, tour desk, laundry, c.c. OK, central

Somnio Hostel, C/ de la Diputació 251, Barcelona; T:932725308, *info@ somniohostels.com/*; $25bed, Kitchen:N, B'fast:$, Pvt.room:Y, Locker:Y, Recep:24/7; Note: bar, lift, tour desk, c.c. ok, central

Hostel New York, C/Gignàs 6, T:933150304, *newyork@ bcnalberg.com/*, $15

Albergue Palau, Albergue Palau, C/ Palau 6, Barcelona; T:934125080, *palau@ bcnalberg.com/*; $15bed, Kitchen:Y, B'fast:Y, Pvt.room:Y, Locker:Y, Recep:24/7; Note: close to supermarket, c.c. ok, linen fee

Arian Y. H., Av. De la Mare de Déu de Montserrat 251, Barcelona; T:696504933, *info@ arianyouthhostel.com/*; $23bed, Kitchen:Y, B'fast:N, Pvt. room:Y, Locker:Y, Recep:24/7; Note: tour desk, laundry, c.c. ok

St. Christophers, Carrer de Bergara 3, Barcelona; T:+34/931751401, *Barcelona@ st-christophers.co.uk/*; $16Bed, Kitchen:Y, B'fast:Y, Pvt.room:Y, Locker:Y, Recep:24/7; Note: resto/club, billiards, wh/chair ok, lift, bag hold, partyyy

360 Hostel Barcelona, Carrer Bailèn 7, Barcelona; T:+34/932469973 *Barcelona@* 360hostel.com/; $28Bed, Kitchen:Y, B'fast:N, Pvt.room:N, Locker:Y, Recep:24/7; Note: café, wh/chair ok, laundry, luggage rm, tour desk, tea/ coffee, nr metro

The Hipstel, Carrer de Valencia 266, Barcelona; T:+34/931745417; *reservations@ thehipstel.com/*; $18Bed, Kitchen:Y, B'fast:Y, Pvt.room:Y, Locker:Y, Recep:24/7; Note: club, bikes, lift, bag hold, tours, shuttle, tea/coffee, pub crawl

Backpackers BCN Diputacio, Diputació 323, ppral.1a; T:934880280, $24bed

Backpackers BCN Casanova, Casanova 52, Barcelona; T:935666725; *bookabed@ backpackersbcn.com/*; $18Bed, Kitchen:Y, B'fast:Y, Pvt.room:N, Locker:Y, Recep:24/7; Note: wh/chair, lift, luggage room, laundry, tea/coffee, a/c

Itaca Hostel, c/ Ripoll 21, Barcelona; T:+34/933019751, *pilimili@ itacahostel. com/*; $13Bed, Kitchen:Y, B'fast:Y, Pvt.room:Y, Locker:Y, Recep:>8p; Note: café/bar, books, luggage room, tour desk, tea/coffee, maps

INOUT Hostel, Carrer Major del Rectoret 2, Barcelona, *inouthostel.com/*, T:+34/932800985, *info@inoutalberg.com*; $11Bed, Kitchen:Y, B'fast:Y, Pvt. room:Y, Locker:Y, Recep:24/7; Note:not ctr, nr metro, pool, resto/bar, billiards, lift, wh/chair ok

Amistat Beach Hostel, c/ Amistat 21-23, Barcelona; T:+34/932213281; *Info@ amistatbeachhostel.com/*; $25Bed, Kitchen:Y, B'fast:Y, Pvt.room:N, Locker:Y, Recep:Y Note:partyyy, wh/chair ok, lift, laundry, luggage rm, tea/coffee, supermkt, nr beach/metro

Black Swan Hostel, Carrer Ali Bei 15, Barcelona; T:+34/932311369; *Info@ blackswanhostel.com/*; $9Bed, Kitchen:Y, B'fast:$, Pvt.room:Y, Locker:Y, Recep:24/7; Note: lift, luggage room, a/c, maps, TV, shuttle

Twentytu Hi-Tech Hostel, Pamplona 114-116, Barcelona; T:+34/932387185, *reservas@ twentytu.com/*; $24Bed, Kitchen:Y, B'fast:Y, Pvt.room:Y, Locker:Y, Recep:ltd; Note: bikes, near center/beach, roof patio

Generator Hostel Barcelona, Carrer de Còrsega 377, Barcelona; *Info@ generatorhostels.com,* T:+34/932200377; $22Bed, Kitchen:N, B'fast:$, Pvt.room:Y, Locker:Y, Recep:24/7; Note: café, billiards, wh/chair ok, lift, laundry, luggage rm, tours

Paraiso Travellers Hostel, Ronda de Sant Pau, 55-57 Ppal 1, Barcelona; *paraisohostel.com/,* T:+34/933299378, *paraisohostel@yahoo.com*; $27Bed, Kitchen:N, B'fast:N, Pvt.room:Y, Locker:Y, Recep:24/7; Note: café, lift, luggage room, maps

Fabrizzios Terrace, C/Girona 49 ppal; *fabrizziosterrace@*, T:664891485, $29

Fabrizzios Guesthouse Barcelona, C/ Consell de Cent 414, 1-1, Barcelona; T:34/676606800, *fabrizziosbarcelona@hotmail.com,* (see FB page); $30Bed, Kitchen:Y, B'fast:Y, Pvt.room:Y, Locker:N, Recep:24/7; Note: cash, café, lift, laundry, tea/coffee

Cool & Chic Hostel, Travessera de Collblanc, 5, Barcelona; T:+34/935097900, *Info@ coolandchichostel.com/*; $17Bed, Kitchen:Y, B'fast:Y, Pvt.room:Y, Locker:Y, Recep:24/7; Note: wh/chair ok, books, maps, laundry, luggage rm, tours, not center

Center Ramblas, Carrer Hospital 63, Barcelona; T:934124069; *reservas@ center-ramblas.com/*; $21Bed, Kitchen:N, B'fast:Y, Pvt.room:N, Locker:Y, Recep:24/7; Note: wh/chair ok, lift, laundry, luggage room, maps, central

Primavera Hostel, Calle Mallorca 330, Barcelona; *primavera-hostel.com/,* T:(+34)931752151; $22Bed, Kitchen:Y, B'fast:$, Pvt.room:Y, Locker:N, Recep:ltd; Note: cash, non-party, near metro

Tailors Hostel, Carrer de Sepulveda 146, Barcelona; *Info@ tailorshostel. com/,* T:+34/932505684; $21Bed, Kitchen:Y, B'fast:$, Pvt.room:N, Locker:N, Recep:24/7; Note: wh/chair ok, lift, laundry, luggage room, tour desk, maps, games

Gracia City Hostel, Carrer de Sant Pere Màrtir 18, Barcelona; *booking@ graciacityhostel.com/*, T:+34/936674115; $14Bed, Kitchen:Y, B'fast:$, Pvt.room:Y, Locker:N, Recep:ltd; Note: café, wh/chair ok, laundry, bag hold, tours, parking

Ideal Hostel, Carrer Unió, 10-12, Barcelona; T:+34/933426177, *idealhostel. com/*; $25Bed, Kitchen:N, B'fast:$, Pvt.room:Y, Locker:Y, Recep:24/7; Note: billiards, wh/chiar ok, laundry, luggage room, tour desk, cash only

Coroleuhouse-BCN, Coroleu 33 Bis, Barcelona; *coroleuhouse-bcn.com/*, T:+34/609318467, *coroleuhouse-bcn@hotmail.com*; $15Bed, Kitchen:Y, B'fast:$, Pvt. room:Y, Locker:N, Recep:ltd; Note: café, luggage rm, coffee/tea, safe dep, not ctr

Hostels Barcelona, Ave Diagonal 578, Barcelona, T:+34/931711450, *WOW@ hostelsbarcelona.es/*; $28Bed, Kitchen:Y, B'fast:Y, Pvt.room:Y, Locker:Y, Recep:24/7; Note: bar/café, billiards, lift, laundry, coffee/tea, c.c. ok, non-central, non-party

Graffiti Hostel, c/ D'Aragó 527, Barcelona, *barcelonatophostels.com/*, T:+34/931863397, *graffiti.hostel@gmail.com*; $14Bed, Kitchen:Y, B'fast:$, Pvt. room:N, Locker:Y, Recep:24/7; Note: bikes, laundry, luggage rm, a/c, tea/cof, not ctr

Annex Rey Don Jaime Hotel, c/ Jaume I #11, Barcelona; *aaeworldhotels. com/*, T:687279306, *bookings@aaereservations*; $30Bed, Kitchen:N, B'fast:Y, Pvt. room:Y, Locker:N, Recep:24/7; Note: Gothic Quarter, lift, bag hold, tour desk, 2 locations?

Serenity Gotic, Ample 24, Main Fl, 2nd door, Barcelona; *serenitybarcelona. com/*, T:+34/620645448, *serenityhostelsbarcelona@yahoo.com*; $12Bed, Kitchen:Y, B'fast:$, Pvt.room:Y, Locker:N, Recep:>10p; Note: cash, nr beach, cntr, hard find, 'rec age14-40'

The Hostel Box Port, Calle Albareda 6-8, Barcelona: $19bed

The Hostel Box Gaudi, c/ Mare de Déu del Coll 59, Barcelona; *info@ thehostelbox.com/*, T:34/934431310; $14Bed, Kitchen:Y, B'fast:$, Pvt.room:N, Locker:Y, Recep:24/7; Note: wh/chair ok, laundry, bag hold, a/c, maps, c.c. ok

Art City Hostel, Rambla de Catalunya 64, 1º-1ª, Barcelona; T:+34/651030431, *facebook.com/artcityhostel/*, $23Bed, *david@artcityhostel.com*, Kitchen:Y, B'fast:$, Pvt. room:Y, Locker:Y, Recep:>12m; Note: cash only, lift, laundry, luggage rm, tea/cof

Sun & Moon Hostel, c/ de Ferran 17, Barcelona, *hostelbcn-sunmoon.com/*, T:+34/932702060, *Info@smhostel.net*; $17Bed, Kitchen:Y, B'fast:Y, Pvt.room:Y, Locker:Y, Recep:24/7; Note: arpt trans, café, wh/chair ok, lift, luggage room, parking

Hostelscat, c/ de Panissars 5, Barcelona; T:+34/936672706, *Info@ hostelscat.com/*; $32Bed, Kitchen:Y, B'fast:Y, Pvt.room:N, Locker:Y, Recep:24/7 Note: wh/chair ok, lift, luggage room, tea/coffee, maps, a/c, near train

Tierra Azul Hostel, c/ de Valencia, 223 Pral. 2, Barcelona; T:+34/935285505, *tierraazulhostel.com/*; $32Bed, Kitchen:Y, B'fast:$, Pvt.room:Y, Locker:N, Recep:24/7; Note: café, lift, laundry, luggage room, tour desk, a/c, books, cash only

After Hostel, Enric Granados 52, Barcelona; *afterhostel.com/*, T:+34/934518541 $26Bed, Kitchen:Y, B'fast:$, Pvt.room:Y, Locker:Y, Recep:24/7; Note: bikes, café/club, laundry, coffee/tea, maps, fax, c.c. ok, near metro, not central

Albergue La Ciutat, C/ Alegre de Dalt n° 66, Barcelona; *laciutat@laciutat.com*, T:+34/932130300; $17Bed, Kitchen:Y, B'fast:$, Pvt.room:Y, Locker:Y, Recep:24/7; Note: wh/chair ok, lift, luggage room, basic

Cool Hostel, 44 La Rambla 2nd Fl, Barcelona; *cool.hostel@gmail.com*, T:933012184, (see FB page); $17Bed, Kitchen:N, B'fast:N, Pvt.room:Y, Locker:N, Recep:24/7; Note: location, location, loca-...

My Bed BCN, c/Sant Germà 15, Barcelona; *mybedbcn.com/*, T:+34/936243978, *info.mybedbcn@gmail.com*; $18Bed, Kitchen:Y, B'fast:$, Pvt. room:Y, Locker:Y, Recep:24/7; Note: luggage room, tour desk, tea/coffee

Albergue Studio Hostel, Carrer Duquessa d'Orleans 56, Barcelona; *Info@ alberguestudio.com/*, T:+34/932050961; $18Bed, Kitchen:N, B'fast:Y, Pvt.room:Y, Locker:Y, Recep:24/7; Note: laundry, luggage rm, tour desk, forex, tea/cof

Bedcelona Gracia, Legalitat 17, Barcelona, T:+34/932196505, *info@*, $18bed

Bedcelona Beach Club, Baluart 106, Barceloneta, Barcelona; T:+34/936673628, *info@ bedcelona.com*; $15Bed, Kitchen:Y, B'fast:$, Pvt.room:Y, Locker:Y, Recep:12n>6p; Note: laundry, luggage rm, tour desk, tea/cof, a/c, c.c. ok, hard find, cozy

Hostel Casa Kessler, c/ Enric Granados, 30 Entresuelo, Barcelona; *Info@ casakesslerbarcelona.com/*, T:+34/935285742; $26Bed, Kitchen:Y, B'fast:$, Pvt. room:Y, Locker:Y, Recep:24/7; Note: café, laundry, bag hold, tours, maps

Hostal Fernando, Carrer Ferran 31, Barcelona; T:+34/933017993, *reservas@ hfernando.com/*; $31Bed, Kitchen:Y, B'fast:Y, Pvt.room:Y, Locker:Y, Recep:24/7; Note: a/c, c.c. ok, Gothic quarter

De Lis Guest House, Carrer de Bailèn 190, Barcelona; T:+34/666899578, *contact@ delisguesthouse.com/*; $33Bed, Kitchen:Y, B'fast:$, Pvt.room:Y, Locker:N, Recep:ltd; Note: arpt trans, lift, laundry, tea/coffee, maps, safe deposit

Pillow One Barcelona, c/Montserrat 13, Barcelona, *pillowonebarcelona. com/*; T:+34/936671081, *pillowonebarcelona@pillowhostels.com*; $17Bed, Kitchen:Y, B'fast:Y, Pvt.room:Y, Locker:Y, Recep:1p>12m; Note: tea/coffee, central, basic

Bon Moustache Hostel, Girona 33, Barcelona; *hola@ bonmoustachehostel. com*, T:+34/936672473; $28Bed, Kitchen:Y, B'fast:$, Pvt.room:Y, Locker:Y, Recep:advise ETA; Note: laundry, luggage room, tour desk, tea/coffee, c.c. ok

AWA Relax, Av de la Rep Argentina 256, (PRAL 1), Barcelona; $31bed

AWA Barcelona Hostel Central, Pelai 11, buzz 'Casa', Barcelona, Spain; T:+33/970440194, *reservations@ awahostels.com/*; $25bed, Kitchen:Y, B'fast:N, Pvt.room:Y, Locker:Y, Recep:24/7; Note: a/c, laundry, good location

AWA Plaza Catalunya Hostel, Diputacio 251, Tercero, Barcelona; T:+33/970440194, *reservations@ awahostels.com/*; $28bed, Kitchen:Y, B'fast:N, Pvt.room:Y, Locker:N, Recep:24/7; Note: a/c, lounge, tours, new

Urbany BCN GO, Gran Via 563; *urbanyhostels.com/*, T:937379618, $17

Barcelona Urbany Hostel, Av de la Meridiana, 97, Barcelona; *info@ barcelonaurbany.com/*, T:932458414, *urbanyhostels.com*; $17bed, Kitchen:Y, B'fast:Y, Pvt.room:Y, Locker:Y, Recep:24/7; Note: pool, a/c, gym, resto/bar, laundry, lift, rooftop

Feetup Mellow Eco Hostel, Aguilar 54, Barcelona; T:933575280, *mellow@*, $23

Feetup Yellow Nest Hostel, Passatge Regente Mendieta 5, T:934490596; *nest@*

Feetup Hostels-Garden House Barcelona, C/ Hedilla 58, Barcelona; *gardenhouse@ feetuphostels.com/*, T:934272479; $17bed, Kitchen:Y, B'fast:$, Pvt. room:Y, Locker:N, Recep:24/7; Note: non-party, far from center

Equity Point Sea, Plaça del Mar 1-4 *infosea@equity-point.com* T:932312045

Equity Point Gothic, c/Vigatans 5, T:932312045, *infogothic@ equity-point.com/*

Equity Point Centric, Passeig de Gràcia, 33, Barcelona; T:932156538, *infocentric@ equity-point.com*; $17bed, Kitchen:Y, B'fast:Y, Pvt.room:N, Locker:Y, Recep:24/7; Note: bar, tour desk, laundry, elevator, terrace

Hostel One Paralelo, c/ Salvà, 62, Barcelona; T:934439885, *hosteloneparalelo@ onehostel.com/*; $23bed, Kitchen:Y, B'fast:$, Pvt.room:N, Locker:Y, Recep:8a>10p; Note: free city tour, swimming pool, A/C, c.c. ok

Hostel One Sants, c/ Casteras 9, Barcelona; T:933324192, *hostelonesants@ onehostel.com/*; $18bed, Kitchen:Y, B'fast:$, Pvt.room:N, Locker:Y, Recep:9a>12m; Note: a/c, c.c. ok, bar, laundry, not central, nr transport

Be Sound Hostel, C/ Nou de la Rambla 91, Barcelona; T:(0034)931850800, *sound@ behostels.com/*; $22bed, Kitchen:Y, B'fast:Y, Pvt.room:N, Locker:Y, Recep:24/7; Note: a/c, c.c. ok, laundry, rooftop drinks

Be Mar Hostel, C/ Sant Pau, 80 Barcelona; *barcelonamar.com/*, T:933248530, *mar@behostels.com*; $19bed, Kitchen:Y, B'fast:Y, Pvt.room:N, Locker:Y, Recep:24/7; Note: laundry, tour desk, city tour, a/c, c.c. surcharge

Be Dream Hostel, Avinguda Alfons XIII, 28, Barcelona; T:933991420, *dream@ behostels.com/*; $17bed, Kitchen:Y, B'fast:Y, Pvt.room:Y, Locker:Y, Recep:24/7; Note: nr beach, 30-day cancel, lounge, laundry, c.c. ok

Sant Jordi' Gracia, c/ Terol 35, Barcelona; T:+34/933424161, *gracia@* $22

Sant Jordi' Diagonal, Diagonal 436, entresuelo, Barcelona; T:932183997, *diagonal@santjordi.org*; $22bed, Kitchen:Y, B'fast:N, Pvt.room:Y, Locker:Y, Recep:9a>12m; Note: tea & coffee, laundry, lounge, c.c. ok

Sant Jordi Arago', Aragó 268 Pral. 1, Barcelona; *santjordihostels.com/*, T:932156743, *arago@santjordi.org*; $22bed, Kitchen:Y, B'fast:N, Pvt.room:N, Locker:Y, Recep:9a>10p; Note: laundry, café, bag hold, small, nr train, good location

Sant Jordi' Mambo Tango, C/ Poeta Cabanyes 23, Barcelona; *santjordihostels.com/*, T:934425164, *mambotango@santjordi.org*; $21bed, Kitchen:Y, B'fast:Y, Pvt.room:N, Locker:Y, Recep:24/7; Note: café & bar, laundry, bag hold, a/c

Sant Jordi Sagrada Familia, C/ Freser, 5 Barcelona; T:934460517, *sagradafamilia@ santjordi.org/*; $15bed, Kitchen:Y, B'fast:N, Pvt.room:Y, Locker:Y, Recep:24/7; Note: party hostel, not central, laundry, elevator

Sant Jordi Alberg, Roger de Lluria 40, piso 1° puerta 2ª, Barcelona; T:+34/933023901, *lluria@ santjordi.org*; $22bed, Kitchen:Y, B'fast:N, Pvt. room:N, Locker:Y, Recep:24/7; Note: party hostel, laundry, TV, tea & coffee

9 Hostels) BILBAO is the capital of Biscay province in Basque country, and is Spain's tenth largest city. Tourism is now a major industry in Bilbao, and its tourist attractions include the Guggenheim Museum. There is also the 14th C. Cathedral of Santiago in Gothic style, the 19th C. Plaza Nueva, San Antonio, Santos Juanes, and San Nicholas.

Ganbara Hostel, Calle Prim 11, Bilbao; *info@ ganbarahostel.com/*, T:944053930; $24bed, Kitchen:Y, B'fast:Y, Pvt.room:N, Locker:Y, Recep:24/7; Note: bike rent, wh/chairs ok, luggage room, laundry, tour info, a/c

Surf Backpackers, Calle Ercilla 11 1° Izq, Vizkaia Bilbao; *surfbackpackers. com*, T:+34(0)944754214, *surfbpsbilbao@gmail*; $21bed, Kitchen:Y, B'fast:Y, Pvt. room:N, Locker:Y, Recep:ltd; Note: café, bikes, luggage rm, a/c, c.c. ok, @ Guggenheim, no sign

Botxo Galery/Y. H. Bilbao, Ave. de las Universidades, Bilbao; T:944134849, *info@ botxogallery.com/*; $21bed, Kitchen:Y, B'fast:Y, Pvt.room:N, Locker:Y, Recep:ltd; Note: whelchairs ok, vending, forex, c.c. ok, a/c, triple bunks, central

Pilpil Hostel, Av. Sabino Arana 14, Bilbao; *Info@ pilpilhostel.com/*, T:T:+34/944345544; $21Bed, Kitchen:N, B'fast:Y, Pvt.room:N, Locker:Y, Recep:24/7; Note: bikes, wh/chair ok, luggage room, tour desk, tea/coffee, maps, books, TV, nr bus

BBK Bilbao Good Hostel, Av. Miraflores, 16, Bilbao; T:+34/944597759; *Info@ bbkbilbaogoodhostel.com/*; $24Bed, Kitchen:N, B'fast:Y, Pvt.room:Y,

Locker:Y, Recep:24/7; Note: café/bar, wh/chair ok, lift, luggage rm, tour desk tea/cof, prkg, far

Bilbao Akelarre Hostel, Morgan Kalea 4, Bilbao; T:+34/944057713, *Info@ bilbaoakelarrehostel.com/*; $22Bed, Kitchen:N, B'fast:Y, Pvt.room:N, Locker:Y, Recep:24/7; Note: café, wh/chair ok, bikes, bag hold, laundry, tours, nr train

Bilbao Central Hostel, Fernandez del Campo 24-2nd fl, Bilbao; *Info@ bilbaocentralhostel.com*, T:+34/946526057; $28Bed, Kitchen:Y, B'fast:Y, Pvt. room:Y, Locker:N, Recep:24/7; Note: wh/chair ok, laundry, tea/coffee, central

Moon Hostel Bio, c/ Luzarra 7, Bilbao; T:+34/944750848, *info@ moonhostelbio.com/*; $20Bed, Kitchen:N, B'fast:$, Pvt.room:N, Locker:Y, Recep:10:30//10p; Note: lift, laundry, c.c. ok

Albergue Aterpetxea Bilbao, Ctra Basurtu-Kastrexana 70, Bilbao; *Info@ alberguebilbao.net/*, T:+34/944270054; $26Bed, Kitchen:Y, B'fast:Y, Pvt.room:Y, Locker:Y, Recep:24/7; Note: wh/chair ok, resto, bikes, laundry, bag hold, tours

4 Hostels) CADIZ is a city of 125,000, in an urban area five times that size, in the far southeast of the country. Founded by Phoenicians as Agadir, it is sometimes considered the oldest city in Europe. It is a peculiar and scenic city on a spit of land surrounded by sea... with declining population. Columbus sailed from here and Francis Drake raided it. Top sights include a unique cathedral, a theater, an old municipal building, an 18th-century watchtower, a vestige of the ancient city wall, and ancient Roman theater.

Cadiz Inn Backpackers, Calle de la Botica 2, Cádiz; T:+34/956262309, *booking@ cadizbackpackers.es/*; $24Bed, Kitchen:Y, B'fast:Y, Pvt.room:Y, Locker:Y, Recep:9a>11:30p; Note:bikes, wh/chair ok, tours, bag hold, tea/coffee, central

Casa Caracol, Suaraez de Salazar 4, Cadiz; *hostel-casacaracol.com/*, T:956261166, *Casacaracol1@gmail.com*; $23Bed, Kitchen:Y, B'fast:Y, Pvt.room:N, Locker:Y, Recep:10a>12m; Note: bikes, wh/chair ok, laundry, bag hold, tours, meals $

La Casa de David, Plaza Jesus Nazareno, 14-2C- 2nd Planta, Cadiz; T:667908935, *david@ hostelcadiz.com*; $30Bed, Kitchen:Y, B'fast:Y, Pvt.room:Y,

Locker:N, Recep:advice ETA; Note:cash, bikes, laundry, tea/coffee, maps, hard find, apt.

Mambo Beach House, Paseo Maritimo s/n, El Palmar, Vejer de la Frontera; *andalucia4you.com/*, T:+34/610306509, *mambobeachhouse@mail.com*; $28Bed, Kitchen:Y, B'fast:Y, Pvt.room:Y, Locker:N, Recep:ltd; 33mi/55km>Cadiz, café, laundry

CALPE is a city of 30,000 only 40mi/67km from Alicante on the central Atlantic coast of Spain. In addition to Roman, Iberian and Arab archeological sites, sites of interest are the Queen's baths, the bird sanctuary, the Gothic Catholic church and the tower of *La Peça*.

Youth Hostel 4YOU, Avda. Ejercitos Espanoles s/n, Calpe, Valencia, *youthhostel4you.com/*, T:+34/965834604; $23Bed, Kitchen:N, B'fast:Y, Pvt. room:Y, Locker:Y, Recep:24/7; Note: resto/bar, wh/chair ok, lift, luggage room

5 Hostels) CORDOBA lies 80 miles (130 km) northeast of Seville on the Guadalquivir River. It, too, was likely Carthaginian in origin. It became capital of Spain's Umayyad Muslims in 756 and grew rapidly thereafter. It was one of the most glorious cities in the world at the start of the previous millennium, full of palaces and mosques, before finally falling to the Christian Castilians in 1236. These days the entire old city is a UNESCO World Heritage site. Main attractions are the Roman Bridge and the Grand Mosque. The caliphs' main palace, the Alcazar, is now in ruins. Other classic buildings include monasteries and churches and the museums of fine art and archeology. Beside the old Moorish quarter there is also a Jewish quarter.

Senses&Colours Anil Hostel, Calle de Barroso 4, Cordoba; T:957491544, *maximo@ sensesandcolours.com/*; $17bed, Kitchen:N, B'fast:N, Pvt.room:Y, Locker:N, Recep:24/7; Note: advise ETA, linen & towel fee, wh/chair ok, a/c, terrace

Senses & Colours Seneca, Calle del Conde y Luque, 7, Cordoba; T:957473234, *seneca@ sensesandcolours.com/*; $18bed, Kitchen:Y, B'fast:N, Pvt. room:Y, Locker:N, Recep:ltd; Note: bar/lounge, tours, c.c. ok, linen/towel fee, Jewish quarter

Cordoba Bed and Be, Calle de José Cruz Conde 22, Córdoba; *cordoba@ bedandbe.com/*, T:+34/661420733; $24Bed, Kitchen:Y, B'fast:Y, Pvt.room:Y, Locker:N, Recep:24/7; Note: arpt trans, café/bar, bikes, books, laundry, luggage room

Albergue Inturjoven Cordoba, Plaza Juda Levi, Cordoba; *hihostels.com/*, T:902510000, *cordoba.itj@juntadeandalucia.es*; $25Bed, Kitchen:N, B'fast:Y, Pvt. room:Y, Locker:N, Recep:24/7; Note: HI, café, wh/chair ok, lift, laundry, luggage rm

Funky Cordoba, Calle Lucano 12, Córdoba; T:+34/957492966, *funkycordoba. com/*, $16Bed, Kitchen:Y, B'fast:N, Pvt.room:Y, Locker:N, Recep:24/7; Note: resto/bar, laundry, luggage room, a/c, central historic area

DENIA is a city of 45,000 halfway between Alicante and Valencia. There is a castle, an ethnologic musem, a ferry to Ibiza, and a huge bonfire of papier mache *fallas* in March.

Denia Meeting Point, Sandunga 50, Denia, Valencia; T:+34/966430935, *Info@ deniameetingpoint.com/*; $28Bed, Kitchen:N, B'fast:Y, Pvt.room:N, Locker:Y, Recep:ltd; Note: bar, wh/chair ok, laundry, bag hold, tour desk, nr ferry/beach/center

ESPINOSA is a village of over 2000 in far northern Spain. It was founded in 1008, has some medieval architecture of note, and some mountain-based tourism.

YH Espinosa de los Monteros, Ctra de Baranda, Espinosa; *hihostels.com/*, T:+34/947120449, *albergueespinosa@hotmail.com*; $18Bed, Kitchen:N, B'fast:Y, Pvt.room:Y, Locker:Y, Recep:10a>8p; Note: 1 hr>Bilbao, resto/bar, pool, laundry, prkng

FISTERRA is a town of 5000 on the westernmost point of Galicia in Spain's northwest, the "land's end" which gives the town its name. It is also the final destination for many pilgrims on the Camino de Santiago, supposedly the burial place of St. James.

Albergue Cabo da Vila, Av. Coruña 13, Finisterre (A Coruña); T:607735474, *alberguecabodavila.com/*, $18Bed, *alberguecabodavila@gmail.com*; Kitchen:Y, B'fast:Y, Pvt.room:Y, Locker:Y, Recep:8>10p; Note: wh/chair ok, laundry, luggage rm

2 Hostels) FUERTEVENTURA is one of the CANARY ISLANDS, second-largest after Tenerife, and a UNESCO Biosphere Reserve. Situated off the coast of Africa, it has pleasant year-round temperatures. There are over 150 beaches, both black sand and white. The population tops 100,000, with many festivals and concerts. Do you like fish?

Surf Riders Fuerteventura, Hierro, 2, Duplex 14, Corralejo, Fuerteventura; T:+34/655182964, *surfridersfuerteventura.com/*; $19Bed, Kitchen:N, B'fast:$, Pvt. room:Y, Locker:N, Recep:9a>10p; Note: cash only, arpt trans, pool, parking, reggae

Sol y Mar (Flag Beach Windsurf & Kitesurf Centre), Corralejo, Fuerteventura *Info@ flagbeach.com/*, T:+34/609029804; $21Bed, Kitchen:Y, B'fast:Y, Pvt.room:Y, Locker:N, Recep:ltd; Note: min 4N, arpt trans, laundry, parking, tea/coffee, central

GERNIKA is a town of over 16,000 in Spain's northern Basque region, famous for the 1937 bombings by Hitler's *Luftwaffe* and Picasso's painting of it. Monday is the town's traditional market and leisure day. There are museums and churches, a peace monument and museum, and a replica of Picasso's masterpiece.

Gernika Lumo Aterpetxea, Kotezubi Bidea, N° 9, Gernika; *hihostels.com/*, T:944650775; *gernika@suspergintza.net*; $35Bed, Kitchen:N, B'fast:$, Pvt.room:N, Locker:N, Recep:9a/7p; Note:resto, bikes, pool, wh/chair ok, lift, tour desk

GIRONA is a city of almost 100,000 in Spain's far northeast Catalan region. There was an important Jewish community and school of Kabbalism in the 12th Century, whose ghetto is now a major tourist attraction. There are also ancient city walls and towers. It is only 62mi/99km from Barcelona. RyanAir lands here.

Equity Point Girona, Plaça Catalunya 23, Girona; *infogirona@ equity-point.com*, T:+34/972417840; $17Bed, Kitchen:Y, B'fast:Y, Pvt.room:Y, Locker:Y, Recep:24/7; Note: bar, wh/chair ok, lift, luggage room, tour desk

GONDOMAR is a town of 14,000 in Spain's northwest Galicia region. There is historic architecture.

Nornas Hostel, Barrio da Igrexa nº15, Gondomar, Galicia, T:+34/986363604, *reservas@ nornashostel.com/*; $Bed, Kitchen:N, B'fast:Y, Pvt.room:N, Locker:N, Recep:10a/8p; Note: bikes, luggage room, wh/chair ok, laundry, tour desk, c.c. ok

10 Hostels) GRAN CANARIA is the second most populous of the Canary Islands, Spain's first overseas colony, and an important stepping-stone to the Americas. One-third of the island is a UNESCO Biosphere Reserve. There is a population of 850,000 of which half that reside in the capital of LAS PALMAS. The climate is subtropical. The city's historic center is scheduled for UNESCO world heritage inclusion. Carnival is good. There are numerous beaches and museums, parks and squares.

Volver Hostel, Las Conchas 11, Puerto de Mogan, Gran Canaria; *write-me@ volverhostel.com/*, T:+34/636154560; $24Bed, Kitchen:Y, B'fast:N, Pvt.room:Y, Locker:Y, Recep:1>7p; Note: min 2N, cash, bikes, books, luggage rm, parking, tea/coffee

Big Fish Hostel Las Palmas, C/ Sargento Llagas 34, Las Palmas; *bigfishhostel.com/*, T:+34/622428830, *bigfishlaspalmas@gmail.com*; $19Bed, Kitchen:Y, B'fast:$, Pvt.room:Y, Locker:Y, Recep:24/7; Note: hot tub, laundry, tea/cof

Downtown House, Domingo J. Navarro 10, Las Palmas de Gran Canaria; T:+34/618089237, *downtown@ houselaspalmas.com/*; $24Bed, Kitchen:Y, B'fast:Y, Pvt.room:Y, Locker:Y, Recep:ltd; Note: bikes, laundry, tea/coffee, cash only

El Warung Cave Hostel, La Cuevita 38, Artenara, Gran Canaria, $19bed

El Warung Beach Hostel, Calle de Portugal, 69, Las Palmas de Gran Canaria; *Info@ elwarung.com*, T:+34/656604290; $17Bed, Kitchen:N, B'fast:Y,

Pvt.room:Y, Locker:Y, Recep:ltd; Note: bikes, supermkt, luggage room, tour desk, parking

Ecohostel Bettmar Canarias, c/Pedro Díaz 20, Las Palmas; T:+34/ 608201108, *Info@ ecohostelcanarias.com/*; $19Bed, Kitchen:Y, B'fast:Y, Pvt. room:N, Locker:Y, Recep:ltd; Note: arpt trans, books, maps, café, bikes, wh/ chair ok, laundry, luggage room

Lua Lua Youth Hostel, Fernando Guanarteme 27, Las Palmas; *Info@ lua-lua.com/*; T:+34/615444037, $17Bed, Kitchen:Y, B'fast:$, Pvt.room:Y, Locker:Y, Recep:ltd; Note: arpt trans, laundry, tour desk, cash only

Blablabla Tasarte, El Lomito 2, Playa de Tasarte, Gran Canaria; T:+34/ 928894375, *blablabla.tasarte@gmail.com* (see FB page), $21Bed, Kitchen:Y, B'fast:$, Pvt.room:Y, Locker:N, Recep:24/7; Note: café, laundry, luggage rm, parking

Pension Ibiza, Nicolas Estevanez #31, Las Palmas de Gran Canaria; *pensionibiza.com/*, T:+34/928263123; $17Bed, Kitchen:N, B'fast:$, Pvt.room:Y, Locker:N, Recep:24/7; Note: lift, near beach/bus, hotel-like, central

Santa Brigida Eco Countryside Hostel, Camino El Tejar (behind 1), Las Meleguinas; *eco.bb.info@gmail.com*, T:+35/628136393, (see FB page); $17Bed, Kitchen:Y, B'fast:Y, Pvt.room:N, Locker:Y, Recep:ltd; Note: min 5N, cash, café, laundry

23 Hostels) GRANADA was a Jewish community before being selected as the capital of Moorish al-Andalus, with the Reconquista in full swing after the fall of Seville in 1248. Nevertheless it was the last bastion of Moorish Spain, lasting until 1492, when the Moors were defeated, then along with the Jews forced to convert or leave. The oldest part of the city is in the northeast Albaicin quarter. The Alhambra "Palace City" was its heart. The Generalife was the palace of the Moorish sultans, and along with the Alhambra and Albaicin, is a UN World Heritage site. Other landmarks include the Cathedral of Granada and the palace of Charles V. The pomegranate ("Granada") is its symbol.

Hostel Almora, Solanilla 7, Niguelas, Granada; *hostelalmora.com/en/*, T:677685800, *hostelalmora@gmail.com*; $18bed, Kitchen:Y, B'fast:$, Pvt.room:Y, Locker:N, Recep:call; Note: linen $, village 50 min ride south of Granada

El Granado, C/ Conde de Tendillas 7, Granada; T:958960259, *info@ elgranado.com/*; $19bed, Kitchen:Y, B'fast:Y, Pvt.room:Y, Locker:Y, Recep:ltd; Note: rooftop terrace, laundry, good location

Rambutan G.H., Vereda de Enmedio 5, Granada; *rambutangranada.com/*, T:958220766, *rambutangranada@hotmail.com*; $17bed, Kitchen:Y, B'fast:Y, Pvt. room:Y, Locker:Y, Recep:24/7; Note: free bikes, great views, long walk from center

Funky Granada, C/ del Conde de las Infantas 15, Granada; T:958800058, *funkygranada.weebly.com/*, $14bed, *funky@altrernativeacc.com*; Kitchen:Y, B'fast:Y, Pvt.room:N, Locker:N, Recep:24/7; Note: bar, city tour, parking, c.c. ok, central

Granada Inn Backpackers, Calle Padre Alcover 10, Granada; *booking@ granadabackpackers.es*, T:+34/958266214; $18Bed, Kitchen:Y, B'fast:Y, Pvt. room:Y, Locker:Y, Recep:24/7; Note: bikes, lift, laundry, bag hold, tour desk, tea/coffee

Oasis Backpackers Hostel Granada, Calle del Correo Viejo 3, Granada; T:+34/958215848, *Granada@ hostelsoasis.com/*; $14Bed, Kitchen:Y, B'fast:N, Pvt. room:Y, Locker:Y, Recep:24/7; Note: café, bar, books, lift, bag hold, laundry, cntr

Makuto Backpackers Hostel, Calle de la Tiña 18, Granada; *makuto.net/*, T:+34/958805876, *Info@makutoguesthouse.com*; $19Bed, Kitchen:Y, B'fast:Y, Pvt. room:Y, Locker:Y, Recep:8a>12m; Note: café, bar, laundry, bag hold, historic dist

Hostel One Granada, Calle de Azhuma 30, Granada; *districthostel1.com/*, T:+34/958521346, *hostelonegranada@onehostel.com*; $15Bed, Kitchen:N, B'fast:Y, Pvt.room:N, Locker:Y, Recep:8a>10p; Note:café/bar, bikes, wh/chair ok, laundry, tea/cof

Fun-da-lucia, Barrio Alto 18, Quentar, Granada; *fundalucia.es/*, T:958485164; $17Bed, Kitchen:Y, B'fast:$, Pvt.room:Y, Locker:N, Recep:advise ETA; Note:8mi-13km>Granada, arpt trans, pool, bikes, laundry, tea/coffee, parking, 'mountain getaway'

White Nest Hostel-Granada, Calle Santísimo San Pedro 4, Granada; *Info@ nesthostelsgranada.com/*; T:+34/958994714; $13Bed, Kitchen:Y, B'fast:$, Pvt. room:Y, Locker:Y, Recep:24/7; Note:café, wh/chair ok, bike, billiards, laundry, bag hold, tea

Polaroid Siesta Hostel, Calle Frailes 28, Granada; *Info@ pshostel.com/*, T:+34/858981040; $18Bed, Kitchen:Y, B'fast:$, Pvt.room:Y, Locker:Y, Recep:ltd; Note:books, bag hold, tea/coffee, supermarket, not central, rooftop views

Funky Meridiano, Calle Angulo 9, Granada, *funkymeridiano. com/* T:+34/958250544; $14Bed, Kitchen:Y, B'fast:Y, Pvt.room:Y, Locker:N, Recep:24/7; Note: laundry, luggage room, tea/coffee, c.c. ok, center

Hotel Nest Style Granada. Plaza del Carmen 29, Granada; *neststylehotels. com/* T:958058708, *booking@neststylegranada.co;* $21Bed, Kitchen:Y, B'fast:$, Pvt.room:Y, Locker:N, Recep:24/7; Note: café, lift, luggage room, tea/coffee, central

Itinere Hostel, C/ Natalio Rivas 1, Granada, *info@ itinerehostel.com/*, T:+34/958994731; $14Bed, Kitchen:Y, B'fast:N, Pvt.room:Y, Locker:Y, Recep:8a>11p; Note: café, lift, laundry, luggage room, tea/coffee, maps, c.c. ok, daily activities

Sweet Albayzin, Calle Horno del Oro 21, Granada; *acasagranada@gmail. com*, T:+34/958073376, (see FaceBook page); $19Bed, Kitchen:Y, B'fast:$, Pvt. room:Y, Locker:N, Recep:ltd; Note:café, bikes, books, laundry, bag hold, maps, tea/cof, rooftop

Hostal Atenas, Gran Via de Colon 38-1, Granada; T:+34/900352708; *Info@ hostalatenas.com/*; $17Bed, Kitchen:N, B'fast:$, Pvt.room:Y, Locker:N, Recep:ltd; Note: historic center, parking, hotel-like

Casa Bombo, Callejón Algibe de Trillo 22, Granada- Albayzin, Granada; T:+34/958290635, *Info@ casabombo.com/*; $25Bed, Kitchen:Y, B'fast:Y, Pvt. room:Y, Locker:Y, Recep:1p>12m; Note: bar, wh/chair ok, laundry, bag hold, tea/coffee, view

Pension Duquesa, C/ Duquesa #10, Granada; *Pensionduquesa-granada. com/*, T:958281983, *duquesagranada@gmail.com;* $19Bed, Kitchen:Y, B'fast:Y, Pvt.room:Y, Locker:N, Recep:24/7; Note: café, bag hold, maps, parking, tea/ coffee, central

Barbieri Granada Hostel, c/Fábrica Vieja 8, Granada; T:+34/958275013, *granada@ barbierihostel.com/*; $14Bed, Kitchen:Y, B'fast:Y, Pvt.room:Y, Locker:Y, Recep:8a>8p; Note: laundry, bag hold, tours, c.c. ok, central

Guesthouse 36, Alhambra s/n, Granada; *guesthouse36.com/*, T:(34)661210326 $14Bed, Kitchen:N, B'fast:N, Pvt.room:Y, Locker:N, Recep:call; Note: very basic

Cuevascoloras, Cuevas Coloradas, Granada; *cuevascoloras.blogspot.com/*, $22Bed, *cuevascoloradas@gmail.com*; Kitchen:Y, B'fast:$, Pvt.room:Y, Locker:N, Recep:advise ETA; Note: arpt trans, café, laundry, tea/coffee, massage, cave in Albaicin

Posada Jose Bocanegra, Cuesta Escoriaza #10, Granada; T:+34/661210328, *hostaljosebocanegra.com/*; $15Bed, Kitchen:Y, B'fast:$, Pvt.room:Y, Locker:N, Recep:2>10p; Note: laundry, tea/coffee, basic

Albergue Inturjoven Granada, Avda Ramon y Cajal 2, Granada; *hihostels. com/*, T:902510000, *granada.itj@juntadeandalucia.es*; $24Bed, Kitchen:N, B'fast:Y, Pvt.room:Y, Locker:N, Recep:24/7; Note: lift, laundry, bag hold, parking, a/c

HUELVA is a city of 150,000 in southwesternernmost Andalusia. It is a maritime city and the resting-place of Columbus's ships. There are festivals for Carnaval, Semana Santa, Columbus, and films. Besides Columbus, Huelva was home to many artists.

Albergue Inturjoven Huelva, Avda Marchena Colombo 14, Huelva; *hihostels.com/*, T:34/955035886, *huelva.itj@juntadeandalucia.es*; $25Bed, Kitchen:N, B'fast:Y, Pvt.room:Y, Locker:N, Recep:24/7; Note: meals, lift, laundry, meals $

2 Hostels) IBIZA is a city of 50,000 on an island of the same name which is not too much bigger. Part of the Balearic Islands, it lies off Spain's Mediterranean coast and is known for its nightlife. Sights include the cathedral of Santa Maria d'Eivissa, the Punic necropolis of Puig des Molins, and the statue of 'Christ, the Sacred Heart of Jesus'.

Hostal Giramundo Ibiza, Carrer Ramon Muntaner 55, Ibiza, Balearic Islands; T:+34/971307640, *Info@ hostalgiramundoibiza.com/*; $25Bed, Kitchen:N, B'fast:Y, Pvt.room:Y, Locker:Y, Recep:8a>1a; Note: resto/bar, minimart, parking, room themes

Hostal Ceibo Ibiza, Medico Jose Costa 2, 5° 4ª, Ibiza, Balearic Islands, T:+34/625925656, *Info@ hostalceiboibiza.com*; $28Bed, Kitchen:N, B'fast:$, Pvt. room:Y, Locker:N, Recep:ltd; Note: central, c.c. ok

IRUN is a Basque city of over 60,000, on the far northern border with France. There are vestiges of the old Roman town of Oiasso here. Border-town b/s dominates the economy.

Albergue Juvenil Martindozenea, Elizatxo Etorbidea 18, Irun, Guipuzcoa; *hihostels.com/*, T:+34/943621042, *albergue@irun.org*; $36Bed, Kitchen:Y, B'fast:Y, Pvt.room:N, Locker:N, Recep:ltd; Note: wh/chair ok, lift, laundry, bag hold

JAEN is a city of 120,000 in south-central Spain in the Santa Catalina hills of an Andalusian province of the same name. It is known as the 'World Capital of Olive Oil.' Nazis bombed here, too, in 1938. The castle is built upon a previous Arab fortress. There are Arab baths, too, plus a Museum of Arts and Popular Customs, the International Museum of Naïf Art, San Andrés's Chapel, and the Provincial Museum of Jaén.

Jaén - Albergue Inturjoven & Spa Jaén, c/ Borja s/n, Jaén; *hihostels.com/*, T:34/955035886, *jaen.itj@juntadeandalucia.es*; $25Bed, Kitchen:N, B'fast:Y, Pvt. room:Y, Locker:N, Recep:24/7; Note: pool, wh/chair ok, lift, laundry, parking

LANZAROTE is the easternmost of the Canary Islands, only 75mi/125km off the coast of Africa, and 600mi/1000km from mainland Spain. The island is volcanic in origin, with a current population or 142,000 and has UNESCO Biosphere Reserve status.

Famara Chill Zone, Calle Roque Del Este 19, Caleta de Famara; *Info@ famarachillzone.com/*, T:+34/638558110; $21Bed, Kitchen:N, B'fast:$, Pvt. room:Y, Locker:N, Recep:ltd; Note: cash only, beach

2 Hostels) LEON is a city of 130,000 in an urban area of a half million in the country's northwest. Once a Roman military camp, it is now a UNESCO world heritage city. It is on the *Camino de Santiago* pilgrimage route. Prominent sites

are the Cathedral, the Basilica of San Isidoro, the Monastery of San Marcos, and the Casa Botines, by Gaudí. Semana Santa is a big deal. It has its own language, in danger of extinction.

Alda Centro Leon Hostel, Calle la Torre, 3, Leon; T:987225594, $20bed

Hotel Alda Casco Antiguo, Cardenal Landzuri, Leon; *aldahostels.es/*, T:987074000; $21Bed, Kitchen:N, B'fast:$, Pvt.room:Y, Locker:N, Recep:24/7; Note: laundry, maps, TV, tour desk, parking, wh/chair ok

LLANES, ASTURIAS is a town of 14,000 on Spain's northern coast. There is a Fiesta on 15 August of the patron saint of the town, *Nuestra Señora del Conceyu,* and three big summer Fiestas: 22 July La Magdalena, 16 August San Roque, and 8 September La Guía. The Battle of Mazuco was fought here in 1937. There are caves and mountains.

Albergue la Estacion, Estacion de Feve s/n, Llanes, Asturias; T:+34/985401458, *alberguelaestacionllanes.net/*, $17Bed, *info@escueladenaturaleza. com*; Kitchen:N, B'fast:$, Pvt.room:N, Locker:Y, Recep:24/7; Note: maps, laundry, tours, tea/coffee

LOGRONO is a city of over 150,000 in the northern La Rioja, famous for wine. Once Roman, then Celt, this was the scene of Basque witch trials during the Inquisition. There are historic churches, museums, and parks. Party on Calles San Juan, Laurel, Portales, and Marques San Nicolas. Fiesta San Mateo is in September, San Bernabe June 11.

Hostel Entresuenos, c/ Portales 12, Bajo esquina, Logroño (La Rioja); T:+34/941271334&5, *info@ hostellogrono.com/*; $26Bed, Kitchen:Y, B'fast:$, Pvt. room:Y, Locker:Y, Recep:advise ETA; Note: wh/chair ok, cash only, a/c, maps

26 Hostels) MADRID is the center of Spanish government and one of the financial capitals of Europe, as well as a center of tourism, but seems far from the Riviera ambience of which Barcelona is one of the capitals. Documented from the ninth century and the Arab era, Madrid rejoined Castile in 1085 and became capital in 1561, capital of an empire that spread around the globe. Today it's one of Europe's largest cities, and has many immigrants

from the countries it once held sway over, giving it a lively cosmopolitan atmosphere.

There are many nightlife and entertainment venues, but it's not the party center that Barcelona is, which may be good. El Prado is one of the best art museums in the world. Others are El Cason del Buen Retiro, Queen Sofia museum, the National Archeological Museum, the Thyssen-Bornemisza Museum, the Royal Academy of Fine Arts of the San Fernando Museum, and the Museum of the Americas. The "*Puerta del Sol*" is one of the busiest and most popular squares. Hostels are good.

Way Hostel, C/Relatores, 17 Madrid, Spain; T:914200583, *reservas@ wayhostel.com/*, $15bed, Kitchen:Y, B'fast:Y, Pvt.room:N, Locker:Y, Recep:24/7; Note: city tour, travel desk, safe deposit, stairs

No Name City Hostel, C/Atocha, 45 Madrid; T:913692919, *info@ nonamecityhostel.com/*; $14bed, Kitchen:Y, B'fast:Y, Pvt.room:N, Locker:N, Recep:24/7; Note: lounge, city tour, laundry, cozy, few power outlets

Los Amigos Sol Hostel, C/Arenal, 26 Madrid; T:915592472, *reservassol@ losamigoshostel.com/*; $26bed, Kitchen:Y, B'fast:Y, Pvt.room:N, Locker:Y, Recep:8a>12m; Note: a/c, c.c. ok, city tour, good location

Equity Point Madrid, C/ de la Cruz, 5 Madrid; T:915323122, *infomadrid@ equity-point.com/*; $13bed, Kitchen:N, B'fast:Y, Pvt.room:Y, Locker:N, Recep:24/7; Note: luggage room, lift, bar, c.c. ok, big hostel, cozy rooms

The Living Roof Hostel Madrid, C/ Costanilla de San Vicente 4, Madrid; *thelivingroofhostel.com/*, T:915230578; $23bed, Kitchen:Y, B'fast:Y, Pvt.room:N, Locker:Y, Recep:24/7; Note: pub crawl, c.c. ok, tours

Barbieri Sol Hostel, C/Victoria 6 piso 2, T:915224198, *bookingsol@*, $14bed

Barbieri Intl. Hostel, C/ Barbieri, 15, Madrid; T:915310258, *booking@ barbierihostel.com/*; $14bed, Kitchen:Y, B'fast:Y, Pvt.room:Y, Locker:N, Recep:24/7; Note: a/c, TV, lounge, c.c. ok

La Posada de Huertas Hostel, C/ Huertas (Centro), 21 Madrid; T:914295526, *info@ posadadehuertas.com/*; $14bed, Kitchen:Y, B'fast:Y, Pvt.room:N, Locker:Y, Recep:24/7; Note: city tour, lounge, laundry, travel desk

Musas Residence, c/Jesus y Maria 12, Madrid; *lasmusashostel.com/*, T:+34/915394984, *Info@ lasmusasresidence.com*; $19Bed, Kitchen:Y, B'fast:N, Pvt. room:Y, Locker:Y, Recep:24/7; Note: lift, laundry, bag hold, tours, tea/cof

U Hostels, Calle Sagasta 22, Madrid; *Info@ uhostels.com/*, T:+34/914450300; $20Bed, Kitchen:N, B'fast:Y, Pvt.room:Y, Locker:?, Recep:24/7; Note: bar/ resto/club, bikes, wh/chair ok, laundry, bag hold, parking, tea/coffee, tours, activities

Living Cat's Hostel, Cañizares 6, Madrid, T:+34/913692807, *Info@ catshostel. com/*; $18Bed, Kitchen:N, B'fast:Y, Pvt.room:Y, Locker:Y, Recep:24/7; Note: bar/ club, wh/chair ok, lift, laundry, bag hold, tour desk, a/c, TV, central, partyyy

Hostel RC Miguel Angel, Plaza de Celenque #1, 4 Izq, Madrid; T:915222355, *reservas@ hostelrcmiguelangel.com/*; $Bed, Kitchen:Y, B'fast:Y, Pvt. room:Y, Locker:Y, Recep:24/7; Note: lift, luggage room, tour desk, a/c, central

360 Hostel Centro, Calle Carmen 16; T:915233192, *madridcentro@,* $19bed

360 Hostel Malasana, Manuela Malasaña 23, 1st, Madrid; T:+34/ 915915579, *madridmalasana@ 360hostel.com/*; $15Bed, Kitchen:Y, B'fast:N, Pvt.room:Y, Locker:Y, Recep:24/7; Note:café, laundry, bag hold, tours, tea/ coffee, not center

Living Mad Hostel, Calle de la Cabeza 24, Madrid, T:+34/915064840, *Info@ madhostel.com/*; $17Bed, Kitchen:N, B'fast:Y, Pvt.room:Y, Locker:Y, Recep:24/7; Note: billiards, wh/chair ok, lift, bag hold, tours, a/c, central

Mucho Madrid, Gran Vía 59, Madrid; T:+34/915592350, *reservas@ muchomadrid.com/*; $25Bed, Kitchen:Y, B'fast:Y, Pvt.room:Y, Locker:Y, Recep:24/7; Note: arpt trans, lift, laundry, bag hold, tea/coffee, tours, maps, a/c

Hostel Era, C/ San Mateo #2-1st Fl, Madrid; T:+34/915314258, *info@ hostelera.es/*; $14Bed, Kitchen:Y, B'fast:$, Pvt.room:N, Locker:N, Recep:24/7; Note: lift, laundry, luggage room, c.c. ok

Hostel Meeting Point, Calle Factor 5, Madrid, *hostelsmeetingpoint. com/* T:+34/915599725; $14Bed, Kitchen:Y, B'fast:N, Pvt.room:N, Locker:Y, Recep:24/7; Note: arpt trans, bikes, laundry, bag hold, tours, tea/coffee, safe dep, central

Madrid Motion Hostel, Calle Mesonero Romanos 7, Madrid; T:+34/915313389, *Info@ motionhostels.com/*; $19Bed, Kitchen:N, B'fast:Y, Pvt. room:Y, Locker:Y, Recep:24/7; Note: café/bar, bikes, arpt trans, lift, laundry, bag hold, tours, central

Room007 Ventura Hostel, Ventura de la Vega, 5, Madrid; *reservas@ room007.com/*, T:914204481; $21Bed, Kitchen:N, B'fast:$, Pvt.room:N, Locker:Y, Recep:24/7; Note: resto/bar, bikes, wh/chair ok, lift, bag hold, tea/coffee, a/c, TV

Backpackers Madrid, San Leonardo 12, Plantas 2ª y 3ª, Madrid; T:915487067, *info@ backpackersmadrid.com*; $11Bed, Kitchen:N, B'fast:$, Pvt. room:Y, Locker:Y, Recep:24/7; Note: resto/bar/club, minimart, lift, laundry, tea/coffee, bag hold, center

Hostal Miralva, c/ Valverde 32 1º Izq., Madrid; T:(+34)913604536, *info@ hostalmiralva.com/*; $18Bed, Kitchen:N, B'fast:N, Pvt.room:Y, Locker:Y, Recep:ltd; Note: lift, luggage room, tour desk

Sol Hostel, calle Bernardino Obregon #25, Madrid; *Info@ solhostel. com/*, T:+34/914686876; $14Bed, Kitchen:Y, B'fast:Y, Pvt.room:Y, Locker:Y, Recep:24/7; Note: arpt trans, café, bar, lift, laundry, luggage room, tour desk, c.c. ok, near museums

Hostal Welcome, Calle de Casas de Miravete 28, Madrid; T:+34/913052712, *hwelcome.com/*;$11Bed, Kitchen:N, B'fast:Y, Pvt.room:Y, Locker:Y, Recep:ltd; Note: laundry, hard find, café, bar, parking $, not central, need car, long-stays

Residencia la Luna, Calle de Aralar 7, Madrid; *residencialaluna.com/*, T:+34/619244969, *residencialaluna@gmail.com*; $24Bed, Kitchen:N, B'fast:Y, Pvt. room:Y, Locker:N, Recep:ltd; Note: laundry, good for arpt & Spanish students

Sleep in Madrid, c/ Lavapies, 32, Madrid; *reservas@ sleepinmadrid. es/*, T:915280679; $13Bed, Kitchen:N, B'fast:Y, Pvt.room:N, Locker:Y, Recep:morning; Note: noon checkout, TV, café, wh/chair ok, bag hold, tours, tea/coffee, central

16 Hostels) MALAGA was under Arab dominance for some 800 years and that's almost appropriate, since it was first settled by their cousin forebear Phoenicians. Combined with the Romans and Spanish who have also ruled

here, it all makes up for one of the more interesting histories in Europe. These days Malaga is better known as Europe's southernmost and warmest city. Tourist attractions include the Roman theatre and the Moorish fortress on Mount Gibralfaro. The cathedral was built in 1528 on the site of a mosque. The provincial museum of art includes works by Pablo Picasso, who was born here. The Moorish castle, Alcazaba, has been turned into a museum and garden.

Oasis Backpacker's Hostel Malaga, c/San Telmo 14, Malaga; *hostelsoasis.com/,* T:952005116; $17bed, Kitchen:Y, B'fast:Y, Pvt.room:N, Locker:Y, Recep:ltd; Note: welcome drink, free city tour, rooftop bar, hard to find, central

Feel City Center, c/Concejal Agustin Moreno 1; T:952218268, *citycenter@,* $13

Feel Hostel Soho Malaga, Calle Vendeja, 25, Malaga; *Sohomalaga@ feelmalagahostel.com,* T:952222832; $13bed, Kitchen:Y, B'fast:Y, Pvt.room:Y, Locker:Y, Recep:ltd; Note: bikes, bar/club, lift, laundry, bag hold, tours, parking

Melting Pot, Av. del Pintor Joaquín Sorolla, 30 Malaga; T:952600571, *malaga@ meltingpothostels.com/;* $21bed, Kitchen:Y, B'fast:Y, Pvt.room:N, Locker:Y, Recep:24/7; Note: arpt trans, bikes, resto/bar, wh/chair, laundry, bag hold, tours

X Hostel Malaga/Picasso's Corner, C/ San Juan de Letrán, 9 Malaga; *picassoscorner.hostel.com/,* T:952212287; $15bed, Kitchen:Y, B'fast:Y, Pvt.room:N, Locker:Y, Recep:24/7; Note: bar, luggage room, c.c. ok, laundry, books

Patio 19, Calle Mariblanca 19, Málaga; T:+34/952223729; *Info@ roomsinmalaga.com/;* $11Bed, Kitchen:Y, B'fast:Y, Pvt.room:Y, Locker:N, Recep:ltd; Note: café, laundry, bag hold, tea/coffee, central, historic house

Malaga Backpackers, c/ Jeronimo Bobadilla #4, Malaga; *Info@ MalagaBackpackers.com/;* $11Bed, Kitchen:Y, B'fast:$, Pvt.room:Y, Locker:Y, Recep:24/7; Note: bar, café, laundry, bag hold, tours, tea/coffee, prkng, not center

Pink House Backpackers, Carretera 2, Malaga; *pinkhousemalaga.com/,* T:+34/952210066, *pinkhousemalaga@gmail.com;* $13Bed, Kitchen:Y, B'fast:$, Pvt. room:Y, Locker:Y, Recep:8:30a//:30a; Note: arpt trans, café, luggage rm, tours

Casa al Sur Terraza, c/Marmoles 28, Malaga; T:+34/951132429, *terraza@*

Casa al Sur, Calle Molinillo del Aceite 5, Málaga, *casa@ casa-al-sur.com/*; T:+34/951132429; $14Bed, Kitchen:Y, B'fast:Y, Pvt.room:Y, Locker:N, Recep:2>10p; Note: wh/chair ok, laundry, bag hold, tea/coffee, cash only

Hostal Vidamia, Calle de Cisneros 7, Málaga, T:+34/951254870, *reservas@ hostalvidamia.es/*; $Bed, Kitchen:?, B'fast:$, Pvt.room:N, Locker:N, Recep:9a//8p; Note: noon checkout, tea/coffee, maps, a/c, resto, laundry, fax, central

Casa Babylon Hostel, c/Pedro de Quejana 3, Malaga; *casababylonhostel.com/*, Skype:casababylonmalaga; $14Bed, Kitchen:Y, B'fast:Y, Pvt.room:Y, Locker:Y, Recep:24/7; Note: arpt trans, bar, café, bag hold, tours, chill terrace, central

Nomadas Hostel, c/Arquitecto González Edo 3, Málaga, *nomadashostel. com/*, T:+34/951993452, *nomadashostelmálaga@gmail.com*; $22Bed, Kitchen:Y, B'fast:Y, Pvt.room:Y, Locker:Y, Recep:2>11p; Note: bar, café, laundry, luggage rm, center

Albergue Inturjoven de Málaga, Plaza Pio XII 6, Malaga; *hihostels.com/*, T:34/955035886, *malaga.itj@juntadeandalucia.es*, $25Bed, Kitchen:N, B'fast:Y, Pvt. room:Y, Locker:Y, Recep:24/7; Note: meals $, laundry, bag hold, wh/chair ok

Alamos 14, Alamos 14, Malaga; *Info@ alamos14.com/*, T:+34/680839277; $16Bed, Kitchen:Y, B'fast:$, Pvt.room:Y, Locker:Y, Recep:24/7; Note: arpt trans, café, tour desk, maps, TV, a/c

Malaga Hostel, C/ Conde de las Navas #1, Malaga; *malagahostel. es/*, T:+34/952296530; $21Bed, Kitchen:Y, B'fast:Y, Pvt.room:Y, Locker:Y, Recep:7a/8p; Note: arpt trans, bikes, café, wh/chair ok, laundry, tea/coffee, bag hold, beach

2 Hostels) MARBELLA is a city of 140,000 on the southernmost Costa del Sol, near Malaga, and sometimes a destination of the jet set, once including King Fahd of Saudi Arabia and a young Bin Laden. Besides the beaches, casinos, corruption, and the Golden Mile of luxury residences, there are an Old City; Dali sculptures; Roman, Punic, and Phoenician ruins, museums, festivals, and… beaches, miles of 'em.

Hostal Plaza San Pedro, c/Juan Ramón Jiménez 21, San Pedro de Alcántara, Marbella; T:+34/674777970, *hostalplazamarbella.com/*; $21Bed, Kitchen:N, B'fast:Y, Pvt.room:Y, Locker:N, Recep:advise ETA; Note: luggage room, tour desk, a/c

Albergue Inturjoven Marbella, c/Trapiche 2, Marbella; *hihostels.com/*, T:34/955035886; *marbella.itj@juntadeandalucia.es*; $25Bed, Kitchen:N, B'fast:Y, Pvt.room:Y, Locker:N, Recep:24/7; Note: pool, bikes, meals $, laundry, parking

SANT LLUIS, MENORCA, is a municipality on the Balearic island of Menorca, the 'lesser' island, in comparison to Majorca, at least. Originally founded by the French, there is a winery. Mayonnaise may originate from the capital city of Port Mahon. Also once ruled by the British, the island is a mélange of cultures, and many summer festivals.

Hostel & Gym Relise, c/Pedro Tudurí, #45, Sant Lluís, Menorca, Baleares T:971150714; *info@ relise.es/*; $26Bed, Kitchen:N, B'fast:$, Pvt.room:Y, Locker:Y, Recep:7a>11p; Note: gym, bag hold, tours, parking, books

MONISTROL DE MONTSERRAT is a town of only 3000 in the far northeast Catalan region of Spain. There are mountains and a Benedictine monastery.

Hostal Guilleumes, c/ Guilleumes 3, Monistrol de Montserrat, Barcelona; T:938284065, *hostal@ guilleumes.com/*; $69Bed, Kitchen:N, B'fast:Y, Pvt. room:Y, Locker:N, Recep:ltd; Note: 1 hr>Barca, resto/bar, wh/chair ok, stairs no lift, quiet

2 Hostels) MURCIA is a city of 440,000 in the country's southeast. It may have some previous roots, but was founded as a Moorish city in 825 AD, complete with irrigation and agriculture. Main sights include the Cathedral, the Bishop's Palace, and the old town. Fests include Holy Week, *Bando de la Huerta* next week, and '3 Cultures' in May.

The Cathedral Hostel, c/ Traperia 19, Murcia; *thecathedralhostel.com/*, T:+34/968930007, *thecathedralhostel@gmail.com*; $21Bed, Kitchen:N, B'fast:Y, Pvt. room:N, Locker:Y, Recep:10a//10p; Note: bikes, wh/chair ok, lift, laundry, tours

Hostel/Albergue La Casa Verde, Carril de la Esparza La Arboleja, Murcia; *Info@ lacasaverdeguesthouse.com/*, T:+34/968295031; $25Bed, Kitchen:N, B'fast:Y, Pvt.room:Y, Locker:Y, Recep: >9p; Note: pool, club, bar, bikes, wh/chair ok, hard find

NERJA, ANDALUCIA is a city of 22,000 on Spain's southern coast, famous for the prehistoric caves of the same name, and the paintings found within. There are Roman and Arab ruins, a hermitage, an aqueduct, historic church of El Salvador, and a viewpoint known as "The Balcony (balcon) of Europe." The town is steep and scenic.

Easy Nerja Hostel, c/ Bronce 25, Nerja; *easynerjahostel.com*, T:+34/670035922, *easynerjahostel@hotmail.com*; $18Bed, Kitchen:Y, B'fast:N, Pvt. room:Y, Locker:Y, Recep:ltd; Note:arpt tran, café, laundry, bag hold, tours, tea/coffee, nr bus/pier/bch

5 Hostels) PALMA DE MALLORCA is capital of the largest of the Balearic Islands, with a population of 400,000, almost half the island's total. The city was Roman, then Byzantine, then Moorish, before becoming fully Spanish. It is now a tourist zoo, with 22M per year. Attractions are the Old City, Arab baths, bronze trash-bins, and...beaches.

Live Mallorca Hostel, Av. del Fra Joan Llabrés 1, Palma de Mallorca; *Info@ livemallorcahostel.com/*, T:+34/607797072; $28Bed, Kitchen:Y, B'fast:Y, Pvt. room:N, Locker:Y, Recep:9a//9p; Note: new (remodel seminary), lift, tours, parking, c.c. ok

Hostal Atlanta, Carrer Terral 50, Llucmajor (Mallorca), Balearic Islands; T:+34/971443280, *stay@ hostal-atlanta.eu/*; $21Bed, Kitchen:N, B'fast:$, Pvt. room:Y, Locker:Y, Recep:>12m; Note: resto/bar, billiards, bikes, wh/chair ok, bag hold, beach

Central Palma YH, Plaza Josep Maria Quadrado 2, Palma de Mallorca; T:+34/971101215, *Info@ centralpalma.com/*; $35Bed, Kitchen:N, B'fast:N, Pvt. room:N, Locker:Y, Recep:24/7; Note: café, bar, lift, bag hold, central, basic

Hostal la Mimosa, c/Suecia 5 & c/Calviá 4, Palma de Mallorca, Illes Balears; T:+34/971400330, *hostalamimosa.com/*; $39Bed, Kitchen:N, B'fast:Y,

Pvt.room:Y, Locker:N, Recep:9a>10p; Note: laundry, not central, pool, bar, terrace

Hostal Terramar, Plaza de la Mediterránea 8, Palma de Mallorca; *hostalterramar.com/*, T:+34/971739931, *hostalterramar@yahoo.es;* $28Bed, Kitchen:Y, B'fast:N, Pvt.room:Y, Locker:N, Recep:ltd; Note: laundry, luggage rm, basic

2 Hostels) PAMPLONA is a city of 200,000 in the far northern Navarre region, most famous for the 'running of the bulls' during the July San Fermin fest. It is near the borders of France and the Basque country. Once a purely Basque town itself, it spent much of its history as a fortified military post trying to hold off one intruder or the other. Main sights are the cathedral and several Gothic churches, city walls, and many parks.

Aloha Hostel, Calle Sangüesa 2, 1st Fl, Pamplona, Navarra; T:+34/648289403, *Info@ alohahostel.es/*; $21Bed, Kitchen:Y, B'fast:Y, Pvt.room:N, Locker:N, Recep:9a>10p; Note: café, bikes, lift, laundry, bag hold, tours, tea/coffee

Hostel Hemingway, c/ Amaya, 26, 1st Left, Pamplona; T:+34/948983884, *Info@ hostelhemingway.com/*; $22Bed, Kitchen:Y, B'fast:Y, Pvt.room:Y, Locker:N, Recep:8a>12m; Note: bikes, laundry

PLASENCIA is a city of almost 42,000 in Spain's hilly border region with Portugal, in the province of Caceres, on the old 'Silver Trail.' It was incorporated in 1186 and served as a bulwark against the Moors, a mission it largely accomplished. There are walls, gates and towers from that era, in addition to a Roman aqueduct and historic cathedrals.

Albergue Santa Ana, Plaza Santa Ana #2, Plasencia, T:927410288, *Info@ alberguesantaana.es/*; $25Bed, Kitchen:Y, B'fast:Y, Pvt.room:N, Locker:Y, Recep:ltd; Note: wh/chair ok, tour desk, parking, a/c, central

RONDA is a city of 37,000 only 62mi/100km from Malaga, in Spain's far south. It was once the scene of vicious battles between Moorish refugees and Spanish forces, then again with Napoleon's forces, then again in the Spanish Civil War. Give it a break. Modern bullfighting originated here. Hemingway and Rilke wrote here. There are Arab baths. The 'new bridge' was completed in 1793. You get the picture.

El Refugio Hostel, Calle de Cerillo, Cartajima, Ronda; *Info@ elrefugiohostel. com/*, T:+34/952180792; $23Bed, Kitchen:N, B'fast:Y, Pvt.room:Y, Locker:N, Recep:24/7; Note: tours, parking, 10mi/15km>Ronda, village, cash, hikes

5 Hostels) SALAMANCA is a city of 150,000 in an urban area of over 200K in the province of the same name in the centre-west of the country. Its old city is a UNESCO world heritage site. Prominent spaces include the Plaza Mayor, old and new cathedrals, Casa de las Conchas, and many others: religious, museums and university. Fests include Holy Week, *Lunes de Aguas* on Sunday following Easter, and "university new year."

Erasmus Home, c/ Jesús 18, Salamanca, T:+34/923710257, *info@ erasmushome.com/*; $20Bed, Kitchen:N, B'fast:$, Pvt.room:Y, Locker:N, Recep:>10p; Note: café/pub, historic center

Revolutum Hostel, Calle Sánchez Barbero 7, Salamanca; T:+34/923217656, *Info@ revolutumhostel.com/*; $25Bed, Kitchen:Y, B'fast:Y, Pvt.room:Y, Locker:Y, Recep:1p>12m; Note: bar, café, wh/chair ok, lift, bag hold, tours, center

Pension San Jose, Calle de Jesús 24, Salamanca; T:+34/923265461, *pension@ pension-sanjose.com/*; $24Bed, Kitchen:N, B'fast:N, Pvt.room:Y, Locker:N, Recep:9a>10p; Note: parking nearby, new, central

Salamanca - Albergue Juvenil, c/Escoto 13-15, Salamanca; *hihostels.com/*, T:+34/923269141, *info@alberguesalamanca.com*; $17Bed, Kitchen:N, B'fast:$, Pvt.room:N, Locker:N, Recep:10a>9p; Note: resto, pool, bikes, laundry, bag hold, prkg

Alda Centro, Paseo Canalejas, 14, Salamanca; *aldacentro.es/* T:+34/633961597 $14Bed, Kitchen:Y, B'fast:Y, Pvt.room:Y, Locker:N, Recep:ltd; Note: laundry, luggage room, tours, tea/coffee, parking, maps, central

10 Hostels) SAN SEBASTIAN is in Basque country, and only a stone's throw from France. Basques are descendants of the aboriginal inhabitants of the region with no known relation to any other peoples or language. If the tourist industry seems a bit tentative, there's a good reason. Until not so long ago

secessionist activity was strong here. It seems like a surfers' town, and it's on my short list. For the cultured among you, the old town contains the Gothic church of San Vicente, the Baroque church of Santa Maria, and the former convent of San Telmo. Hostel quality is probably not up to big-city standards, probably the sketchiest in all of Spain here. Choose carefully.

Roger's House, C/ Juan de Bilbao 13-3°, S. Sebastian; *hostel-rogers-house. com/*, T:943433856, *rogershouse@hotmail.es*; $25bed, Kitchen:Y, B'fast:$, Pvt. room:N, Locker:Y, Recep:8a>12m; Note:bikes/boards, sports yes party no, café, cozy, old town

Pension Goiko, C/ del Puerto, 6 Portu Kalea, San Sebastián; *pensiongoiko. com/*, T:943431114, *pensiongoiko@hotmail.com*; $29bed, Kitchen:Y, B'fast:Y, Pvt. room:Y, Locker:N, Recep:24/7; Note: old town, close to beach, c.c. ok, bike rent

Hospedaje Kati, C/ Fermin Calbeton Kalea, 21 San Sebastián; *hospedajekati. com/*, T:943430487; $27bed, Kitchen:N, B'fast:N, Pvt.room:N, Locker:N, Recep:24/7; Note: advise arrival time, near beach, homestay flat

Surf Backpackers, Narrica 23-2nd right, San Sebastian; *surfbackpackers. com/*, T:943425511, *surfbackpackers@gmail.com*; $21bed, Kitchen:Y, B'fast:N, Pvt. room:Y, Locker:Y, Recep:24/7; Note: café, bikes, laundry, bag hold, tea/coffee, central

Urban House/Lolo Etxea, Alameda del Blvd 26; *urbanhousehostel@gmail.com*

Urban House Hostel, Plaza de Gipuzkoa 2, Donostia-San Sebastián, T:+34/943428154, *info@   urbanhousesansebastian.com/*; $24Bed, Kitchen:Y, B'fast:Y, Pvt.room:Y, Locker:N, Recep:10a>10p; Note: bikes, lift, luggage rm, tea/cof, teen spirit

Enjoyss, 31 de Agosto 16-1st, San Sebastian; *Reservas@   enjoyss.com/*, T:943431228; $31Bed, Kitchen:Y, B'fast:Y, Pvt.room:Y, Locker:N, Recep:10a>10p; Note: café, bag hold, tours, tea/coffee, maps, books, old town

Green Nest Hostel, Camino de Uba 43, San Sebastian; T:+34/943457117, *nesthostelsansebastian.com/*, $22Bed, *booking@greennestdonostia*; Kitchen:Y, B'fast:$, Pvt.room:Y, Locker:Y, Recep:24/7; Note: resto, wh/chair ok, lift, laundry, bag hold, far

San Fermin, Fermin Calbeton Kalea 23, Donostia-San Sebastián; *hostelsanfermin.com/*, T:+34/943425491; $34Bed, Kitchen:N, B'fast:$, Pvt.

room:Y, Locker:N, Recep:8a>12m; Note: hot tub, café, wh/chair ok, lift, bag hold, central

San Sebastian Roos Bed & Brekky, Calle Inigo 5 -1a, San Sebastian; *rooshostel@hotmail.com*, T:(0034)652756638, *rooshostel.blogspot.com/*; $30Bed, Kitchen:N, B'fast:Y, Pvt.room:N, Locker:Y, Recep:ltd; Note: bikes, café, lift, old town

2 Hostels) SANTANDER is a city of 180,000 on the far northern coast and capital of Cantabria. It was and is an important port for trade and recreation. Sights include the cathedral, regional museum, 'El Sardinero' district, Palacio de la Magdalena, and more.

Hostel B&B&B, C/ Mendez Nuñez #6, 1st, Santander; *hostelsantander. com/*, T:+34/942227817, *hostel.b.b.b@googlemail.com*; $28Bed, Kitchen:N, B'fast:Y, Pvt.room:Y, Locker:Y, Recep:4>11p; Note: no party, 12n checkout, lift, tours, nr bus

Surf to Live House, Calle Cayuso 33, Somo, Santander; *Info@ surftolive. com/*; $36Bed, Kitchen:N, B'fast:Y, Pvt.room:N, Locker:N, Recep:24/7; Note: arpt trans, bikes, small beach town outside Santander

7 Hostels) SANTIAGO DE COMPOSTELA is a city of 95,000 in the country's far northwest (Galician) A Coruna province, with roots in Rome and once a Suebi stronghold. For some 1000 years it has been a pilgrimage destination for the cult of St. James. Bring *sleeping* (bag). The city's old town is a World Heritage Site.

Roots & Boots Hostel, Rua Campo do Cruceiro do Gaio 7, Santiago; *Info@ rootsandboots.es/*, T:+34/699631594; $14Bed, Kitchen:Y, B'fast:Y, Pvt.room:N, Locker:Y, Recep:24/7; Note: pool, café, bikes, minimart, bag hold, laundry, maps

Albergue Acuario, C/ Estocolmo 2, Santiago; *reservas@ acuariosantiago. com/*, T:+34/981575438; $17Bed, Kitchen:Y, B'fast:$, Pvt.room:N, Locker:Y, Recep:9a>12m; Note: resto, mkt, bikes, laundry, bag hold, tours, tea/coffee, parking, wh/chair ok

O Fogar de Teodomiro, Praci'a de Algalia de Arriba, 3, Santiago; *Info@ fogarteodomiro.com/*, T:+34/981582920; $21Bed, Kitchen:Y, B'fast:N, Pvt. room:N, Locker:Y, Recep:ltd; Note: bar, bag hold, tours, meals, maps, laundry

Hostel Santo Santiago, Rúa do Valiño 3, Santiago; *elsantosantiago.com/*, T:+34/657402403, *elsantosantiago@gmail.com*; $17Bed, Kitchen:N, B'fast:$, Pvt. room:N, Locker:N, Recep:ltd; Note: resto, wh/chair ok, bag hold, tours, cash

Albergue la Magdalena; Av La Merced 60, Sarria; *sarria@*, T:982533568, $14

Albergue Seminario Menor, Av Quiroga Palacios s/n, Santiago De Compostela; *santiago@ alberguesdelcamino.com/*, T:+34/881031768; $14Bed, Kitchen:Y, B'fast:$, Pvt.room:N, Locker:Y, Recep:2>11p; Note: tours, parking, laundry

Hostal La Salle, St behind Santa Clara, no #, Santiago; *hostallasalle.com/*, T:(+34)981585667, *hostallasalle@terra.es*; $24Bed, Kitchen:N, B'fast:$, Pvt. room:N, Locker:N, Recep:24/7; Note: wh/chair ok, lift, bag hold, tours, fax

SEGOVIA is a city of 57,000 in central Spain and capital of the province of the same name. Once Celtic, then Roman, then abandoned to the Moors, it regained status as a center of Jews and textiles, no connection. Today it is a UNESCO world heritage city, with Roman aqueduct, Alcazar, Walls of Segovia, and Gothic cathedral. There are museums and festivals. Holy Week is big. Day trips from Madrid are popular.

Duermevela Hostel, Calle de los Gascos 7, Segovia; T:+34/921047004, *reservas@ duermevelahostel.com/*; $26Bed, Kitchen:Y, B'fast:$, Pvt.room:Y, Locker:Y, Recep:.9p; Note: café, wh/chair ok, laundry, bag hold, tours, tea/coffee, c.c. ok

24 Hostels) SEVILLE (Sevilla) is another part of Spain, older and with a much different history. The city is some 3000 years old and has one of Europe's largest "old towns" to prove it. This is where the Moors from North Africa ruled for over 500 years until the mid-13th century, and it still maintains much of that ambience to this day. This is also where trade from the New World

flowed during Spain's Golden Age. The Alcazar and the Cathedral, both UNESCO World Heritage sites, are major tourist attractions.

The Alcazar, begun by the Almohads in 1181, is the finest surviving example of Moorish architecture in the city. The cathedral was previously a mosque and the minaret still survives as bell tower. The adjacent Casa Lonja houses the General Archive of the Indies, a treasure trove of info on Spain's colonial period. The city museum houses paintings of the Sevilla School.

Five miles (8 km) northwest of the city are the ruins of the Roman city of Italica. There are numerous celebrations and festivals, of which the one during Holy Week (*Semana Santa*) is probably most important. The April Fair celebrates the Andalusian countryside. Sevilla is home to flamenco, and performances are frequent and lively. Hostel quality is high, and the tendency is toward partying, if not quite Barcelona. It's easy to get lost in the old quarter, especially at night, so carry your hostel's business card with you. You can always flag a cab. That's what I did.

Traveler's Inn Seville, Plaza Alfalfa, 11, Seville; *travelersinnseville.com/*, T:954216724; $14bed, Kitchen:Y, B'fast:Y, Pvt.room:Y, Locker:Y, Recep:24/7; Note: café, bikes, laundry, bag hold, tea/coffee, tours, pub crawl, a/c, c.c. ok, maps

The Garden Backpacker, Calle Santiago, 19 Seville; T:954223866, *reservas@ thegardenbackpacker.com/*; $20bed, Kitchen:Y, B'fast:Y, Pvt.room:N, Locker:Y, recep:24/7; Note: bar, city tour, laundry, bag hold, free sangria, wh/chair ok

Sevilla District 1 Hostel, C/ Angostillo 6, Seville; T:+34/954221615, *hostelonesevillacentro@ onehostel.com/*; $13bed, Kitchen:Y, B'fast:$, Pvt.room:Y, Locker:Y, Desk hr:8a>10p; Note: a/c, city tour, laundry, bikes

Hostel One Sevilla Alameda, C/ Jesús del Gran Poder 113, Seville; T:954909622, *hostelonesevilla.com/*; $14bed, Kitchen:Y, B'fast:N, Pvt.room:Y, Locker:Y, Recep:8a>10p; Note: café, bikes, wh/chair ok, laundry, bag hold, not ctr

The Spot Central Hostel, C/ Adriano, 6 Seville; *hi@ thespotcentralhostel. com/*, T:955295837; $14bed, Kitchen:Y, B'fast:Y, Pvt.room:Y, Locker:Y, Recep:24/7; Note: café, bar, bikes, wh/chair ok, bag hold, tours, central, cambio, minimart, a/c

Feetup Hostels-Samay Sevilla, Ave. de Menéndez Pelayo 13, Sevilla; T:955100160, *sevilla@ samayhostels.com/*; $13bed, Kitchen:Y, B'fast:$, Pvt. room:Y, Locker:N, Recep:24/7; Note: café, wh/chair ok, lift, laundry, bag hold, tours, terrace

Sevilla Inn Backpackers, C/ Angeles 11 (cnr. Mateos Gago), Seville; *booking@ sevillabackpackers.es/*, T:954219541; $13bed, Kitchen:Y, B'fast:Y, Pvt. room:Y, Locker:Y, Recep:24/7; Note: bar, tours, bag hold, terrace, free sangria, paella

Oasis Urban Lodge, C/ Bajeles 18, Sevilla; *reception.lodge@*, T:955542821

Oasis Backpackers' Palace, C/ Almte Ulloa 1; *reception.palace@*, T:955262696

Oasis Backpacker's Hostel, C/ de la Compañía 1, Sevilla; *oasissevilla.com/*, T:954293777, *sevilla@ hostelsoasis.com/*; $16bed, Kitchen:Y, B'fast:Y, Pvt.room:Y, Locker:Y, Recep:24/7; Note: bar, coffee/tea, tours, pool, a/c, bikes, hard find

Sevilla Urbany Hostel, Maria Coronel 12, Seville; *sevillaurbany.com/*, T:+34/954227949; $10bed, Kitchen:Y, B'fast:Y, Pvt.room:N, Locker:Y, Recep:8a>11p; Note: bar, bikes, wh/chair ok, lift, bag hold, tour desk, a/c

Grand Luxe Hostel, Don Remondo 7, Seville, *Info@ grandluxehostel. com/*, T:+34/955326546; $18Bed, Kitchen:Y, B'fast:$, Pvt.room:Y, Locker:Y, Recep:24/7; Note: gym, bikes, wh/chair ok, lift, laundry, bag hold, tours, tea/ coffee

Nuevo Suizo, Calle del Azofaifo 7, Sevilla; T:+34/954229147, *Info@ nuevosuizo.com/*; $20Bed, Kitchen:N, B'fast:Y, Pvt.room:Y, Locker:Y, Recep:24/7; Note: c.c.+4%, bag hold, tours, central, no party, no lift

The Architect Hostel, C/ Joaquin Guichot 8, 1ˢᵗ Fl, Seville; *reservas@ thearchitectbackpacker.com/*, T:+34/955324640; $15Bed, Kitchen:N, B'fast:Y, Pvt. room:N, Locker:Y, Recep:24/7; Note: lift, tours, maps, central, roof terrace

Feeling Sevilla Hostel, c/Imaginero Castillo Lastrucci 8, Sevilla; T:+34/955261414, *reservas@ feelingsevillahostel.com/*; $11Bed, Kitchen:Y, B'fast:Y, Pvt.room:Y, Locker:Y, Recep:24/7; Note: central, laundry, café bikes, wh/chair ok, lift

Triana Backpackers, c/ de Rodrigo de Triana 69, Sevilla; T:+34/954459960, *trianabackpackers.com/*, $18Bed, *SevillaTriana@gmail.com/*; Kitchen:N, B'fast:Y, Pvt.room:Y, Locker:Y, Recep:24/7; Note: hot tub, pool, café, bikes, laundry, bag hold

Soho Boutique Hostel, Calle Sales y Ferré 18, Sevilla; *sohoboutiquehostel. com/*, T:+34/955293148, *sohoboutiquehostel@gmail.com*; $13Bed, Kitchen:Y, B'fast:Y, Pvt.room:Y, Locker:Y, Recep:ltd; Note: gym, lift, bag hold, tea/coffee,

Hostel Trotamundos, Calle Bailén 12, Seville; T:+34/672100299, *Info@ hosteltrotamundos.es/*; $17Bed, Kitchen:Y, B'fast:Y, Pvt.room:N, Locker:Y, Recep:ltd; Note: cash, café, bikes, laundry, bag hold, tours, tea/coffee, c.c. ok, no party

Cathedral Backpackers Hostel, Calle Arfe 36, Seville, T:+34/954221040, *Info@ cathedralbackpackershostel.com/*; $19Bed, Kitchen:Y, B'fast:Y, Pvt.room:Y, Locker:Y, Recep:8a>9p; Note: café, bikes, lift, bag hold, tours, a/c

Pension Lis Dos, Olavide 5, Seville; *reservas@ pensionlisdos.com/* T:+34/954560228; $15Bed, Kitchen:N, B'fast:Y, Pvt.room:Y, Locker:N, Recep:24/7; Note: central, luggage room, laundry, maps, a/c

La Caja Habitada, Calle Crédito 20, Sevilla; *lacajahabitada.es/*, T:+34/954902445, *lacajahabitada@gmail.com*; $14Bed, Kitchen:Y, B'fast:Y, Pvt. room:N, Locker:Y, Recep:24/7; Note: bar, café, wh/chair ok, bag hold, tours

Hostal Dona Pepa, Juan De Vera 20, Sevilla; *hostaldonapepa.com*, T:+34/ 954413628; $15Bed, Kitchen:N, B'fast:$, Pvt.room:Y, Locker:N, Recep:ltd; Note: a/c, parking $, central, near train, hard find

HI Albergue Inturjoven Sevilla, C/ Isaac Peral 2, Sevilla; *hihostels.com/*, T:34/955035886, *sevilla.itj@juntadeandalucia.es*; $25Bed, Kitchen:N, B'fast:Y, Pvt.room:Y, Locker:N, Recep:24/7; Note:meals $, laundry, bag hold, parking, near U

HI Albergue Inturjoven Constantina, C/ Cuesta Blanca, Constantina; T:34/955035886, *constantina.itj@juntadeandalucia.es*; $25Bed, Kitchen:N, B'fast:Y, Pvt.room:Y, Locker:N, Recep:24/7; Note: ntl park, pool, meals $, lift, laundry, prkng

2 Hostels) TARIFA is a town of 18,000 on Spain's — and Europe's — southernmost tip. Once a Roman town, it was also the starting point of Moorish incursion onto the peninsula in 710. There are Roman ruins, medieval walls, Guzman castle, and the Gothic church of St. Matthew. There are also ferries to Morrocco, though Algeciras has most. Strong winds mean turbines, winsurfers and kitesurfers. There are also birds and whales.

Melting Pot Hostel, c/ Turriano Gracil 5, Tarifa, Cádiz; T:+34/956682906, *Info@ meltingpothostels.com/*; $18Bed, Kitchen:Y, B'fast:Y, Pvt.room:Y, Locker:Y, Recep:ltd; Note: arpt trans, bar, minimart, bikes, laundry, bag hold, tours, beach

Pension Facundo, Calle de la Batalla del Salado 47, Tarifa, Cádiz, *pensionfacundo.com/*, T:+34/956684298; $14Bed, Kitchen:Y, B'fast:Y, Pvt. room:Y, Locker:N, Recep:24/7; Note: resto/bar, laundry, parking, TV, no-party

TAULL is a village of less than 300 in the northwest of Spain's Catalonia region, in the Valley of Boi. It has two Romanesque churches.

Albergue Taull, Av Feixanes 5-7, Ctra de Pistas de Boí-Taüll, Taüll, Lleida, T:+34/973696252, *Info@ alberguetaull.com/*; $25Bed, Kitchen:N, B'fast:Y, Pvt. room:N, Locker:Y, Recep:24/7; Note: café, laundry, tea/coffee, parking, books

5 Hostels) TENERIFE is the largest and most populous of the Canary Islands, with a population of 900,000. El Teide is the local volcano, with national park, and one of the world's highest. There are Guanche (pre-Spanish) archeological sites, Guimar Pyramids, and 'Castillo de San Andres'. SANTA CRUZ is the capital, a city of 222,000. It has one of the largest Carnavals in the world, plus many museums, and sculpture spaces.

`Los Amigos Backpackers Hostel, C/ Giralda 9, El Medano, Tenerife; *reservassol@ losamigoshostel.com/*, T+34/915592472; $20Bed, Kitchen:Y, B'fast:Y, Pvt.room:Y, Locker:Y, Recep:ltd; Note: arpt trans, pool, bikes, café, luggage rm, prkng

Albergue Mamio Verde, C/ Los Olivos 39, Pino Alto, Tenerife; *Info@ mamioverde.com/*, T:+34/653736704; $17Bed, Kitchen:N, B'fast:$, Pvt.room:N,

Locker:N, Recep:24/7; Note: resto/bar, pool, billiards, laundry, tours, animals, nature

Casa Grande Hostel, C/ Galo Ponte 7, El Médano, Santa Cruz de Tenerife, T:+34/922176376, *Info@ casagrandehostel.com/*; $21Bed, Kitchen:Y, B'fast:Y, Pvt.room:N, Locker:Y, Recep:24/7; Note:café, bar, bikes, laundry, coast village

Lagarto Backpackers, Camino del Guincho 108, La Barranquera, Tenerife; *lagartobackpackers.com/*, T:+34/922545487, *lagartotenerife@hotmail.com*; $17Bed, Kitchen:Y, B'fast:Y, Pvt.room:Y, Locker:Y, Recep:24/7; Note:café/bar, bikes, pool, rural

Tenerife Surf House, Paseo Los Cardones 77, Playa De Las Americas, Tenerife; *tenerifesurfhouse.es/*, T:34/922790676, *tenerifesurfhouse@gmail.com*; $21Bed, Kitchen:N, B'fast:Y, Pvt.room:N, Locker:Y, Recep:24/7; Note: bar, gym, laundry

2 Hostels) TOLEDO is a city of 84,000 in the center of Spain, 45mi/70km south of Madrid, and capital of the province of the same name. It is a UNESCO world heritage site, especially for the mixed legacy of its Christians, Jews, and Muslims. Thus right here, from Islamic libraries, much of the West's own Greek and Roman heritage was recovered. When the capital of Castile was moved, so was much of its importance. Sights include the Castillo de San Servando, the Alcazar fortress, and the Synagogue.

Oasis Hostel Toledo, c/ Cadenas 5, Toledo; T:+34/925227650, *Toledo@ hostelsoasis.com*; $19Bed, Kitchen:N, B'fast:$, Pvt.room:Y, Locker:Y, Recep:ltd; Note: resto/bar, lift, laundry, bag hold, tours, meals, maps, books

Albergue Los Pascuales, Cuesta de Pascuales 8, Toledo; T:+34/925282422, *alberguelospascuales.com/*; $18Bed, Kitchen:N, B'fast:Y, Pvt.room:N, Locker:Y, Recep:12n>9p; Note: laundry, hard find, central, c.c. ok

TORREMOLINOS is a city of 68,000 on Spain's southern Costa del Sol, famous for LGBT night life. But the Phoenicians were here first; the Romans built roads; then Moors built the Towers that give the city its name. British tourists and ex-pats flock here. It is only 8mi/13km from Malaga.

Casa Castilla, C/ Manila 3, Torremolinos, Málaga; *pensioncastilla.com/*; $20Bed, Kitchen:Y, B'fast:Y, Pvt.room:Y, Locker:N, Recep:24/7; Note: café, bikes, bag hold, tea/coffee, central

TOSSA DE MAR is a town of 6000 on Spain's far northeast Catalonian coast, 60mi/100km to Barcelona to the south and France to the north. There are prehistoric, Iberian, and Roman remains, and the medieval church atop Mt. Guardi. It has Catalonia's best medieval Old Town and three major beach areas.

Mana Mana Hostel, c/ Sant Telm 9, Tossa de Mar, Catalonia, *Info@ manamanahostel.com/*, T:+34/972342549; $21Bed, Kitchen:N, B'fast:$, Pvt.room:Y, Locker:Y, Recep:2>8p; Note: bar, bikes, laundry, bag hold, tours, c.c. ok

11 Hostels) VALENCIA is Spain's third city and third region, with its own language and own history, spanning all the same major periods as the others — Roman, Visigoth, Arab, and Reconquest. El Cid briefly liberated it from the Moorish Almoravids late in the 11th century, but it did not become a full part of the Aragon crown until 1238, then united with the Castile of Ferdinand and Isabella in 1479. It is famous for its *paella* and its annual festival is the Fallas in March. The *fallas* are huge satirical monuments made of papier-mache and wax that are constructed over the course of a year.

Valencia has plenty of classic architecture and landscapes, some of which rate World Heritage status. Major landmarks include the Valenciana Cathedral and the Towers of the old city. Others are Lonja de la Seda (Silk Exchange), the Palacio de la Diputación, the Ayuntamiento (Town Hall), and the 18th C. Neoclassical Palacio de Justicia. Hostel quality seems generally good; unlike elsewhere, most are not chains.

Feet-up Hostels-Hilux Valencia, Cadirers 11-1st, Valencia; *feetuphostels. com/*, T:+34(0)963914691; $22bed, Kitchen:Y, B'fast:Y, Pvt.room:Y, Locker:Y, Recep:24/7; Note: laundry, c.c. ok, central, café, bikes, laundry, bag hold, tours, books, maps

Home Backpackers, Plaza de Vicente Iborra, 46 Valencia; T:963913797, *homehostelsvalencia.com/*; $17bed, Kitchen:Y, B'fast:N, Pvt.room:N, Locker:Y, Recep:24/7; Note: bikes, wh/chair ok, lift, laundry, bag hold, tours, tea/cof

Home Youth Hostel, C/ Lonja 4, Valencia; *homeyouthhostel.com/*, T:963916229; $24bed, Kitchen:Y, B'fast:N, Pvt. room:Y, Locker:Y, Recep:24/7; Note: laundry, bikes, c.c. ok, a/c, near central market, bag hold, tours, tea/coffee

Russafa Youth Hostel, C/ Padre Perera, 5 Valencia; T:963289460, *info@ russafayouthhostel.com/*; $25bed, Kitchen:N, B'fast:Y, Pvt.room:Y, Locker:Y, Recep:24/7; Note: stairs, c.c. ok, min 3N, tea/coffee, maps

Center Valencia Y. H., C/ Samaniego, 18 Valencia; T:963914915, *info@ center-valencia.com/*; $17bed, Kitchen:Y, B'fast:Y, Pvt.room:N, Locker:Y, Recep:24/7; Note: lift, bikes, a/c, laundry, tours, wh/chair ok, central, quiet, café, bag hold

Purple Nest Hostel Valencia, Plaza Tetuán #5, Valencia; T:+34/963532561, $17

Red Nest Hostel Valencia, Calle Paz 36, Valencia; T:+34/963427168, *Info@ nesthostelsvalencia.com/*; $17Bed, Kitchen:zN, B'fast:N, Pvt.room:Y, Locker:Y, Recep:24/7; Note: bar/café, bikes, billiards, lift, laundry, bag hold, tours, tea/cof

River Hostel Valencia, Plaza de Temple, 6, Valencia; T:+34/963913955, *hola@ riverhostelvalencia.com/*; $13Bed, Kitchen:Y, B'fast:N, Pvt.room:Y, Locker:Y, Recep:24/7; Note: bikes wh/chair ok, lift, bag hold, tours, parking

QuartYouthHostel, c/ Guillem de Castro 64, Valencia; T:+34/963270101, *reservas@quarthostel.com*, $17Bed, *facebook.com/QuartYouthHostel*, Kitchen:Y, B'fast:Y, Pvt.room:Y, Locker:Y, Recep:ltd; Note: café, wh/chair ok, laundry, bag hold

Albergue de Valencia, c/ de Balmes 17, Valencia; T:+34/963925100, *albergue@ alberguedevalencia.com/*; $17Bed, Kitchen:Y, B'fast:Y, Pvt.room:Y, Locker:Y, Recep:ltd; Note:café, bikes, wh/chair ok, lift, laundry, bag hold, tours

Innsa Hostel, Calle Baja 48, Valencia; *Info@ innsahostel.com/*, T:+34/653977522; $17Bed, Kitchen:N, B'fast:Y, Pvt.room:Y, Locker:N, Recep:24/7; Note: luggage room, laundry, c.c. ok

VIGO is a city of 300,000 in the Galician far east, largest in the region and 14th in Spain. This was the site of an important Roman fort. Today there are the 'Casco Vello' historic centre), a modern centre, Príncipe & Urzaiz Street commercial area, Celtic Castro ruins, Cathedral of Santa Maria de Vigo, many museums, and… beaches, of course.

Kaps Vigo Hostel, Estrada Provincial, 12, Vigo, Pontevedra, *kaps.es/*, T:+34/986110010, *reservas@hostelvigo.com/*, $17Bed, Kitchen:Y, B'fast:$, Pvt. room:Y, Locker:Y, Recep:24/7; Note: arpt trans, bikes, wh/chairs ok, lift, laundry, maps, parking

ZARAGOZA is a city of 700,000 in the northeast of the country. Landmarks are the Basílica del Pilar, La Seo Cathedral and the Aljafería Palace, which form part of the Mudéjar Architecture of Aragon, a UNESCO World Heritage Site. The *Fiestas del Pilar* are held in October. There is a Moorish castle Aljaferia and a basilica.

Albergue Zaragoza, c/ de los Predicadores 70, Zaragoza; T:+34/976282043, *Info@ alberguezaragoza.com;* $22Bed, Kitchen:Y, B'fast:Y, Pvt.room:Y, Locker:Y, Recep:24/7; Note: café, wh/chair ok,, lift, laundry, bag hold, tours

Part II: Alps and The Italian Peninsula

4) Austria

The territory that is now Austria (*Osterreich*) was originally settled in the historical period by Celts, including one of Northern Europe's first high cultures at Hallstatt. After the fall of the Roman Empire, it is first documented as a German area in the *Ostarrichi* document of 996, when it was a Bavarian prefecture. Most of Austrian history, though, is about the Habsburgs, the ruling dynasty for over six hundred years, who were not only the royalty of Austria but also Holy Roman Emperors, with one exception.

The Habsburgs accumulated land through marriage far and wide, and in those years Austria was one of the most powerful kingdoms in the world, and much more important than the land now known as Germany itself. Only the Ottoman Turks presented a real challenge, and they were repulsed at the Battle of Vienna in 1683. That all changed with the Napoleonic wars and the dissolution of the Holy Roman Empire. Germany began to unite and the question of Austria's role was paramount, it ultimately opting out.

Instead the Austrian Empire of the Habsburgs joined with the Kingdom of Hungary to form Austria-Hungary, another far-flung empire of many nationalities—with some eight official languages—in an age of rising nationalism. When Archduke Franz Ferdinand (no, not them) was killed by a Serb nationalist in Sarajevo, the WWI was on, and the Empire was lost. WWII was no better, of course, as right-hand man to native son Hitler.

So Austria has fallen a long way from its glory days, but that's probably good, since empires and monarchies are distinctive only as anachronisms of an age long gone. These days Austria, like neighbor Switzerland, is one of the wealthiest and most livable countries in the world, and life is good. The Euro is currency, German is the language, and the phone code is +43.

2 Hostels) BAD GASTEIN is a spa town of 6000 in the Austrian state of Salzburg, at the northern rim of Hohe Tauern national park. The rich and famous have bathed here since the Middle Ages, and with the arrival of the railway in the last century so has everyone else. Paracelsus studied the water here; Marie Curie found radon, the basis of many subsequent therapies, with mixed results. There are pagan traditions. It's cheap now, too.

Junges Hotel Bad Gastein, Ederplatz 2, Bad Gastein; T:+43(0)64342080, *office@ hostel-badgastein.at*; $28Bed, Kitchen:N, B'fast:Y, Pvt.room:Y, Locker:N, Recep:8a//10p; Note: resto/bar, parking, bikes, fax, games, cable TV, skiing

Euro Youth Hotel Krone, Bahnhofsplatz 8, Bad Gastein; *info@ euro-youth-hotel.at/*, T:+43(0)64342330; $24Bed, Kitchen:N, B'fast:Y, Pvt.room:Y, Locker:Y, Recep:24/7; Note: pool, resto/bar, lift, parking, bikes, tours, wh/chair ok

BAD ISCHL is a spa town of 14,000 in the Salzkammergut region. With roots in Europe's earliest Hallstatt culture, the town is fully attested from the medieval period. Franz Joseph signed the declaration of war against Serbia here in 1914. His Kaiservilla is a tourist sight now. Other sights include the Kongresshaus, the Kurhaus, and... baths.

YH Bad Ischl, Am Rechensteg 5, Bad Ischl; *jgh.badischl@oejhv.or.at*, T:+43/613226577, *jugendherbergsverband.at/herbergen/badischl/*; $30Bed, Kitchen:Y, B'fast:Y, Pvt.room:Y, Locker:N, Recep:8a/7p; Note: bikes, meals, wh/chair ok

FELDKIRCH is a beautiful well-preserved medieval city, with castle, on the Austrian western border with Leichtenstein. Besides the castle, historic buildings include the Gothic parish church of Sankt Nikolaus, the town hall, and Sankt Johannes' Church. The bus system contains a "nightline" that services local drinkeries.

Hostel Feldkirch-Levis, Reichstr. 111, Feldkirch-Levis; *hihostels.com/*, T:0552273181, *feldkirch@jungehotels.at*; $20bed, Kitchen:Y, B'fast:$, Pvt.room:Y,

Locker:Y, Recep:7a>11p; Note: bar, parking, tours, bag hold, wh/chair ok, walk>train

2 Hostels) GRAZ is a city of a quarter mil 95mi/155km southwest of Vienna, and Austria's second-largest city. It dates back to the Middle Ages and probably before. The old quarter is a UNESCO world heritage site. Arnold the Governator is from here.

JUFA, Idlhofgasse 74, Graz; T:+43/57083210, *info@ jufa.at/en/*; $32Bed, Kitchen:N, B'fast:Y, Pvt.room:Y, Locker:N, Recep:ltd; Note: HI mem, central, resto/bar, wh-chair ok, bikes, parking, lift

A&O Graz Hauptbahnhof, Eggenberger Straße 7, Graz; T:+43/160206173801, *aohostels.com/de/*; $32Bed, Kitchen:Y, B'fast:N, Pvt. room:Y, Locker:Y, Recep:24/7; Note: 15min>ctr at train stn, lift, bar, billiards, parking, laundry

IMST is a town of over 11,000 in Austria's far Alpine west, with a history as a market town going back to the Middle Ages. Today it is a center of luge racing.

Romedihof Backpacker Hostel, Brennbichl 41, Karrösten / Imst; T:+43(0)664/2221210, *info@ romedihof.at/*; $26Bed, Kitchen:Y, B'fast:N, Pvt. room:Y, Locker:N, Recep:ltd; Note: fireplace, parking

3 Hostels) INNSBRUCK has hosted the Winter Olympics more than once. Emperor Maximilian I used to live here. Landmarks include the Hofburg and the Franciscan, or Court, church. There are four major museums: Ferdinandeum, Tirolean Folk Art Museum; Museum of the Imperial Rifles; and the collections of the archduke Ferdinand II, in the Castle Ambras. Innsbruck is one of Europe's prime resorts, the Alps, baby.

Doug's Mtn Hideaway, Mühlwiese 12, Fulpmes, Tirol; T:+43/6509686865, *chaletexperiences.com/*; $46Bed, Kitchen:Y, B'fast:Y, Pvt.room:Y, Locker:N, Recep:ltd; Note: ski, arpt trans, bar, hot tub, gym, laundry, luggage room, cinema

YH Innsbruck Reichenauerstraße 147, A-6020 Innsbruck Tyrol; T:0512346179, *office@ youth-hostel-innsbruck.at/english/*; $31Bed, Kitchen:Y, B'fast:Y, Pvt.room:N, Locker:Y, Recep:7a//11p; Note: billiards, bag hold, parking, laundry, not central

Y.H. Nikolaus Glockenhaus, Weiherburggasse 3, Innsbruck; T:0512286515, *innsbruck@ hostelnikolaus.at;* $25 bed, Kitchen:N, B'fast:N, Pvt. room:Y, Locker:N, Rercep:9a>10p; Note: close to center, good views, WiFi $

2 Hostels) KITZBUHEL is a ski resort of 8000 residents, 62mi/100km east of Innsbruck. There is also an historic old town. It has a rep for high-end tourism, but... you know.

Snowbunnys, Bichlstraße 30, Kitzbuhel; *hostel@ snowbunnys.co.uk/,* T:+43/6767940233; $25Bed, Kitchen:Y, B'fast:Y, Pvt.room:Y, Locker:N, Recep:>10p; Note: arpt trans, bikes, parking, laundry, cats, central, no parties, outdoor activities

Alp King Hostel, Dorf 44, Ellmau; T:+43/6503721053, *alpking.com/* $26Bed, Kitchen:N, B'fast:Y, Pvt.room:Y, Locker:Y, Recep:ltd; Note: bar, pool, billiards, lift, parking, skiing, central

LINZ is a city of 200,000 in upper Austria near the Czech border. The Romans called it Lentia and it was later an important Holy Roman city. Kepler taught math here. Hitler lived here. There is a 'culture mile' of music and arts. There is a major street fest every July and an Ars Electronica Center and Festival.

YH Linz, Stanglhofweg 3, Linz; *linz; jgh.linz@oejhv.or.at*, T:+43/732664434, *jugendherbergsverband.at/,* $33Bed, Kitchen:N, B'fast:Y, Pvt.room:Y, Locker:Y, Recep:8a.8p; Note: wh-chair ok, bikes, parking, luggage room, central, buffet b'fast

MONDSEE is a lake in upper Austria, on the border with Salzburg province, with fish.

YH Mondsee, Krankenhausstraße 9, Mondsee; *jugendherbergsverband. at/*, T:+43/62322418; *jgh.mondsee@oejhv.or.at*; $30Bed, Kitchen:N, B'fast:Y, Pvt. room:Y, Locker:N, Recep:8a//7p; Note: water sports on lake, lift, parking, wh/chair ok

6 Hostels) SALZBURG is best known for Mozart and *The Sound of Music*. There's more than that, though. The Old Town is a UNESCO World Heritage site. It includes the Residenzplatz, with a gallery of 16th-19th C. paintings, and the cathedral. Near Monchsberg (Monks' Hill) is the Benedictine Abbey of St. Peter and the Franciscan Church. The great fortress of Hohensalzburg crowns the hill. At times the tourists outnumber the locals.

YoHo Intl. Youth Hostel, Paracelsusstraße 9, Salzburg; T:0662879649, *office@ yoho.at/*; $24 bed, Kitchen:Y, B'fast:$, Pvt. room:Y, Locker:Y, Recep:24/7; Note: bar, bike hire, laundry, luggage room, c.c. ok, afternoon kitchen

Meininger Salzburg City Center, Fürbergstraße 18, Salzburg; T:0720883414, *meininger-hotels.com/*; $30Bed, Kitchen:Y, B'fast:$, Pvt. room:Y, Locker:N, Recep:24/7; Note: lift, A/C, bag hold, parking, not central, hotel-like

JUFA Salzburg, Josef-Preis-Allee 18, Salzburg; *bookingcenter@ jufa. eu/*, T:+43/57083613; $25Bed, Kitchen:N, B'fast:Y, Pvt.room:N, Locker:Y, Recep:24/7; Note: resto/bar, bikes, wh'chair, tour desk, laundry, lift, near old town

Heinrichhaus Hostel-Salzburg, Eduard-Heinrich-Straße 2, Salzburg; T:+43/662625976, *heinrichhaus@hostel-salzburg.at*; $31Bed, Kitchen:N, B'fast:Y, Pvt. room:Y, Locker:Y, Recep:24/7; Note: resto/bar, far, parking

Muffin Hostel, Hegigasse 9, A-5020, Salzburg; *salzburg@ salzburghostel. com*, T:+43/6646367635; $28Bed, Kitchen:Y, B'fast:$, Pvt.room:Y, Locker:N, Recep:24/7; Note: bikes, pool, bar, laundry, parking, tour desk

Kolpinghaus Salzburg, Adolf-Kolping-Straße 10, Salzburg; T:+43/66246610, *info@ kolpinghaus-salzburg.at/*; $30Bed, Kitchen:Y, B'fast:$, Pvt.room:Y, Locker:N, Recep:ltd; Note: summer only, bikes, resto, gym, lift, laundry, wh-chair OK

ST.GILGEN is a village of 4000 on the Wolfgangsee in Salzburg's Salzkammergut region, dating from 1376. There are lake tours, mountains, and historic architecture.

YH St. Gilgen, Mondseerstrasse 7, St. Gilgen; *jgh.stgilgen@oejhv.or.at*; T:+43/62272365, *jugendherbergsverband.at/*; $30Bed, Kitchen:N, B'fast:Y, Pvt. room:Y, Locker:N, Recep:8a//7p; Note: parking, water sports

23 Hostels) VIENNA is the capital and largest city of Austria, and home to fully one-fourth of Austria's eight-million-plus people. With Celtic roots and Roman rearing, it finally bore fruit as the city of the Habsburgs and *de facto* capital of the Holy Roman Empire, then Austria-Hungary. Perhaps more importantly, it was a world center of art and culture, particularly known for the music of Brahms, Mahler, and Strauss, but also for the analytic psychology of Freud, and the philosophy of Wittgenstein.

The loss of empire and two world wars didn't change all that. Today its role as a center of culture extends to alternative culture, too. Notable landmarks include St. Stephan's Cathedral in the center, Church of the Augustinians, the Church of Maria am Gestade, and the Church of the Friars Minor, all dating from the 14th century. Even older is St. Ruprecht's. Secular buildings include the Imperial Palace, or Hofburg, with many museums. Vienna has the world's oldest zoo. For some reason hostels here like cash.

Hostel Ruthensteiner, Robert-Hamerling-Gasse 24, Vienna; T:018932796, *info@ hostelruthensteiner.com/*; $25 bed, Kitchen:Y, B'fast:$, Pvt.room:Y, Locker:Y, Recep:24/7; Note: cash, bar, bikes, bag hold, tours, near train, walk>town

Palace Hostel Schlossherberge, Savoyenstrasse 2, Vienna, *hostel.at/en/*, T:014810300, *shb@hostel.at*; $32bed, Kitchen:N, B'fast:Y, Pvt. room:Y, Locker:Y, Recep:ltd; Note: bag hold, laundry, parking, towel fee, mansion above city, far

Strawberry Y. H. Vienna, Mittelgasse 18, Vienna; *strawberryhostels.com/*, T:0159979660, *strawberryhostels@hotmail.com*; $29bed, Kitchen:Y, B'fast:N, Pvt. room:Y, Locker:N, Recep:24/7; Note: no bunks, laundry, bag hold, tours, cash, central

Do Step Inn, Felberstrasse 20, Vienna; T:019823314, *office@ dostepinn.com/*; $24bed, Kitchen:Y, B'fast:N, Pvt.room:Y, Locker:N, Recep:ltd; Note: lounge, laundry, luggage room, close to train

Westend City Hostel, Fügergasse 3, Vienna; T:015976729, *info@ westendhostel.at/*; $27bed, Kitchen:Y, B'fast:Y, Pvt.room:Y, Locker:Y, Recep:24/7; Note: cash only, laundry, lift to 10pm, bag hold, deposit p.p. for key

MyMOjOvie, 77 Kaiserstrasse, Apt. 8, Fl 3, Vienna; T:+43/6765511155, *accommodation@ mymojovie.at/*; $36Bed, Kitchen:Y, B'fast:Y, Pvt.room:Y, Locker:Y, Recep:ltd; Note: lift, bag hold, tours, laundry, jobs board

Happy Hostel, Kurzgasse 2, Vienna; T:+43/12082618, *info@ happyhostel. at/*; $24Bed, Kitchen:Y, B'fast:N, Pvt.room:Y, Locker:Y, Recep:24/7; Note: wheelchair ok, laundry, luggage room

Hostel Hütteldorf, Schloßberggasse 8, Wien; T:+43/1877150, *jgh@ hostel. at/*; $18Bed, Kitchen:Y, B'fast:Y, Pvt.room:Y, Locker:Y, Recep:24/7; Note: resto, bikes, lift, billiards, bag hold, tours, far, on hill, HI member

Vienna City Hostel, Dampfgasse 8, Vienna, *office@ viennacityhostel.at*, T:+43/15058843; $21Bed, Kitchen:Y, B'fast:$, Pvt.room:N, Locker:Y, Recep:24/7 Note: bikes, lift, tours, parking, laundry, bag hold, central to Hbf, safe dep

Alibi Hostel, Wilhelm-Exner-Gasse 4, Vienna; T:+43/810101890, *alibi@ alibihostel.com/*; $22Bed, Kitchen:Y, B'fast:N, Pvt.room:Y, Locker:N, Recep:24/7 Note: lift, wh'chair ok, parking, tours, bag hold, night life

Believe-it-or-not-Vienna, Myrthengasse 10, Apt.14, Vienna; T:+43/ 15264658, *believe-it-or-not-vienna.at/*; $36Bed, Kitchen:Y, B'fast:Y, Pvt.room:N, Locker:Y, Recep:ltd; Note: central, parking, many provisions, min 2N, artsy, jobs board

A&O Wien Stadthalle, Lerchenfelder Gürtel 9-11, T: +43/14930480-3900

A&O Wien Hauptbahnhof, Sonnwendgasse 11, Vienna; T:+43/ 160206173800, *aohostels.com/en/wien/*; $17Bed, Kitchen:N, B'fast:$, Pvt.room:Y, Locker:Y, Recep:24/7; Note: bar, billiards, laundry, tours, parking, bag hold, lift, linen $

JUFA Wien City, Mautner-Markhof-Gasse 50, Vienna; T:+43/57083700, *wien@ jufa.eu/*; $35Bed, Kitchen:N, B'fast:Y, Pvt.room:Y, Locker:N, Recep:24/7: Note: arpt trans, resto/bar, lift, wh/chair ok, tours, bag hold, a/c, safe dep

Hostel Wien-Brigittenau, Adalbert Stifter Str. 73, Vienna; *oejhv.at/*, T:01/3328294, *jgh.1200wien@chello.at/*; $25Bed, Kitchen:N, B'fast:Y, Pvt.room:Y, Locker:Y, Recep:24/7; Note: HI, far, resto, bikes, billiards, parking, lift, wh/chair ok

Jack's Hostel, Lerchenfelder Gürtel 26-28/4-8, Vienna; T:+43/6764008346, *reservations@ jackshostel.com/*; $22Bed, Kitchen:Y, B'fast:N, Pvt.room:Y, Locker:Y, Recep:7a>11p; Note: arpt trans, laundry, tours, bag hold, wh/chair ok, lift, metro

A&T Holiday Hostel, Leibnizgasse 66, Vienna; T:+43/16070727, *office@ athostel.com/*; $20Bed, Kitchen:Y, B'fast:N, Pvt.room:Y, Locker:Y, Recep:24/7; Note: café/bar, billiards, lift, wh/chair ok, laundry, tours, parking, maps, hotel-like

Wombats Vienna-the Naschmarkt, Rechte Wienzeile 35, Vienna

Wombats Vienna-the Lounge, Mariahilfer Strasse 137, Vienna

Wombats Vienna-the Base, Grangrasse 6, Vienna; T:+43/18972577, *office@ wombats-vienna.at/*; $18Bed, Kitchen:Y, B'fast:N, Pvt.room:Y, Locker:Y, Recep:24/7; Note: bar, billiards, lift, meals, laundry, luggage rm, Westbahnhof

Meininger Wien Downtown Sissi, Schiffamtsgasse 15; T:+43(0)720882066

Meininger Wien Downtown Franz, Rembrandtstraße 21; T:+43(0)720882065

Meininger Hotel Wien City Center, Columbusgasse 16, Wien, Österreich; T:+43(0)720881453, *welcome@ meininger-hotels.com/*; $29Bed, Kitchen:Y, B'fast:N, Pvt.room:Y, Locker:N, Recep:24/7; Note: bar, bikes, lift, wh-chair ok, near metro

WILDSCHONAU is a municipality of 4000 in the Kitzbuhel Alps, and consisting of four 'church villages': *Niederau, Oberau, Auffach,* and *Thierbach.*

Once a mining town, it now focuses on 'gentle' tourism, low-key and family-friendly.

Apsley Ski Lodge, 191 Wildschönauerstrasse, Niederau, Wildschonau; T:+43(0)533921608, *apsleyski.com*; $36Bed, Kitchen:n, B'fast:Y, Pvt.room:Y, Locker:N, Recep:ltd; Note: bar, pool, minimart, parking, hot tub, TV, luggage room

ZELL AM SEE is a town of almost 10,000 in Salzburg state, 62mi/100km east of Innsbruck, located on Lake Zell (hence the name), and comprised of five villages. The old center dates back to the Roman era. It is picturesque and lively.

Junges Hotel Zell am See, Seespitzstraße 13, Zell am See; T:+43(0)65425718, *seespitz@ hostel-zellamsee.at/*; $36Bed, Kitchen:N, B'fast:$, Pvt.room:Y, Locker:Y, Recep:8a>10p; Note: resto/bar, gym, minimart, billiards, laundry, bag hold, hot tub

ZILLERTAL is an area only 24 mi/40km from Innsbruck, consisting of mountains and valleys, the Ziller River... and singing families. With remnants from the Stone Age, there are Illyrian digs from the Bronze Age. Records start from the early Middle Ages.

Bluebird Mountain Hostel, Gattererberg 17, Stummerberg; T:+43/6503611378, *info@ bluebirdmountainhostel.com/*; $26Bed, Kitchen:Y, B'fast:N, Pvt.room:Y, Locker:N, Recep:24/7; Note: laundry, bag hold, cash only

5) ITALY

Italy is arguably the oldest country of Europe proper, inheritor to much of the culture of ancient Greece. As such it carries a lot of historical baggage, so

Italy tends to chug along in the slow lane in terms of change and innovation. Still few countries can claim such a place of importance in both remote history and the modern world, China being the other obvious exception. Proto-Italy in the early years of the Common Era controlled much of the ancient known world from its base in Rome, and is one of the world's dozen largest economies in the modern one. Its maritime republics in Venice, Genoa, and elsewhere helped bring Europe out of the Middle Ages and launch the Age of Discovery.

The Renaissance happened in Florence first. The lines that divide Europe into three parts — Latin, German, and Slavic — all converge on and around the borders of Italy. Then there's the line that divides past from present. It still runs well north of Sicily. For the traveler it's both eye candy and mental floss, and its status as a top tourist draw is a mixed blessing. While the high-rollers may wax nostalgic over their candlelight dinners and their instant friends in the countryside, the budget travelers have cause for concern.

For one thing, hostels in Italy are hardly of the highest quality and websites funky or non-existent. More importantly, short-changing seems to be the national sport. Other guides won't tell you that. I will; and I don't say it lightly. You've been warned. Think you'll learn Italian language to avoid those problems? Ha! Better avoid tourist sites, too. Euro is the currency. Telephone country code is +39.

AGEROLA is a town of over 7000 on Italy's lower west coast, only 21mi/35km from Naples, and bordering Amalfi.

Beata Solitudo, Piazza Generale Avitabile, Agerola; *beatasolitudo.it/*, T:+39/0818025048, *beatasol@tiscalinet.it*; $21Bed, Kitchen:Y, B'fast:Y, Pvt.room:Y, Locker:Y, Recep:24/7; Note: gym, laundry, parking, tea/coffee, need car

ALGHERO is a city of 44,000 on the isle of Sardinia's northwest coast. It was the site of prehistoric Ozieri and Nuraghe cultures. Sights include the Palazzo Carcasonna, the Alghero Cathedral, the churches of St. Francis and St. Michael, the Madonna del Santo Rosario, the Torre del Portal, the Tower dell'Esperò Reial, and the Palazzo D'Albis.

HI Hostal de l'Alguer, Via Parenzo 79, Fertilia Province of Sassari; *algherohostel.com/*, T:+39/079930478, *alghero@aighostels.it*; $21Bed, Kitchen:N, B'fast:Y, Pvt.room:Y, Locker:N, Recep:ltd; Note: resto/bar, bikes, wh/chair ok, not cntr

2 Hostels) AMALFI is a town of over 5000 and long a favorite of British tourists. Its history goes back to the Middle Ages as capital of a maritime duchy of the same name, and prominent trading power in Byzantine and Arab ports. Maritime law of the era originated here. A *tsunami* destroyed it in 1343. It is a UNESCO world heritage site. There are churches, museums, and fests such as St. Andrew's and Byzantine new year.

A Scalinatella Hostel, 5 Piazza Umberto I, Atrani; T:+39/089871492, *Info@ hostelscalinatella.com/*; $42Bed, Kitchen:N, B'fast:Y, Pvt.room:Y, Locker:N, Recep:ltd; Note: resto/bar, laundry, picturesque village, walk to Amalfi

Le Palme Amalfi, Via Salita dello Spinale, Amalfi; *info@ lepalmeamalfi. com/*, T:0898304548; $63Bed, Kitchen:N, B'fast:Y, Pvt.room:Y, Locker:N, Recep:ltd; Note: laundry, a/c, many stairs, splendid views

ANCONA is a city of over 100,000 and capital of the province of the same name, located, 170mi/280km northeast of Rome. Though a port, it can get chilly this far north. Founded by Greeks, one of its earliest products was 'Tyrian purple' (*murex* snail) dye. Now it's a good place to catch a ferry to Croatia or Greece. Sights include the Ancona Cathedral, the National Archeological Museum, the Municipal Art Gallery, the arch of Trajan, 'Lazzaretto' the original Pentagon, and numerous historic churches.

Ostello Ancona, 7 Via Lamaticci, Ancona; *ostelloancona.it/*, T:+39/07142257, *Ancona@aighostels.it*; $25Bed, Kitchen:N, B'fast:$, Pvt.room:N, Locker:N, Recep:ltd; Note: resto, lift, bag hold, tours, near train, midday lockout, basic

ASCOLI PICENO is a city in east-central Italy with 50,000 folks in an urban area of 100,000, and on the edge of two national parks. Its historic square has fifty towers. Then there are the Cathedral of Sant'Emidio, the Tempietto di Sant'Emidio alle Grotte, the Tempietto di Sant'Emidio Rosso, and many more.

People dress up in Renaissance costume the first Sunday in August. Sounds like fun.

HI Ostello de Longobardi YH, Via Soderini 26, Palazzetto Longobardo, Ascoli Piceno; *hihostels.com/*, T:+39/0736259191, *longobardoascoli@libero.it*; $21Bed, Kitchen:N, B'fast:N, Pvt.room:Y, Locker:Y, Recep:24/7; Note: maps, medieval bldg

BARI has a population over 300,000 out of an urban area with a million. It was once a major Roman port, and still is. During the Byzantine era the trade was heavy in white slaves, mostly for Mediterranean Muslim countries. Ferries now carry tourists to Greece. A Greek pidgin is still spoken in the port. Sights include the *Basilica di San Nicola*, Bari Cathedral, Petruzelli Theatre, the Swabian Castle, the Russian church, and much more.

Santa Claus Apartments for Holidays, Strada Arco San Pietro 4, Bari; *Info@ hostelbari.com/*, T:+39/3381744695; $28Bed, Kitchen:N, B'fast:Y, Pvt. room:Y, Locker:N, Recep:10:30a/10p; Note: bag hold, tea/coffee, different places/prices (confirm)

BERGAMO is a city of 120,000 only 25mi/40km north of Milan. The Alps start just north of here. The lower city is modern and industrial. The upper city is historic and scenic. A funicular connects the two. Once a part of the medieval Lombard League, now it's part of the European Football League, American football, that is, the contrary s-o-b's.

Ostello di Bergamo, Via Ferraris 1, Bergamo; *ostellodibergamo.it/*, T:+39/035361724, *hostelbg@libero.it/*; $27Bed, Kitchen:N, B'fast:Y, Pvt.room:Y, Locker:Y, Recep:ltd; Note: arpt trans, bikes, wh/chair ok, lift, parking, not central

4 Hostels) BOLOGNA was founded by Celts then Eruscans. Almost a reluctant Roman colony, it fared well after the fall, opening the world's first university in 1088. Always radical politically, it abolished feudal serfdom and even allowed women to study at the university level. More recently the Italian resistance was based here in WWII and the Communist Party of Italy in the 1970's. The city maintains a medieval feel, highlighted by the (leaning) "two towers" of

Asinelli and Garisenda. Notable palaces of the era are the Palazzi Comunale, Podesta', Mercanzia, Re Enzio, and Palazzo Bevilacqua. Churches include S. Petronio, S. Domenico, S. Pietro, Sta. Maria del Servi, and S. Stefano. If you want to cross northern Italy from east to west, change trains here.

Hostel Due Torri San Sisto, Via Viadagola 5, Bologna; *hihostels.com*, T:+39/051501810, *bologna@aighostels.com*; $23bed, Kitchen:N, B'fast:Y, Pvt. room:Y, Locker:Y, Recep:24/7; Note: arpt trans, café, mart, wh/chairs ok, parking, noon lockout

Il Nosadillo, via Nosadella, 19, Bologna; T:+39/0517162926, *ilnosadillo@ gmail.com*; $28Bed, Kitchen:Y, B'fast:Y, Pvt.room:Y, Locker:N, Recep:2>8p; Note: cash only, laundry, tea/coffee

Centro Turistico Città di Bologna, Via Romita, 12/4 Bologna; T:051325016, *hotelcamping.com/*; $24Bed, Kitchen:N, B'fast:$, Pvt.room:Y, Locker:N, Recep:24/7; Note: br, café, gym, pool, bag hold, wh/chair ok, laundry, not central

Centro Europa Uno, Via Emilia 297, San Lazzaro di Savena, Prov. Bologna; T:+39/0516258352, *ricettivo@ centroeuropauno.it/*; $28Bed, Kitchen:N, B'fast:Y, Pvt.room:N, Locker:Y, Recep:3>8p; Note: resto, wh/chair ok, parking, maps, not central

BRENO is an Italian town of 5000 in the far northern foothills of Lombardy. There is a castle, an archeological museum, and numerous historic churches. They have a dialect.

Casthello, via Corno Cerreto, Breno; *ostellodivallecamonica@gmail.com*, T:0364327992, *ostellodivallecamonica.com/*; $28Bed, Kitchen:N, B'fast:Y, Pvt. room:Y, Locker:N, Recep:2>8p; Note: cash, bar/café, billiards, lift, laundry, wh/chair ok, bag hold

BRINDISI is a city of 90,000 and Italy's other Adriatic port, besides Ancona and Bari. Being on Italy's southeastern-most boot-heel, it is the main one for Greece, and a ferry terminal, too. Like much of southern Italy, it was Greek before it became Roman. There are castles, Roman columns, cathedrals, parks, and wetlands. The semi-pagan cult of Tarantismo here uses exorcism by non-stop dancing and music; sounds good. There are American soldiers here, and British pensioners, too.

Hostel Carpe Diem YH, Via Nicola Brandi 2, Brindisi; *hostelcarpediem. it/*, T:3200891305, *hostelbrindisi@hotmail.com*; $24Bed, Kitchen:N, B'fast:$, Pvt. room:Y, Locker:Y, Recep:24/7; Note: pool, bar, café, gym, bag hold, parking, not central, basic

CABRAS is a town of 9000 on the west coast of the island of Sardinia, 55mi/90km northwest of Cagliari. There are the remains of a medieval castle, and plenty of beaches.

Hostel Oasi Marina, Loc. F. Meiga, S.P. 6 S. Giovanni di Sinis, Cabras; *hosteloasimarina.it/*, T:0783310101, *hosteloasimarina@gmail.com*; $35Bed, Kitchen:N, B'fast:Y, Pvt.room:Y, Locker:N, Recep:11a>11p; Note: resto/bar, bikes, wh/chair ok

CAGLIARI is a city of 150,000 in an urban area of a half mil on the southern end of the island of Sardinia. It was once inhabited by ancient Phoenicians, then their cousin Carthaginians, before the Romans and their cousin Byzantines. Pisa, Spain, and Austrian Habsburgs all took turns before Italy got it right. The old-town hilltop castle and city walls still stand. There are cathedrals, sanctuaries, parks, museums, clubs and pubs and... beaches, of course.

HI Hostel Marina, Piazza San Sepolcro 2, Cagliari; *hihostels.com/*, T:+39/070670818, *cagliari@aighostels.it*; $31Bed, Kitchen:N, B'fast:Y, Pvt. room:Y, Locker:N, Recep:24/7; Note: bar, café, wh/chair ok, lift, luggage room, central

4 Hostels) CATANIA is a city of almost 300,000 on the east coast of Sicily. It was originally a Greek city until submitting to Rome after the Frst Punic War. It was then subsequently Islamic, Norman, and Spanish, until becoming part of modern Italy. Its claim to fame is proximity to volcanic Mt. Etna. The main sight is the elephant made of lava. Yep. Historic architecture includes the Greek-Roman Theatre, the Odeon Amphitheatre, the Greek Acropolis

of Montevergine, the Roman Aqueduct, Roman Forum, Christian basilicas, Catacombs, and more. The fest of St. Agatha is Feb. 5. ENNA is a historic city of 28,000 in the center of the island at 3000ft/930mt.

C. C. Ly Hostel Enna, Via Vulturo 3, Enna; T:0935072257, *infoenna@*

C. C. Ly Hostel Catania, Piazza Giovanni Falcone 3, Catania; T:0957462399; *Info@ ccly-hostel.com/*; $28Bed, Kitchen:Y, B'fast:Y, Pvt.room:N, Locker:Y, Recep:ltd; Note: café, bikes, lift, arpt trans, wh/chair ok, laundry, bag hold, parking, tours, nr train

Agora Hostel, Piazza Currò, 6, Catania, (Mt Etna), Sicily; *Info@ agorahostel. it/*, T:0957233010; $23Bed, Kitchen:Y, B'fast:Y, Pvt.room:Y, Locker:Y, Recep:24/7; Note: resto/bar, wh/chair ok, laundry, bag hold, parking, tea/coffee, tours, partyy

Villaggio Europeo, Viale Kennedy 91, Catania, T:+39/095591026, *Info@ villaggioeuropeo.it/*; $20Bed, Kitchen:Y, B'fast:$, Pvt.room:Y, Locker:N, Recep:24/7; Note: pool, resto/bar, billiards, wh/chair ok, bag hold, parking, minimart

LAMPORECCHIO is a town of 7000 in Italy's Tuscany region, 18mi/30km west of Florence, and known for its Communists, anise-flavored wafers, and Chianti wine.

Heart of Tuscany Hostel, Via Vecchia Maremmana 3, Lamporecchio; *Info@ heartoftuscanyhostel.com/*, T:+39/3775407275; $29Bed, Kitchen:Y, B'fast:Y, Pvt. room:Y, Locker:N, Recep:9a//11p; Note: shuttle, pool, gym, resto/bar, bikes, parking

6 Hostels) CINQUE TERRE is that rugged part of the Italian Riviera composed of five 'lands': Monterosso al Mare, Vernazza, Corniglia, Manarola, and Riomaggiore. The hillsides are traditionally terraced, and the entire area is a UNESCO world heritage site. Trains and ferries provide the best connections. The wines are good... or so I hear.

Ostello Tramonti, Via Fabio Filzi 110, Biassa; *ostellotramonti.it/*, T:0187758507, *ostellotramonti@cdh.it*; $28Bed, Kitchen:N, B'fast:$, Pvt.room:Y, Locker:Y, Recep:7//1a; Note: resto, wh/chair, lift, lndry, prkng, 1a curfew, noon lockout

Cinque Terre Holidays, Via Colombo 94, Riomaggiore, Cinque Terre; *cinqueterreholidays.it/*, T/F:0187760073, *robertofazioli@libero.it*; $35Bed, Kitchen:Y, B'fast:$, Pvt.room:Y, Locker:N, Recep:10:30a>5p!; Note:dorm>35y.o, bikes, resto, lndry

Ostello di Corniglia, Via alla Stazione 3, Corniglia; *ostellocorniglia.com/*,

T/F:39/0187812559, *ostellocorniglia@gmail.com*; $31Bed, Kitchen:N, B'fast:$, Pvt.room:Y, Locker:Y, Recep:3>10p; Note: café, laundry, prkng, 1-3p lockout, 365 steps

Mar-Mar, via Malborghetto 4, Riomaggiore, *5terre-marmar.com/*, T:+39/0187920932, *marmar.riomaggiore@gmail.com*; $42Bed, Kitchen:Y, B'fast:Y, Pvt.room:N, Locker:N, Recep:>7p; Note: cash only, apartment, near train

Hostel 5 Terre, Via B. Riccobaldi 21, Manarola, La Spezia; T:0187920039, *Info@ hostel5terre.com/*; $31Bed, Kitchen:N, B'fast:$, Pvt.room:N, Locker:Y, Recep:10a//8p; Note: resto/bar, wh/chair ok, lift, bag hold, shuttle, uphill, 5-min shower

Ostello Ospitalia del Mare, Via S. Nicolò, Levanto; *Info@ ospitaliadelmare. it/*, T:(+39)0187802562; $32Bed, Kitchen:N, B'fast:Y, Pvt.room:N, Locker:Y, Recep:10a//6p; Note: wh/chair ok, lift, laundry, bag hold, maps, books

2 Hostels) COMO is a city of 85,000 near Italy's far northern Swiss border, on the beautiful lake of the same name. There is a small medieval castle and numerous historic cathedrals, churches, museums, and fountains. Boats connect the villages on the lake. There was a silk industry here not long ago. Now many people work in nearby Switzerland. MENAGGIO is a town of 3000 on the western end of the lake, complete with guitar fest.

HI Lake Como YH La Primula, Via IV Nov 106, Menaggio; *hihostels. com/*, T:034432356, *info@lakecomohostel.com*; $28Bed, Kitchen:N, B'fast:Y, Pvt. room:Y, Locker:Y, Recep:5>11p; Note: resto/bar, bikes, billiards, wh/chair ok, laundry

Respau Eco Hostel, Via Santa Brigina e Respaù, Como; T:+39/3467249131, *info@ cascinarespau.it/*; $25Bed, Kitchen:N, B'fast:$, Pvt.room:Y, Locker:Y, Recep:10:30//10p; Note: resto/bar, bag hold, tours, shuttle, uphill, nature rez

COSENZA is a city of 70,000 in an urban area of a quarter mil, in the southern Calabria region of Italy. It was variously contested by Romans, Goths, Saracens, Lombards, Normans, and Spanish. There was a renaissance-era Sicilian school of philosophy here. There is a castle, cathedrals, museums, and an open-air museum of famous sculptures.

Ostello re Alarico, Via Giuseppe Marini Serra, Cosenza; *ostellorealarico.com/*, T:+39/3281149430, *ostelloalarico@libero.it*; $24Bed, Kitchen:Y, B'fast:Y, Pvt.room:Y, Locker:N, Recep: advise ETA; Note: bikes, tea/coffee, cash only, uphill

CREMONA is a city of 70,000 in the Italian northern Lombardy region, and famous for its luthiers, including Antonio Stradivari himself. The Celts were here before the Romans, though legends tell of even earlier peoples. There are many historic churches and buildings, including museums. But music is the big deal here, and long has been, especially Renaissance and Baroque.

Ostello L'Archetto, Via Brescia 9, Cremona; *info@ ostellocremona. it/*, T:+39/0372080281; $32Bed, Kitchen:Y, B'fast:$, Pvt.room:Y, Locker:Y, Recep:5:30>9:30p; Note: bikes, wh/chair ok, tea/coffee, bag hold

FERRARA is a city of 130,000 in Italy's northeast, 30mi/50km from Bologna. It is a UNESCO world heritage city for its 14th-15th Century architecture. This was an important Renaissance cultural center, especially for its school of painters. There are 5.5mi/9km of Renaissance-era city walls still standing, a castle, many palaces, and countless churches. There has been a Jewish community here for hundreds of years, responsible for the 1553 Ferrara Bible. Festivals include Palio, Buskers, and Balloons.

Ostello Ferrara, Corso Biagio Rossetti 24, Ferrara; T:+39/0532201158, *Info@ ostelloferrara.it/*; $27Bed, Kitchen:N, B'fast:Y, Pvt.room:Y, Locker:Y, Recep:24/7; Note: resto/bar, bikes, wh/chair ok, lift, bag hold, mart, tours, parking

32 Hostels) FLORENCE (Firenze) is where you go when you've grown tired of Rome. If Rome is the political capital of Italy, then Florence is the cultural capital. Much of the Renaissance happened right here, in the Florence of Dante and Petrarch, Leonardo and Michelangelo, Macchiavelli and the Medici. Here

sits the highest ratio of art to audience in the world. The Florentine dialect is the standard for Italian. Catch it on a warm day in the off-season, and you just might think you've died and gone to heaven.

The entire city is a UNESCO world heritage site. Everything is of tourist interest, e.g. the Palazzo Vecchio, the Loggia del Lanzi, the Uffizi, the Duomo, the Medici Palace, the Strozzi Palace, the Pitti Palace, the Boboli Gardens, and much more. Florence is still a center of craftsmanship, with guilds dating back to the Middle Ages, the Ponte Vecchio (old Bridge) being one of the traditional markets for goldsmiths and jewelers. Then there's the sublime Tuscan countryside. Hostel quality is pretty good.

Academy Hostel, Via Ricasoli, 9, Stairs B, 1st Fl, Florence; T:0552398665, *info@ academyhostel.eu/*; $41bed, Kitchen:Y, B'fast:Y, Pvt.room:Y, Locker:Y, Recep:24/7; Note: lift, tea/coffee, noon lockout, wh/chair ok, bag hold, laundry

Ostello Gallo D'Oro, Via Cavour, 104 Florence; T:0555522964, *info@ ostellogallodoro. com/*; $39bed, Kitchen:Y, B'fast:Y, Pvt.room:Y, Locker:Y, Recep:24/7; Note: wh/chair ok, lift, bar, tours, bag hold, laundry, c.c. ok, tea/cof

HI Ostello del Chianti, V. Roma 137, Tavarnelle Val di Pesa, Firenze; T:0558050265, *ostello@ ostellodelchianti.it/*; $23bed, Kitchen:N, B'fast:$, Pvt. room:Y, Locker:Y, Recep:ltd; Note: bikes, 15mi/23 km south, wh/chair ok, bag hold, parking

Florence Youth Hostel, Via della Condotta, 4 Florence; T:3293980218, *florence-youth-hostel.com/*, $39bed, *florenceyouthostel@gmail.com*; Kitchen:N, B'fast:N, Pvt.room:Y, Locker:N, Recep:>10p; Note: café, mart, 10-2 lockout, cash

Locanda Daniel, Via Nazionale, 22, Firenze; *locandadaniel.it/*, T:+39/ 055211293; $31bed, Kitchen:Y, B'fast:$, Pvt.room:Y, Locker:N, Recep:24/7; Note: no bunks, call check-in, bag hold, laundry, tours, a/c, cc ok

David Inn, Via Ricasoli 31, Florence; *davidinn.it/*, T:+39/055213707; $33bed, Kitchen:Y, B'fast:N, Pvt.room:N, Locker:N, Recep:9a>12m; Note: hard to find, cash only, b.y.o. towels, luggage room, tour desk, café, lift

PLUS Camping Michelangelo, Viale Michelangiolo 80; T:0556811977

PLUS Florence, Via S Caterina D'Alessandria15, Florence; *plushostels.com/*, T:0556286347; $23bed, Kitchen:N, B'fast:$, Pvt.room:Y, Locker:Y, Recep:24/7; Note: resto/bar/café, wh/chair ok, lift, pool, sauna, gym, ATM, a/c, c.c.

Maison (The Queen's), Via C. Cavour 15, Florence; *bbmaison.hostel. com/*, T:3494093023; $17bed, Kitchen:Y, B'fast:$, Pvt.room:Y, Locker:N, Recep:8:30a>11p; Note: advise ETA, maps, near supermkt, central, stairs, basic

Hostel Santa Monaca, Via Sta. Monaca 6, Florence; T:055268338, *info@ ostellosantamonaca.com/*; $23bed, Kitchen:Y, B'fast:N, Pvt.room:N, Locker:Y, Recep:ltd; Note: hard find, noon lockout, bag hold, TV, bikes, laundry, forex

Il Giglio Guesthouse, Viale Fratelli Rosselli 74, Florence, *ilgiglioguesthouse. it/*, T:+39/3475300438; $37Bed, Kitchen:Y, B'fast:Y, Pvt.room:N, Locker:N, Recep:9a>9p, advise ETA; Note: tea/coffee, maps, absentee staff, near train, central

HostelArchi Rossi, Via Faenza 94, Florence; T:+39/055290804, *Info@ hostelarchirossi.com/*; $30Bed, Kitchen:N, B'fast:Y, Pvt.room:Y, Locker:Y, Recep:24/7; Note: resto/bar, wh/chair ok, lift, laundry, bag hold, tours, near train, central

Emerald Palace, Via Dell' Ariento 2, Florence; T:+39/3291862260; $38bed

Emerald Fields, Via Guelfa 59, Firenze, *hostel-florence-emeraldfields. com/*, T:39/3291862260, *antonio.palace@gmail.com*; $31Bed, Kitchen:N, B'fast:Y, Pvt.room:Y, Locker:Y, Recep:8a>12m; Note: hot tub, café, bag hold, nr train, cash

Alex House, Borgo de' Greci13, Florence; T:+39/3493600709, *Info@ alexhouse.it/*; $63Bed, Kitchen:N, B'fast:$, Pvt.room:Y, Locker:N, Recep:1>7p; Note: lift, luggage room, tour desk, central

Hostel 7 Santi, Viale dei Mille 11, Florence: *7santi.com/*, T:0555048452; $23Bed, Kitchen:N, B'fast:$, Pvt.room:Y, Locker:Y, Recep:24/7; Note: resto/ bar, wh/chair ok, laundry, tea/coffee, tours, not central

Soggiorno Pitti, Piazza de' Pitti 8, Florence; T:+39/0553921483; *Info@ soggiornopitti.com/*; $28Bed, Kitchen:N, B'fast:$, Pvt.room:Y, Locker:N, Recep:9a>9p; Note: café, lift, luggage room, tour desk

Riverbanks Hotels, via Volta dei Tintori 1, Firenze; T:+39/3489771630, *info@ riverbankshotels.com/*; $35Bed, Kitchen:Y, B'fast:$, Pvt.room:Y, Locker:N, Recep:24/7; Note: cash only, resto/bar, bag hold, mart, tours

Santa Croce Firenze, Via Ghibellina 87, Florence; T:+39/0552342230, *reservations.santacrocefirenze@ baglionihotels.com/*; $16Bed, Kitchen:Y, B'fast:N, Pvt.room:Y, Locker:N, Recep:(close Fri/nt>Sat/nt); Note: bikes, café, laundry, tea/cof

Hotel Ottaviani, Piazza degli Ottaviani 1, Florence; T:+39/0552396223; *Info@ hotelottaviani.com/*; $16Bed, Kitchen:Y, B'fast:$, Pvt.room:Y, Locker:N, Recep:1:30>10p; Note: resto, bikes, lift, bag hold, parking, tea/cof, tours, @train

Tasso Hostel Florence, Via Villani 15, Florence; T:+39/0550602087, *Info@ tassohostelflorence.com/*; $35Bed, Kitchen:Y, B'fast:Y, Pvt.room:Y, Locker:Y, Recep:24/7; Note: bar, café, lift, wh/chair ok, laundry, central, tours, bag hold, tea/cof

Fattoria Bassetto, Via delle Città 3, Certaldo, Florence; T:+39/0571668342, *reservations@ fattoriabassetto.com/*; $31Bed, Kitchen:Y, B'fast:Y, Pvt.room:Y, Locker:N, Recep:ltd; Note: pool, bikes, bag hold, parking, 1 hr>Florence

Academy Hostel, Via Ricasoli 9, Florence; T:+39/0552398665, *Info@ academyhostel.it/*; $42Bed, Kitchen:N, B'fast:Y, Pvt.room:N, Locker:Y, Recep:24/7; Note: laundry, lift, bag hold, tours, tea/coffee, central, maps, books

New Hostel Florence, Via Jacopo Peri 3, Florence, *newhostelflorence.com/*; T:0555272220, *newhostelflorence@gmail.com*; $17Bed, Kitchen:N, B'fast:N, Pvt. room:Y, Locker:N, Recep:ltd; Note: café, laundry, bag hold, parking, tours, ctr

Ciao Hostel Florence, Via Guido Monaco 34, Florence; T:+39/055321018, *ciaohostelflorence.com/*; $30Bed, Kitchen:Y, B'fast:N, Pvt.room:Y, Locker:N, Recep:9a>10p; Note: lift, tours, central

Florence Dance Hostels, Via Nazionale, 22, Florence; T:3398639548, *florencedancehostels.com/*, $20Bed, *florencedancehostels@gmail.com*; Kitchen:Y, B'fast:$, Pvt.room:Y, Locker:N, Recep:8a>8p; Note: bag hold, tea/cof, cash only

Hotel Genzianella, Via Cavour 112, Florence, *Info@ hotelgenzianella. com/*, T:+39/0342925092; $23Bed, Kitchen:N, B'fast:Y, Pvt.room:Y, Locker:N, Recep:24/7; Note: bar, café, wh/chair ok, lift, bag hold, tea/coffee, tour desk

Rocco Florence, Via del Sole 5, Florence; *reservations@ roccoflorence.com/*, T:3891462725; $20Bed, Kitchen:N, B'fast:$, Pvt.room:Y, Locker:N, Recep:9a>3p; Note: cash only, arpt trans, bikes, bag hold, minibar, parking, central, basic

HI Villa Camerata YH, Viale Augusto Righi 4, Florence; *hihostels.com/*, T:+39/055601451, *firenze@aighostels.it*; $27Bed, Kitchen:N, B'fast:Y, Pvt. room:N, Locker:N, Recep:24/7; Note: café, bar, wh/chair ok, laundry, parking, tours, not ctr

Soggiorno Primavera, via J. Peri 2, Firenze; *primaverainflorence.com/*, T:0553215078, *soggiornoprimavera@libero.it*; $24Bed, Kitchen:N, B'fast:$, Pvt. room:Y, Locker:N, Recep:9a/6p M-F; Note: bag hold, tea/coffee, central

Albergo Paola, Via Faenza 56, Florence; *Info@ albergopaolafirenze.com/*, T:055289999; $27Bed, Kitchen:N, B'fast:$, Pvt.room:Y, Locker:N, Recep:ltd; Note: luggage room, tour desk, central

Camping il Poggetto, Via Il Poggetto 143, Troghi, Florence, *Info@ campingilpoggetto.com/*; T:+39/0558307323; $18Bed, Kitchen:N, B'fast:$, Pvt. room:Y, Locker:N, Recep:3>9p; Note: pool, resto/bar, mart, bag hold, parking, 1hr>Florence

2 Hostels) GENOA is a city of 600,000 in Italy's far northwest, in an urban area of a million and a half, and a UNESCO world heritage site for its old town. With Torino and Milano it forms an economic triangular powerhouse. After Etruscans, Greeks, Ligurians, Rome, Ostrogoths, and Lombards, Genoa came into its own in the Middle Ages as the prime maritime rival to Venice on the other side of the peninsula. Columbus was from here. It was a Renaissance center of art. France annexed it briefly. Main sights are the old city, city walls, lighthouse, Doge's palace, countless churches and palaces.

HI Genoa YH, Via Giovanni Costanzi 120, Genova; *hihostels.com/*, T:0102422457, *hostelge@iol.it*; $27Bed, Kitchen:N, B'fast:$, Pvt.room:Y, Locker:Y, Recep:24//7; Note: bar, wh/chair ok, lift, laundry, parking, bag hold, lockout, not ctr

Manena Hostel, Vico alla Chiesa della Maddalena 9/1, Genoa; T:+39/0108608890, *manenahostel.it/*; $30Bed, Kitchen:Y, B'fast:$, Pvt.room:Y,

Locker:Y, Recep:8a//10p; Note: bar, café, laundry, bag hold, tour, tea/coffee, cntr

2 Hostels) ISCHIA is a volcanic island with a population of 62,000. Last eruption was in 1302. Thermal spas are big biz. There is a castle, gardens, a ferry, and tourist overload.

Paradise Beach Hostel, C. Vittorio Emanuele 46, Casamicciola Terme; *info @ paradisebeachhostel.com/*, T:+39/3382700427; $25Bed, Kitchen:N, B'fast:Y, Pvt.room:Y, Locker:N, Recep:10a>11p; Note: bar, café, bag hold, pool

Ring Hostel, via Gaetano Morgera #72, Ischia Island; *Info@ ringhostel. com/*, T:+39/081997424; $23Bed, Kitchen:N, B'fast:Y, Pvt.room:Y, Locker:Y, Recep:ltd; Note: resto/club, bikes, laundry, bag hold, parking, tea/cof, billiards

3 Hostels) LAKE GARDA is one of Italy's largest lakes, located halfway between Milan and Venice. The climate is mild for such a northern latitude. There are sulfur springs.

Backpackers Villa, Via Vespucci 41, Brenzone; *backpackers-gardasee.com/*, T:+39/3661980557, *kitevilla@ymail.com*; $34Bed, Kitchen:N, B'fast:Y, Pvt. room:Y, Locker:Y, Recep:ltd; Note: cash only, arpt trans, bar, bikes, laundry, bag hold, shuttle

OstelloRiva, PiazzaCavour14, RivadelGarda, Trentino; T:+39/0464554911, *Info@ ostelloriva.com/*; $25Bed, Kitchen:N, B'fast:Y, Pvt.room:N, Locker:Y, Recep:3>10p; Note: pool, resto, wh/chair ok, laundry

Campione Del Garda Via R. Cozzaglio 1, Campione del Garda; T:+39/0365/791102, *booking@ campioneunivela.it*; $35Bed, Kitchen:N, B'fast:Y, Pvt.room:Y, Locker:N, Recep:2>7p; Note: resto/bar, gym, lift, wh/chair ok

LAKE MAGGIORE is a lake that Italy shares with Switzerland, and the most western of the lakes in the region. It has a Mediterranean climate. There is a 'Spirit of Woodstock' Festival in Mirapuri. VERBANIA is a city of 31,000 only 57mi/91km from Milan.

HI Verbania YH, Via Alle Rose 7, Verbania; *hihostels.com/*, T:+39/0323501648, *ostelloverbania@gmail.com*; $30Bed, Kitchen:N, B'fast:Y, Pvt. room:Y, Locker:Y, Recep:3>7p; Note: café, bar, parking, wh/chair ok

LAKE TRASIMENO is located in the Umbria region, between the Tiber and Po Rivers. With no inlets or outlets, it is salty and muddy. There are three islands in the lake, and ruined castles surrounding it. Then there is the Vernazzano leaning tower.

Fattoria il Poggio, Isola polvese s/n, San Feliciano, Lake Trasimeno; *Info@ fattoriaisolapolvese.com/*, T:(+39)0759659550; $25Bed, Kitchen:N, B'fast:Y, Pvt. room:N, Locker:Y, Recep:24/7; Note: pool, resto/bar, bikes, wh/chair ok, lift, cash

LERICI is a town of over 10,000 in La Spezia province on the Italian Riviera. It is connected to Cinque Terre by ferry. Percy Shelley drowned here. There is a castle.

Hostel Ameglia, via Circonvallazione 3, Ameglia La Spezia; T:018765517, *hostelameglia.it/*; $35Bed, Kitchen:N, B'fast:$, Pvt.room:Y, Locker:N, Recep:3:30>8p; Note: lift, parking, tea/coffee, 1 hr>La Spezia

LUCCA is a city of 88,000 in Tuscany, famous for its intact city walls. Then there is the Casa di Puccini and opera festival every year, several piazzas, the ducal palace, the Roman amphitheatre, and many churches and museums. The Lucca Summer Festival brings out some of pop music's top acts. There are fests for jazz, comics and film, too.

Ostello San Frediano, Via della Cavallerizza 12, Lucca; *Info@ ostellolucca. it/*, T:0583469957; $28Bed, Kitchen:N, B'fast:Y, Pvt.room:Y, Locker:Y, Recep:24/7; Note: bar, café, lift, luggage room, parking, historic bldg

MACERATA is a city of 43,000 in east-central Italy. The historic city is on top of a hill, the modern one below, with elevator connecting the two. The central plaza dates from the Renaissance, and there are several palaces and cathedrals. The opera festival is big.

Ostello Asilo Ricci, Via Dell'Asilo 36, Macerata; *ostelloasiloricci.jimdo. com/*, T:0733270020, *asiloricci.ostello@gmail.com*; $23Bed, Kitchen:N, B'fast:Y, Pvt.room:N, Locker:N, Recep:ltd; Note: resto, lift, laundry

MANTOVA (Mantua) is a city of 48,000 in north-central Italy, in the province of the same name. It pre-dates even the Etruscans in the region, and has been battled over by all the usual suspects, most recently France and Austria. Today it is a cultural hub, with artistic and architectural masterpieces, including many palaces, and the Palazzo Te.

Ostello del Mincio, via Porto 25, Rodigo, Mantova; *Info@ ostellodelmincio. it/*, T:3409300509; $28Bed, Kitchen:N, B'fast:$, Pvt.room:Y, Locker:Y, Recep:9a//7:30p; Note: arpt trans, bar, café, bikes, lift, wh/chair ok, bag hold, parking, tours

MAZARA DEL VALLO is a city of over 50,000 in the westernmost part of the island of Sicily. It dates back to the Phoenicians of the 9th Century BC and contains a central *Kasbah* to this day. Fishing is the main business. The main sights are the Greek sculpture *Dancing Satyr*, the Norman Arc 1073 castle ruins, many churches and piazzas.

Sporting Club Village, C.da Bocca Arena, Mazara del Vallo; T:0923947230, *sportingclubvillage.com/*; $24Bed, Kitchen:N, B'fast:$, Pvt.room:Y, Locker:N, Recep:ltd; Note: arpt trans, pool, bar, café, bikes, laundry, parking, tours

17 Hostels) MILAN was settled by Celts and served a term as capital of the Western Roman Empire between 286 and 402, before rising to modern international prominence in the same pre-Renaissance wave that also elevated London and Paris. These days it's the business and financial center of Italy and best known for its fashion industry and its major trade fairs. Milan is the crossroads for this region, with direct connections to most of the major countries of Europe, and of course, the rest of Italy.

The Swiss border at Chiasso is only a day trip away, but almost like another dimension. Tourist sights include paintings by Leonardo and Raphael and the Gothic Milan Cathedral. The Duomo is the third largest church of Europe and a fine example of Gothic architecture. The Pinacoteca di Brera is one of the largest art galleries in Italy, and the Teatro alla Scala is one of the great theatres of the world. Many hostels here are up to modern European standards and expectations, not just cheap hotels with dorms. The airport is at MALPENSA.

Malpensa Fiera Milano Hostel, Via Sampietro 22, Malpensa; *Info@ malpensahostel.com/*, T:+39/0223164327; $28Bed, Kitchen:Y, B'fast:Y, Pvt. room:Y, Locker:Y, Recep:5p>; Note: arpt trans, bar, café, wh/chairs, laundry, bag hold, tea/coffee

The Monastery Hostel, Via Bertoni, 3, Milano; T:0265560201, *info@ themonasteryhostel.it/*; $21bed, Kitchen:Y, B'fast:Y, Pvt.room:Y, Locker:Y, Recep:24/7; Note: lift, TV, travel desk, bag hold, laundry, a/c, c.c. ok, tea/coffee

Ostello Olinda, Via Ippocrate, 45, Milan; T:0264445219, *ostello@ olinda. org/*; $27bed, Kitchen:Y, B'fast:N, Pvt.room:Y, Locker:Y, Recep:10a>8p; Note: wh/chair ok, resto/bar, parking, bag hold, laundry, TV, not central, tea/coffee

Hotel San Tomaso, Viale Tunisia 6, Milan; *hotelsantomaso.com/*, T:0229514747, *hotelsantomaso@tin.it*; $32bed, Kitchen:N, B'fast:$, Pvt.room:Y, Locker:N, Recep:24/7; Note: bar, café, lift, bag hold, c.c.+5%, central, tours

Hotel Central Station, Via Giovanni B. Sammartini 15, Milan; T:0267071766, *info@ hotelcentralstation.com/*; $42bed, Kitchen:N, B'fast:N, Pvt. room:Y, Locker:N, Recep:24/7; Note: 5-day cancel, @arpt trans/train, lift, bag hold, parking

Hostel 3, Via Ignazio Ciaia 5, Milan; T:0239820435, *info@hostel3.it*; $17bed, Kitchen:N, B'fast:$, Pvt.room:Y, Locker:N, Recep:24/7; Note: café, minibar, balcony, luggage room, c.c. ok, far from center

Hotel Galla, Via Privata Galla Placidia 5, Milan; T:0239561321, *info@ hotelgalla.it/*; $28bed, Kitchen:N, B'fast:N, Pvt.room:Y, Locker:N, Recep:24/7; Note: luggage room, c.c. ok, not center, near train, tea/coffee

Hostel Mr. Mido, Via Carlo Goldoni, 84, Milan; T:0239443510, *info@ hostelmistermido.com/*; $27bed, Kitchen:Y, B'fast:$, Pvt.room:Y, Locker:N, Recep:ltd; Note: bar, tours, ATM, bag hold, laundry, TV, c.c. ok

Hostel HI Piero Rotta, Via Salmoiraghi 1, Milan; *hostelmilan.org/*, T:0239267095, *milano@aighostels.com*; $30bed, Kitchen:N, B'fast:Y, Pvt.

room:Y, Locker:Y, Recep:24/7; Note: café, wh/chair ok, bag hold, parking, day lockout

Star Hostel, Via Varesina 63, Milan; *star.hostel@yahoo.com*, T:0233003653, (see FB page); $16Bed, Kitchen:N, B'fast:$, Pvt.room:Y, Locker:N, Recep:24/7; Note: non-ref $, lift, laundry, bag hold, tours, linen fee $, not central

Hostel Colours, Via Desiderio 24, Milan; *Info@ hostelcolours.com/*, T:+39/0236744492; $25Bed, Kitchen:N, B'fast:Y, Pvt.room:Y, Locker:Y, Recep:24/7; Note: bar, wheelchair ok, luggage room

Zebra Hostel, viale Regina Margherita 9, Milan; *zebrahostel.it/*, T:+39/0236705185, *zebrahostel@aruba.it*; $35Bed, Kitchen:Y, B'fast:Y, Pvt. room:Y, Locker:Y, Recep:24/7; Note: billiards, bikes, café/bar/club, bag hold, mart, tea/coffee

Hotel Adelchi, Via Francesco Ingegnoli 20, Milan; T:+39/022892970, *Info@ hoteladelchi.it/*; $28Bed, Kitchen:N, B'fast:$, Pvt.room:Y, Locker:N, Recep:ltd; Note: luggage room, parking, WiFi $

Milan Hostel Emmy, Via Fra Galgario 4, 4th fl, Milan; T:+39/0245488118, *Info@ milanhostelemmy.com/*; $14Bed, Kitchen:N, B'fast:$, Pvt.room:Y, Locker:N, Recep:3>10p; Note: very basic, linen $

Hostel Central Station, Viale Lunigiana 4, Milan; T:+39/0226145050, *Info@ hostelincentralstation.com/*; $31Bed, Kitchen:N, B'fast:$, Pvt.room:Y, Locker:N, Recep:ltd; Note: bag hold, tea/coffee, near train station/airport, res area

Hotel Alba, Viale Porpora 132, Milan; *Info@ hotelalbamilano.it/*, T:+39/0223161796; $28Bed, Kitchen:N, B'fast:$, Pvt.room:Y, Locker:N, Recep:ltd; Note: café, bag hold, tea/coffee, near Lambrete station

B&Brera, Via Bramante 35, Milan; *Info@ bbbrera.it/*, T:+39/3396501253; $31Bed, Kitchen:Y, B'fast:Y, Pvt.room:Y, Locker:N, Recep:>10:30p; Note: laundry, close 3>7p, cash only, E20 key dep, Chinatown near metro

MODENA is a city of 186,000 with ancient roots but best known today for its automotive accomplishments: Ferrari, Lamborghini, Maserati, etc. Still, it is a UNESCO world heritage city, for its 1099 cathedral. Other sights include the Ducal Palace, the 1046 Town Hall, the Museum Palace of the city's main museums, and countless churches.

HI San Filippo Neri YH, Via S. Orsola 48/52, Modena; *hihostels.com/*, T:+39/059234598, *modena@aighostels.com*; $26Bed, Kitchen:Y, B'fast:Y, Pvt. room:Y, Locker:Y, Recep:24/7; Note: wh/chair ok, lift, bag hold, parking, nr train/center

MONTAGNANA is a town of almost 10,000 in north Italy's Padova province. There are medieval walls, San Zeno Castle, Town Hall, Gothic Cathedral and Palazzo.

HI Città Murata YH, Via Circonvallazione Nord 239, Montagnana; *hihostels. com/*, T:04291760453, *info@ostellodimontagnana.com*; $28Bed, Kitchen:N, B'fast:Y, Pvt.room:Y, Locker:Y, Recep:ltd; Note: bikes, café, billiards, wh/chair ok

13 Hostels) NAPLES (Napoli) is another part of Italy and another part of Europe, the most southern part: more old-fashioned, maybe a bit grimier, maybe a bit cheaper, and maybe even friendlier, so that's not all a bad thing. Naples was still speaking Greek when Rome was speaking Latin, and was a major point of diffusion for Greek culture into Latin. The post-Roman medieval enemies in these parts were Arabs, Norman Sicilians and Ottomans. The historic center is one of Europe's largest and is a UNESCO site.

If that's not enough there's another world right below it of catacombs, mines, and geothermal springs. Sights include nearby Mt. Vesuvius and the ruined city of Pompeii. Everything Neapolitan comes from here, and so does pizza. Naples has its own Duomo, a Castel Nuovo, a Royal Palace, and the National Archeological Museum, as well as the National Museum and Gallery of Capodimonte. Hostels here get generally good marks, and quality seems better than the main tourist markets up north.

Hostel Giovanni's Home, Via Sapienza, 43, Naples; T:08119565641, *info@ giovannishome.com/*; $25bed, Kitchen:Y, B'fast:N, Pvt.room:N, Locker:N, Recep: 8a>12m; Note: 2N min. stay, cash only, bag hold, laundry, tours, a/c, c.c. ok

Hostel of the Sun, Via Guglielmo Melisurgo 15, Naples; T:0814206393, *info@ hostelnapoli.com/*; $25bed, Kitchen:Y, B'fast:Y, Pvt.room:Y, Locker:Y, Recep:24/7; Note: bar, bikes, wh/chair ok, laundry, lift, tea/cof, nr ferry/bus, bag hold

Robby's House B&B, Via San Nicola dei Caserti #5, Naples; *robbyshouse. com/*, T:+39/081454546, *robbyshouse@libero.it*; $21bed, Kitchen:N, B'fast:Y, Pvt. room:Y, Locker:N, Recep:24/7; Note: laundry, luggage room

La Controra Hostel, Piazzetta Trinità alla Cesarea 231, Naples; T:0815494014, *info@ lacontrora.com/*; $21bed, Kitchen:N, B'fast:Y, Pvt.room:N, Locker:Y, Recep: 24/7; Note: bikes, wh/chair ok, bar/café, laundry, bag hold, tours, lift, parking, tea/cof

6 Small Rooms, Via Diodato Lioy 18, Naples; T:+39/0817901378, *info@ 6smallrooms.com/*; $24bed, Kitchen:Y, B'fast:Y, Pvt.room:Y, Locker:Y, Recep: 8a>12m; Note: central, tea/coffee, lots of stairs, bag hold, laundry, TV, c.c. ok

Hostel Mancini, Via P. S. Mancini 33, Napoli; T:0815536731, *info@ hostelpensionemancini.com/*; $21bed, Kitchen:Y, B'fast:Y, Pvt.room:Y, Locker:Y, Recep:24/7; Note: laundry, nr train, bag hold, lift, tours, TV, tea/cof, parking

Fabric Hostel & Club, Via Bellucci Sessa 22, Portici, Naples; *fabric-hostel. ory.it/*, T:0817765874, *ristfradiavolo@gmail.com*; $21bed, Kitchen:Y, B'fast:$, Pvt. room:Y, Locker:Y, Recep:8a>2a; Note:arpt trans, resto/bar, wh/chair ok, lift

Welcome Inn Hostel, Via Santa Teresa degli Scalzi, 8 Naples; T:08119579762, *info@ welcomeinn.it/*; $21bed, Kitchen:Y, B'fast:Y, Pvt.room:Y, Locker:N, Recep:24/7; Note: café, wh/chair ok, lift, parking, resto/bar, tours, bag hold

Hostel Bella Capri, Via Guglielmo Melisurgo 4, Naples; T:+39/0815529265, *info@ bellacapri.it/*; $25bed, Kitchen:Y, B'fast:Y, Pvt.room:Y, Locker:Y, Recep:24/7; Note: bar, tours, forex, stairs, by port, bag hold, laundry, lift, tea/coffee

Art Hostel, Vico Luperano 7, Naples; *arthostel.org/*; T:+39/08119572400; $21bed, Kitchen:N, B'fast:Y, Pvt.room:Y, Locker:N, Recep:ltd; Note: restaurant, tour desk, bag hold, hard to find, central, a/c

Naples Pizza Hostel, Via San Paolo ai Tribunali 44, Naples; T:08119323562, *info@ naplespizzahostel.com/*; $23bed, Kitchen:Y, B'fast:Y, Pvt.room:Y, Locker:N, Recep:24/7; Note: advise ETA, bag hold, laundry, c.c. ok, central

AIG Hostel Mergellina, Via Salita della Grotta, Naples; T:+39/0817612346, *napoli@ aighostels.com/*; $21bed, Kitchen:N, B'fast:Y, Pvt.room:Y, Locker:Y, Recep:24/7; Note: resto, lift, parking, bag hold, laundry, c.c. ok

I Fiori di Napoli B&B, Via Francesco Girardi 92, Naples; T:+39/08119577083, *Info@ ifioridinapoli.it/*; $35Bed, Kitchen:N, B'fast:Y, Pvt.room:Y, Locker:N, Recep:ltd; Note: central, laundry, hard to find, stairs

NOTO is a city of 24,000 in southernmost Sicily, 20mi/32km southwest of Syracuse. It is a UNESCO world heritage site for its cathedral. The old town lies 5mi/8km north of the modern one on top of Mount Alveria. It is famous for the Sicilian Baroque style of architecture. There are catacombs. There is good wine, and a flower festival in May.

HI Il Castello YH, Via Fratelli Bandiera 1, Noto; *hihostels.com/*, T:+39/3208388869, *info@ostellodinoto.it*; $25Bed, Kitchen:N, B'fast:Y, Pvt. room:Y, Locker:N, Recep:24/7; Note: bar, arpt trans, bikes, pool, wh/chair ok, lift, bag hold

5 Hostels) PALERMO is a city of 650,000 on the north coast of Sicily, in an urban area twice that size. It dates back to 734 BC and the Phoenicians. After decades of struggle against Mafia influence, it is now a major tourist center. The festival of patron Saint Rosalia is July 15. Sights include the Cathedral, the Palazzo dei Normanni, the city walls, Capuchin catacombs, the solar observatory and countless others.

Your Hostel, Via Gagini #61, Palermo; *Info@ yourhostel.it/*, T/F:+39/ 091320436; $28Bed, Kitchen:Y, B'fast:$, Pvt.room:Y, Locker:Y, Recep:8a>11p; Note: arpt trans, bikes, wh/chair ok, lift, laundry, bag hold, parking

Ai 4 Canti, Piazza del Ponticello 1, Palermo; *aiquattrocanti.hostel.com/*, T:3392660963, *facebook.com/ai.hostel/*; $21Bed, Kitchen:Y, B'fast:N, Pvt.room:Y, Locker:N, Recep: advise ETA; Note: cash, bar, bikes, laundry, bag hold, tea/ cof, ctr

PalazzoSavona, Via Schioppettieri, 8 Palermo; T:+39/0916114731, *info@ palazzosavona.com/*; $27Bed, Kitchen:$, B'fast:$, Pvt.room:Y, Locker:N, Recep:8:30//8p; Note: central, a/c, TV, historic bldg, nr train, bag hold, tours

A Casa di Amici , via Volturno,6, Palermo; *Info@ acasadiamici.com/*, T:+39/091584884; $21Bed, Kitchen:Y, B'fast:Y, Pvt.room:Y, Locker:N, Recep:8a>10p; Note: arpt trans, café, bikes, laundry, bag hold, tea/coffee, tours, parking, 2 bldg

HI Baia del Corallo YH, Via Plauto 27, Palermo; *hihostels.com/*, T:+39/0916797807, *palermo@aighostels.it*; $20Bed, Kitchen:N, B'fast:$, Pvt. room:Y, Locker:N, Recep:7:30a//11p; Note: resto/bar, laundry, bag hold, parking

5 Hostels) PERUGIA is a city of 168,000 in the center of the country, about equidistant from Rome and Florence. It was once a major Etruscan city and later, an artistic center. It is also famous for chocolate, especially 'kisses'. Sights include the Cathedral of St. Lorenzo, the Church and Abbey of St. Pietro, the Palazzo del Priori, and countless others. Festivals include the Eurochocolate Festival in October and Umbria Jazz Festival in July.

Ostello Perugia, Via Bontempi 13, Perugia; T:+39/0755722880; *ostello@ ostello.perugia.it/*; $24Bed, Kitchen:Y, B'fast:$, Pvt.room:Y, Locker:Y, Recep:3:30>12m; Note: wh/chair ok, bag hold, tea/coffee, lockout, center

Perugia Farmhouse, Strada Torre Poggio 4, Perugia; *bookings@ perugia-farmhouse.it/*, T:3395620005; $25Bed, Kitchen:Y, B'fast:Y, Pvt.room:Y, Locker:Y, Recep:24/7; Note: pool, bar, bikes, chairs, bag hold, tours, parking, laundry, rural

HI Mario Spagnoli YH, Via Cortonese 4, Perugia; *hihostels.com/*, T:0755011366, *perugia1@aighostels.it*; $25Bed, Kitchen:Y, B'fast:Y, Pvt.room:Y, Locker:Y, Recep:ltd; Note: arpt trans, bikes, billiards, café, wh/chair ok, laundry

Ostello Ponte Felcino, Via Maniconi 97, Ponte Felcino, Perugia; T:0755913991, *Info@ ostellopontefelcino.com/*; $25Bed, Kitchen:N, B'fast:Y, Pvt. room:Y, Locker:Y, Recep:ltd; Note: resto/bar, bikes, whchair ok, lift, laundry, far, hard find

La Casa Sul Lago, Viale del Lavoro 25, Torricella Di Magione, Perugia; *lacasasullago.com/*, T:3406804907; $23Bed, Kitchen:Y, B'fast:Y, Pvt.room:Y, Locker:Y, Recep: close 3>7p; Note: arpt trans, pool, hot tub, bikes, resto/bar

2 Hostels) PIACENZA is a city of 100,000 in Italy's north-central Emilia-Romagna region. It is something of a crossroads, just as it was in the Middle Ages between the Holy Roman Empire and Rome. There are many historic palaces, including the Farnese and Communale. There are also piazzas, churches, basilicas, and museums.

Hostel Don Zermani, Via Zoni 38/40, Piacenza; T:+39/0523712319 *info@ ostellodipiacenza.it/*; $27Bed, Kitchen:N, B'fast:Y, Pvt.room:Y, Locker:N, Recep:8a//11p; Note: wh/chair ok, lift, laundry, bag hold, parking, not central

Ostello Le Tre Corone, Via Mazzini 59, Calendasco, Piacenza; T:+39/0523772894, *info@ trecorone.it*; $14Bed, Kitchen:N, B'fast:$, Pvt.room:Y, Locker:N, Recep:3>9p; Note: pool, resto/bar, wh/chair ok, laundry, parking, rural

6 Hostels) PISA was a Roman port and after the fall managed to fend off the Lombards, Arabs, and Franks well enough to emerge as a major naval power at the turn of the last millennium, behind only Venice and Genoa. It is on the west coast half-way between Rome and Milan or Turin, so a convenient stopover point for travelers. In addition to its famous leaning tower, and favorite son Galileo, the entire city is something of a museum in its own right, like much of Italy. Got religion? There are the notable old churches of San Pierino, San Frediano, San Sepolcro, San Nicola, San Francesco, Santa Catarina, and others. There are also medieval and Renaissance palaces.

Hostel Pisa Tower, Via Piave, 4 Pisa; *info@ hostelpisatower.it*, T:+39/0505202454; $25bed, Kitchen:N, B'fast:$, Pvt.room:Y, Locker:Y, Recep:2p>1a; Note: bag hold, lockout, café, bike rent, tours, laundry, tea/ coffee

A Casa Doina Tower, Largo del Parlascio 10, Pisa; *bbacasadoina.it/*, T:+39/91671184, *tower@bbacasadoina.it*; $33bed, Kitchen:Y, B'fast:N, Pvt. room:Y, Locker:N, Recep: advise ETA; Note: cash only, a/c, parking, balcony, tower views

Walking Street Hostel, Corso Italia, Pisa; *walkingstreethostel.com/*, T:+39/30648737, *infopisahostel@gmail.com*; $17bed, Kitchen:Y, B'fast:N, Pvt.

Room:N, Locker:Y, Recep:ltd; Note: café, parking, wh/chair ok, tours, laundry, bag hold, lift

Hostel Pisa, Via Corridoni 29, Pisa; T:+39/0505201841, *hostelpisa.com/;* $11Bed, Kitchen:Y, B'fast:$, Pvt.room:Y, Locker:Y, Recep:24/7; Note: dorm age>40, billiards, bikes, wh/chair ok, laundry, bag hold, tours, arpt trans, lift, nr arpt/train

Welcome Bed and Breakfast, Via Matteucci 30, Pisa; T:+39/3477730237, *Info@ welcomebedandbreakfast.it/;* $35Bed, Kitchen:N, B'fast:$, Pvt.room:Y, Locker:N, Recep:2P>12m; Note: cash only, laundry, not central

Rifugio delle Poiane, Rifugio Delle Poiane Podere Torignano, Pisa; *rifugiodellepoiane.it/,* T:3409210378, *rifugiodellepoiane@yahoo.it;* $56Bed, Kitchen:Y, B'fast:Y, Pvt.room:Y, Locker:N, Recep:ltd; Note: wh/chair ok, resto, far, need car

PISTOIA is a city of 90,000 in Italy's central-northwest Tuscany region, 19mi/30km northwest of Florence. Celts, Ligurians, and Eruscans pre-dated the Romans there. It started manufacturing pistols in the 16th Century. There is a Piazza del Duomo, Cathedral of San Zeno, Palazzo dei Vescovi, and countless historic churches.

Villa Michelina, Via Puccini 80, Pistoia; T:057350444, *Info@ villamichelina. it/;* $25Bed, Kitchen:Y, B'fast:$, Pvt.room:Y, Locker:Y, Recep:9a>7p; Note: arpt trans, bikes, wh/chair ok, laundry, bag hold, central

3 Hostels) POMPEI is a city of over 25,000 in the southern region of Naples, famous, of course, for the Roman remains buried under Mt. Vesuvius, a UNESCO world heritage site. The modern city has some sights of its own, including a shrine of pilgrims' interest.

Otello Deluxe Hostel, Via Duca d'Aosta 15, Pompei; *Info@ otellopompei.it/,* T:0810582826; $18Bed, Kitchen:N, B'fast:$, Pvt.room:Y, Locker:N, Recep:24/7; Note: 24/7; arpt trans, resto/bar, bag hold, parking, tours, central

Easy Bed Hostel, Via Diomede 6, Pompei; *easybedpompei@gmail.com,* T:+39/3464692195, *facebook.com/PompeiHostel/;* $30Bed, Kitchen:N, B'fast:Y,

Pvt.room:Y, Locker:N, Recep:24/7; Note: arpt trans, resto, pool, prkng, tours, cash only

Hostel Brikette, via G. Marconi 358, Positano, *hostel-positano.com/*, T:089875857, *info@brikette.com*; $32Bed, Kitchen:N, B'fast:N, Pvt.room:Y, Locker:Y, Recep:24/7; Note: central, lockout, arpt trans, bar/café, laundry, bag hold, tours

PRAIA A MARE is 7000 people lined up along 1mi/2km of beach in Italy's southern Calabria region. There is a Byzantine tower, and caves, too.

Onda Road, Via Boccioni 13, Praia a Mare; *calabriahostel.com/*, T:3470736169, *bookyourbed@hotmail.com*; $27Bed, Kitchen:N, B'fast:Y, Pvt. room:N, Locker:Y, Recep:24/7; Note: 18-35 y.o, arpt trans, bikes, café, wh/ chair ok, parking, not ctr

RAVENNA is a city of 160,000 on Italy's northeast coast. Little-known to most non-historians, this was the last capital of the Roman Empire, from 402-476, after which it served as capital for Ostrogoths, Byzantines, and Lombards. There are eight UNESCO world heritage sites here, plus a Ravenna Festival of classical music, churches, museums.

HI Ravenna–Dante YH, Via Aurelio Nicolodi 12, Ravenna; *hihostels.com/*, T:0544421164, *hostelravenna@hotmail.com*; $25Bed, Kitchen:N, B'fast:Y, Pvt.room:Y, Locker:N, Recep:24/7; Note: bar, café, wh/chair ok, billiards, bikes, far, lockout

REGGIO EMILIA is a city of 170,000 in north-central Italy. The old town is hexagonal. It is known for socialism, Parmigiano cheese and Lambrusco wine. There are countless historic buildings, churches and palaces.

Student's Hostel della Ghiara, Via Guasco #6, Reggio nell'Emilia; T:+39/0522452323, *Info@ ostelloreggioemilia.it/*; $25Bed, Kitchen:N, B'fast:Y, Pvt. room:Y, Locker:Y, Recep:24/7; Note: bikes, resto/bar, wh/chair ok, bag hold

6 Hostel) RIMINI was the home of Federico Fellini and is the quintessential modern Adriatic beach town. You don't come here looking for culture and

history, though there is plenty here. You come here looking for fun. The beach, which has been privately claimed and developed into mini-estates, has got to be seen to be believed. During the summer the city provides bar-hop buses (or so I hear), so very civilized. Rimini is the jumping-off point to visit the independent Republic of San Marino, too. Besides the beach, there are the Roman ruins at the Arch of Augustus, the Roman bridge and the Malatesta Temple. It gets crowded in high season.

Jammin' Party Hostel, Viale Derna, 22 Rimini, Italy; T:0541390800, *info@ hosteljammin.com/*; $17bed, Kitchen:Y, B'fast:Y, Pvt.room:Y, Locker:Y, Recep:24/7; Note: dorm17-45, bar/club, wheelchair ok, luggage ok, a/c, laundry, tours, lift, bikes

Sunflower City Backpacker, Via Dardanelli 102, Rimini; T:054125180

Sunflower Surf Youth Hotel, Via Siracusa 8, Rimini

Sunflower Beach Backpacker Hostel, Viale Siracusa 25, Rimini; *info@ sunflowerhostel.com/*, T:0541373432, $21bed, Kitchen:Y, B'fast:Y, Pvt.room:Y, Locker:Y, Recep:24/7; Note: café/resto/bar/club, tours, bag hold, laundry, parking

Rimini Hostel - Migani Spiaggia, Via Monti, 7, Rimini; T:+39/3288428216

Rimini Hostel (Benvenuti), Viale Praga, 40, Rimini, T:+39/0541381614, *Info@ riminihostel.com/*; $20Bed, Kitchen:N, B'fast:Y, Pvt.room:Y, Locker:N, Recep:24/7; Note: lift, luggage room, parking, not central, near beach

RIVOLI is a city of 50,000 in Northwestern Italy's Piedmont region, 8mi/14km west of Torino (Turin). There is a castle, the Conte Verde House, Piazza Piozzo, and more.

Ostello Rivoli, Viale Papa Giovanni Xxiii 25, Rivoli, Torino; *keluar.it/*, T:+39/0119503728, *info@ostellorivoli.it*; $31Bed, Kitchen:N, B'fast:Y, Pvt.room:Y, Locker:N, Recep:ltd; Note: resto/bar, wh/chair ok, lift, laundry, bag hold

47 Hostels) ROME (Roma) is frequently called "the eternal city." I don't know about that, but certainly it has stood at the crossroads of history for more than 2000 years, as the capital of the Kingdom, the Republic, and then the Empire.

That all came tumbling down in 476, but the tradition carried on through the Middle Ages with Rome as the seat of the Catholic Church, and popes as the heads of state instead of emperors.

In the 19th century, secular Rome became the capital of the new united Italian republic. The sights are too many to mention. Unlike most cities where landmarks are generally divided between churches and museums, here we have the added categories of castles and fountains, plazas and steps. Everything either dates before 400 or after 1400. For a thousand years or more, almost nothing was built and Rome's population dropped from as much as a million to as little as 20,000.

The Colosseum is the main reminder of the Classic Age, but aside from that and the Pantheon and the Roman Forum, the Renaissance era comprises most of what you see, including the Spanish Steps, Trevi Fountain, St. Peter's Basilica, and much much more, such as the Sant'Angelo Bridge and Castel Sant'Angelo, the Church of San Girolamo degli Schiavoni, the Palazzo Farnese, The Lateran Palace, the Tempietto, etc. Even so, it's not so huge, and very walkable. Summer can get crowded. In fact Rome gets so many tourists that it's hard to be a hostel purist. Standards here aren't as high as northern Europe. Persevere, and book far in advance.

Dreaming Rome Hostel, Via Cuma n°2, Roma; *dreamingromehostel. com/*, T:+39/3403916423; $35bed, Kitchen:Y, B'fast:Y, Pvt.room:Y, Locker:Y, Recep:24/7; Note: arpt trans, café, parking, lift, bag hold, laundry, tours, terrace, 2N min.

Lodi Hotel, Via Oristano 14, Rome; *lodihotelrome.com/*, T:+39/067014643; $20bed, Kitchen:N, B'fast:Y, Pvt.room:Y, Locker:Y, Recep:24/7; Note: café, parking, bag hold, not central, pay cash, dorm age limit 50, tours, tea/ coffee

Twin Cities Rome Hostel, Viale Leonardo da Vinci 223, Rome; T:3349491461, *info@ twincitieshostel.it/*; $13bed, Kitchen:Y, B'fast:N, Pvt.room:Y, Locker:Y, Recep:>12m; Note: not central, bag hold, resto, 2N min, arpt trans, laundry, tea/cof

Litus Roma Hostel, Lungomare P. Toscanelli 186, Rome; T:065697275, *info@ litusroma.com/*; $36bed, Kitchen:N, B'fast:Y, Pvt.room:Y, Locker:N, Recep:24/7; Note: bar, parking, tours, laundry, bag hold, on beach near arpt.

Funny Palace, Via Varese 33, Roma; *info@ funnyhostel.com/*, T:0644703523; $28bed, Kitchen:Y, B'fast:Y, Pvt.room:Y, Locker:Y, Recep:>11p; Note: pay cash, bag hold, advise late arrival, near Termini stn, lift, laundry, tours

Pop Inn Hostel, Via Marsala 80, Roma; T:3483073735, *info@ popinnhostel.com/*; $27bed, Kitchen:N, B'fast:Y, Pvt.room:Y, Locker:Y, Recep:24/7; Note: café, lift, TV, luggage rm, tours, a/c, WiFi $, parking

Hostel Alessandro Palace & Bar, Via Vicenza 42; T:+39/064461958, $27

Hostel Alessandro Downtown, Via Carlo Cattaneo 23, Rome; T:0644340147, *info@ hostelsalessandro.com/*; $24bed, Kitchen:N, B'fast:Y, Pvt. room:N, Locker:Y, Recep:24/7; Note: HI chg, lift, TV, tours, bag hold, laundry, WiFi $, arpt trans

Hotel Beautiful, Via Napoleone III #35; *hostelbeauty.net/*, T:064465890

Hotel Beautiful 2, Via Milazzo 14, Ground Fl, Rome; *hotelbeautiful.net/*, T:0644703927, *Solomonhotels@gmail.com*; $21bed, Kitchen:N, B'fast:Y, Pvt. room:Y, Locker:Y, Recep:24/7; Note: lift, tours, laundry, bag hold, nr Termini stn, central

Conte House Roma, Via Merulana, No. 191 Roma; T:+39/0670453886, *info@ contehouse.com/*; $39bed, Kitchen:Y, B'fast:Y, Pvt.room:Y, Locker:N, Recep:24/7; Note: advise ETA, lift, tours, parking, a/c, c.c. ok, bag hold

The Yellow, Via Palestro, 44 Rome; *yellowhostel.com/*, T:0649382682, *questions@the-yellow.com*, $17bed, Kitchen:N, B'fast:$, Pvt.room:Y, Locker:Y, Recep:24/7; Note: resto/bar, bag hold, tours, lift, c.c. ok, near Termini, party

Ares Rooms, Via Domenichino 7, Rome; T:064744525, *info@ aresrooms.com/*; $40bed, Kitchen:N, B'fast:Y, Pvt. room:Y, Locker:N, Recep:24/7;Note: luggage room, c.c. , tour desk, safe deposit, lift to 5th Fl, central

Mosaic Hostel, Via Cernaia 39, Rome; *info@ hostelmosaic.com/*, T:0698937179; $31bed, Kitchen:N, B'fast:Y, Pvt.room:Y, Locker:Y, Recep:24/7; Note: lift, bag hold, a/c, c.c. ok, close to Termini, arpt trans, tours

Legends Hostel, Via Curtatone 12, Rome; *info@ legendshostel.com/*, T:0683393297; $20bed, Kitchen:N, B'fast:Y, Pvt.room:Y, Locker:Y, Recep: 24/7; Note: lockout 10a>3p, age 18-40, café, lift, few sockets, laundry, a/c, c.c. ok, bag hold

Plus Camping Roma, Via Aurelia 831 (km 8, 2), Rome; *plushostels. com/*, T:+39/066623018; $11bed, Kitchen:N, B'fast:$, Pvt.room:Y, Locker:N, Recep:7a>11p; Note: 1hr>city, resto/bar/club, pool, tours, a/c, arpt transfer, billiards, parking

Freedom Traveler Hostel, Via Gaeta, 23, Rome; T:0648913910, *info@ freedom-traveller.it/*; $22bed, Kitchen:Y, B'fast:$, Pvt.room:Y, Locker:Y, Recep:24/7; Note: restaurant, tours, bag hold, lift, a/c, c.c. ok, central, tea/coffee

Rome City Hostel, Viale Ippocrate 91, Rome; T:0644362722, *info@ romecityhostel.com/*; $27bed, Kitchen:Y, B'fast:Y, Pvt.room:Y, Locker:Y, Recep:24/7; Note: arpt trans, lift, parking, tours, luggage room, a/c

Ottaviano Hostel, Via Ottaviano 6, Rome; T:0639738138, *info@ pensioneottaviano.com/*; $17bed, Kitchen:N, B'fast:N, Pvt.room:N, Locker:Y, Recep:7a>10p; Note: cash, dorm 13-40 y.o, tours, lift, bag hold, tea/cof, lockout

Carlito's Way Hotel and Hostel, Via Villafranca 10; T:064440384

Hostel des Artistes, Via Villafranca 20, Rome; T:064454365, *info@ hostelrome.com/*; $25bed, Kitchen:N, B'fast:$, Pvt.room:Y, Locker:Y, Recep:24/7; Note: bar, tours, bag hold, dorm age >36, arpt trans, lift, parking, bikes

Youth Station Hostel, Via Livorno 5, Rome; T:0644292471, *info@ youthstation.it/*; $21bed, Kitchen:Y, B'fast:N, Pvt.room:Y, Locker:Y, Recep: 24/7; Note: age limit 30, tours, arpt trans, bag hold, not central

Camping Tiber, Via Tiberina, km 1400, Rome, *campingtiber.com/*, T:+39/0633610733; $13Bed, Kitchen:N, B'fast:$, Pvt.room:Y, Locker:N, Recep:ltd; Note: resto/bar, pool, market, parking, not central

Comics Guesthouse, viale Giulio Cesare 38, Roma; T:+39/0694379873, *Info@ comicsguesthouse.it/*; $25Bed, Kitchen:N, B'fast:$, Pvt.room:Y, Locker:Y, Recep:2>10p; Note: café, lift, laundry, bag hold, tours, tea/coffee, central

B&T Rooms, Via Dei Mille 9, Roma; T:+39/06490111; *info@ btrooms.com/*; $28Bed, Kitchen:N, B'fast:Y, Pvt.room:Y, Locker:N, Recep:24/7; Note: arpt trans, bag hold, laundry, tea/coffee, WiFi $

Hotel Lella, Via Palestro 9, Rome, *hotellella.net/*, T:+39/0642020488, *solomonhotels@gmail.com*; $24Bed, Kitchen:N, B'fast:N, Pvt.room:Y, Locker:N, Recep:24/7; Note: central, hotel not hostel

Hotel Papa Germano, Via Calatafimi 14, Rome; T:+39/06486919, *Info@ hotelpapagermano.com/*; $28Bed, Kitchen:N, B'fast:$, Pvt.room:Y, Locker:N, Recep:24/7; Note: bag hold, tours, maps, pay cash, central

Hotel Ivanhoe Rome, Via Urbana 92a, Roma; *hotelivanhoerome.com/*, T:06486813, *info@hotelivanhoe.it*; $27Bed, Kitchen:N, B'fast:$, Pvt.room:Y, Locker:Y, Recep:24/7; Note: pay cash, airport transfers, central

Four Seasons Hostel Rome, Via Carlo Cattaneo 23, Rome; T:0699345100, *Info@ fourseasonshostelrome.com/*; $24Bed, Kitchen:N, B'fast:$, Pvt.room:N, Locker:Y, Recep:24/7; Note: café, arpt trans, lift, laundry, bag hold, parking, tea/cof

La Controra, Via Umbria 7, Rome; T/F:+39/0815494014, *info@ lacontrora. com/*; $39Bed, Kitchen:N, B'fast:Y, Pvt.room:Y, Locker:Y, Recep:ltd; Note: café, lift, bag hold, tea/coffee, tour desk, central

M&J Place Hostel Rome, Via Solferino 9, Rome; *mejplacehostel.com/*, T:+39/064462802, *mejhostelrome@gmail.com*; $14Bed, Kitchen:Y, B'fast:$, Pvt. room:Y, Locker:Y, Recep:24/7; Note:arpt trans, resto/bar, bikes, bag hold, prkng

Ciak Hostel, Viale Manzoni 55, Rome; T:+39/0677076703, *info@ ciakhostel. com/*; $14Bed, Kitchen:Y, B'fast:Y, Pvt.room:Y, Locker:Y, Recep:24/7; Note: arpt trans, café, bag hold, parking, tea/coffee, tour desk

Hotel Cervia, Via Palestro 55, Rome; *Info@ hotelcerviaroma.com*, T:06491057 $25Bed, Kitchen:N, B'fast:$, Pvt.room:Y, Locker:N, Recep:24/7; Note: arpt trans, café, bar, luggage room, tour desk, central

Seven Hills Village, Via Cassia 1216, Rome; *sevenhills.it/*, T:+39/0630310826 $10Bed, Kitchen:N, B'fast:$, Pvt.room:Y, Locker:N, Recep:8a/9p; Note: resto/ bar, pool, billiards, minimart, parking, arpt trans, ages 18-35, rural, shuttle to train

Roman Holidays Hostel, Via Volturno 27, Rome; T:+39/064873638, *info@ roman-holidays-hostel.com/*; $18Bed, Kitchen:Y, B'fast:N, Pvt.room:Y, Locker:Y, Recep:ltd; Note: lift, bag hold, tea/coffee, tours, lockout, central

Prima Base Hostel, Via Osimo 61, Rome; *hostelprimabase.com/*, T:0641229928, *hostelprimabase@gmail.com*; $23Bed, Kitchen:N, B'fast:N, Pvt. room:Y, Locker:Y, Recep:ltd; Note: arpt trans, bag hold, parking, not central

Sunshine Hostel, Via Giolitti, 208, Rome; *Info@ touristsunshine.com/*, T:0670305837; $23Bed, Kitchen:N, B'fast:N, Pvt.room:N, Locker:Y, Recep:call; Note: luggage room, tea/coffee, central

Sandy Hostel, Via Cavour 136, Rome; T:+39/064884585, *Info@ sandyhostel.com*; $17Bed, Kitchen:N, B'fast:N, Pvt.room:Y, Locker:Y, Recep:7a>10;30; Note: lift, luggage room, stairs, cash, central

Hotel Positano, Via Palestro 49, Rome; *Info@ hotelpositano.it/*, T:+39/06490360; $28Bed, Kitchen:N, B'fast:N, Pvt.room:Y, Locker:N, Recep:24/7; Note: bikes, lift, bag hold, minimart, tours, age limit 35 y.o, central

Hotel il Papavero, Via Castelfidardo 50, Rome; T:+39/064464664, *Info@ hotelilpapavero.com/*; $21Bed, Kitchen:N, B'fast:N, Pvt.room:Y, Locker:N, Recep:24/7; Note: arpt trans, bag hold, parking, pool, tours, central, WiFi $

Hostel Roma Inn 2000, Via Agostino Depretis 65, Rome; T:+39/064740378, *marioromainn@ tiscalinet.it/*, $23Bed, Kitchen:N, B'fast:$, Pvt.room:Y, Locker:N, Recep:24/7; Note: bar, café, lift, laundry, bag hold, tours, cash only, WiFi $

Roma Scout Center, Largo dello Scautismo 1, Roma; T:+39/0644231355, *romascoutcenter.it/*; $31Bed, Kitchen:N, B'fast:Y, Pvt.room:N, Locker:N, Recep:24/7; Note: cash only, resto/bar, wh/chair ok, lift, bag hold, parking

Hostel Andrew, Via Palestro 44, Rome; T:+39/0644341033, *Info@ hostelandrew.com*; $17Bed, Kitchen:Y, B'fast:N, Pvt.room:Y, Locker:Y, Recep:ltd; Note: lift, luggage room, maps, central

Residenza Giustiniani, Via Gaeta 64, Rome; T:+39/0699330842, *Info@ residenzagiustiniani.com/*; $20Bed, Kitchen:N, B'fast:$, Pvt.room:Y, Locker:Y, Recep:24/7; Note: resto, lift, bag hold, tour desk

Poliziano Inn, Via Angelo Poliziano 27, Roma; T:+39/3737518663, *Info@ polizianoinn.com/*; $17Bed, Kitchen:N, B'fast:Y, Pvt.room:Y, Locker:N, Recep:ltd; Note: arpt trans, lift, laundry, basic

HI Zagarolo Wiki YH, Via Colle Casette 34 (Pren. Nva Km 71), Zagarolo; T:+39/095200054, *info@ wikihostel.it/*, $28Bed, Kitchen:Y, B'fast:Y, Pvt.room:Y, Locker:N, Recep:ltd; Note: pool, hot tub, gym, resto/bar, bikes, parking, 40min>Rome

Central Station Inn, Via San Francesco D'Assisi 11, Ciampino Rome; T:+39/0660657787, *Info@ centralstationinn.com/*; $31Bed, Kitchen:N, B'fast:N, Pvt.room:Y, Locker:Y, Recep:24/7; Note: @LCC arpt, pool, resto, bag hold, tours

ROVERETO is a town of 38,000 in north-central Trentino province. Historically it was an independent buffer region. There is a castle, war museum, Museum of Modern and Contemporary art, and one huge bell.

Ostello Rovereto, Via Scuole18, Rovereto Trento; T:+39/0464486757, *segretaria@ ostellorovereto.it/*; $28Bed, Kitchen:N, B'fast:Y, Pvt.room:Y, Locker:Y, Recep:2>10p; Note: bar, bikes, wh/chair ok, lift, laundry, bag hold, parking

2 Hostels) SALERNO is a city of 132,000 and the main one close to the southwestern tourist Amalfi Coast. It is famous as the center for revival of medical science in west Europe. It was heavily damaged in WWII. There is a castle, old town, promenade, palaces, churches, museums and countless other sights..

HI Ave Gratia Plena YH, Via Canali, Salerno; *hihostels.com/*, T:089234776, *info@ ostellodisalerno.it/*; $23Bed, Kitchen:N, B'fast:$, Pvt.room:Y, Locker:Y, Recep:24/7; Note: resto/bar, wh/chair ok, lift, laundry, bag hold, parking, hist. convent

Hostel Koine, Via Luigi Guercio Tra. Napoletano 10, Salerno, *hostelkoine. it/*, T:+39/0897414038; $18Bed, Kitchen:N, B'fast:$, Pvt.room:N, Locker:Y, Recep:24/7; Note: bikes, wh/chair ok, bag hold, tours, long-stays

SAN MARTINO DI CASTROZZA is a mountain resort village of almost 600 in the northeast Trentino province. It sits up at almost 5000ft/1500meters.

Ostello Dolomiti, Via Laghetto 43, San Martino di Castrozza; T:0439769166, *Info@ ostellodolomiti.com/*; $45Bed, Kitchen:N, B'fast:Y, Pvt.room:Y, Locker:N, Recep:ltd; Note: Paneveggio Natl Park/mts, arpt trans, resto/bar, hike/ski

SAN VINCENZO is a coastal town of 7000 in Tuscany, 62mi/100km southwest of Florence.

Ostello Gowett, Via San Silvestro 34, San Vincenzo, Livorno; T:0565838192, *Info@ ostellogowett.it/*; $36Bed, Kitchen:N, B'fast:Y, Pvt.room:Y, Locker:N, Recep:24/7; Note: cash only, arpt trans, resto/bar, bikes, tours, lift

SERMONETA is a walled hill town of 8500 in central Italy, with castle, abbey, and Romanesque cathedral.

San Nicola Hostel, Via G. Matteotti 1, Sermoneta; *sannicola-hostel.com/*, T:077330381, *sannicolahostel@libero.com*; $17Bed, Kitchen:Y, B'fast:N, Pvt.room:Y, Locker:N, Recep:ltd; Note: handicap facilities, restored convent, quiet, cats

SIENA is a city of over 50,000 in Tuscany. Its historic center is a UNESCO world heritage site. That includes the cathedral, the Piazza del Campo, Piazza Salembini, much art and more. The Palio is a traditional medieval horse race, held twice in the summer.

Siena Hostel, Via Fiorentina, 89 Siena; T:+39/05771698177, *Info@ sienahostel. it/*; $27Bed, Kitchen:N, B'fast:Y, Pvt.room:Y, Locker:N, Recep:3>11p; Note: bar, bikes, wh/chair ok, lift, bag hold, tours, not central

8 Hostels) SORRENTO is a small tourist town and ferry port on the Bay of Naples. It shares much of the same history as Naples. Holy Week festivities are one of the main attractions. There is a cathedral, the 14th century cloister of St. Frances of Assissi, and the Correale di Terranova Museum.

Seven Hostel, Via Iommella Grande 99, Sant'Agnello, Naples; T:0818786758, *reservations@ sevenhostel.com/*; $24bed, Kitchen:Y, B'fast:Y, Pvt. room:Y, Locker:Y, Recep:24/7; Note: lift, rooftop resto/bar, tours, laundry, forex, bag hold, not central

Ulisse Deluxe Hostel, Via del Mare 22, Sorrento; T:0818774753, *info@ ulissedeluxe.com*; $28bed, Kitchen:N, B'fast:$, Pvt.room:Y, Locker:N, Recep:24/7; Note: arpt trans, pool, lift, bar, wh/chairs ok, parking, bag hold, tours, gym, central

Ostello Le Sirene, Via degli Aranci, 160, Sorrento, Naples; T:0818072925, *info@ hostellesirene.com/*; $32bed, Kitchen:Y, B'fast:Y, Pvt.room:Y, Locker:N, Recep:24/7; Note: cash, bar/café, tours, bikes, lift, laundry, central, bag hold, prkg

Hotel Florida, Vico Primo Rota 3, Sant'agnello, Sorrento, Naples; T:0818783844, *Info@ htlflorida.com/*; $21Bed, Kitchen:N, B'fast:N, Pvt.room:Y, Locker:N, Recep:24/7; Note: pool, resto/bar, bag hold, parking, tours, arpt trans,

Village Camping Santafortunata, Via Capo 39/a, Sorrento, Naples; *santafortunata.com/*, T:+39/0818073579; $27Bed, Kitchen:N, B'fast:Y, Pvt. room:Y, Locker:N, Recep:3p>12m; Note: cash, arpt trans, pool, billiards, resto/bar, walk>town

Porto Salvo, Via Nuovo Rione Cappuccini 11, Sant'Agnello di Sorrento; T:0818774887, *info@ portosalvosorrento.com/*; $15Bed, Kitchen:N, B'fast:Y, Pvt. room:Y, Locker:N, Recep:ltd; Note: arpt trans, resto/bar, laundry, bikes, hot tub, prkng

Mami Camilla, Via Cocumella 6, Sant'agnello, Naples; T:+39/0818782067; *Info@ mamicamilla.com/*; $21Bed, Kitchen:N, B'fast:$, Pvt.room:Y, Locker:N, Recep:ltd; Note: minibar, books, a/c, not central, cooking school

Hotel Londra, Via Cocumella, Sant'agnello, Naples; T:+39/0815329554, *Info@ hotelondra.com/*; $21Bed, Kitchen:N, B'fast:N, Pvt.room:Y, Locker:N, Recep:24/7; Note: resto/bar, pool, luggage room

SYRACUSE is a city of 123,000 on the east coast of Sicily, and the chief Greek city there. It is 33mi/53km south of Catania. Its history dates back to the Corinthians, and endured Cathaginians, Romans, Franks, Normans and Arabs. The earthquake of 1693 introduced a new era, most of which remains. There are a temple of Apollo; Baroque cathedral; Montalto, Bellomo, and Parisio Palaces, and more.

LoL Hostel, Via Francesco Crispi 92, Syracuse; T:+39/0931465088, *Info@ lolhostel.com/*; $27Bed, Kitchen:Y, B'fast:Y, Pvt.room:Y, Locker:Y, Recep:24/7; Note: arpt trans, café, bar, wh/chair ok, laundry, bag hold, tea/cof, prkng, tours, @bus/trn

4 Hostels) TAORMINA is a town of 11,000 in eastern Sicily. There are a Roman theater and reservoir, and medieval cathedral and palaces.

Hostel Gianni House, 47 Via Pergusa, Giardini Naxos, Sicily; *giannihouse. com/*, T:+39/094256756, *giannihouse@gmail.com*; $24Bed, Kitchen:Y, B'fast:Y, Pvt.room:Y, Locker:Y, Recep:ltd; Note: cash, bikes, bar, café, laundry, parking, tea/cof, bag hold

Hostel Taormina, Via Circonvallazione 13, Taormina; *hosteltaormina.com/*, T:3491026161, *hosteltaormina@libero.it*; $25Bed, Kitchen:Y, B'fast:Y, Pvt.room:Y, Locker:Y, Recep:1>10p; Note: arpt trans, café, bag hold, tours

Taormina Odyssey, Via Paternò di Biscari 13, Taormina; T:+39/094224533, *Info@ taorminaodyssey.com/*; $27Bed, Kitchen:Y, B'fast:Y, Pvt.room:Y, Locker:N, Recep:>6p; Note: parking, luggage room

Borgo Case Vacanze, via Roma 1, Letojanni (5 km>Taormina); *info@ caseborgovacanze.it/*; T:+39/094237091; $32Bed, Kitchen:Y, B'fast:N, Pvt. room:Y, Locker:N, Recep:advise ETA; Note: cash, bag hold, tea/coffee, parking

3 Hostels) TURIN (Torino) is another of those places rich in culture and history, yet barely on the tourist map of Italy, even though it was the site of the winter Olympics in 2006. Torino has it all – industry, natural beauty, art, history – but few tourists yet. It is the home of Fiat and the shroud of Turin, housed in the Santa Sindone Chapel of the cathedral of San Goiovanni Batista. Other notable churches include La Consolata and the basilica of Superga, the royal burial church. Palaces include the Madama Palace, the Carignano Palace, and the Royal Palace. There is a Museum of Antiquities, an Egyptian Museum, and a Gallery of Modern Art. East-west trains pass through; it's worth a stop.

Hostel TO, Via Modane 17, Turin; T:+39/011331176, *info@ hostel.to/*; $27bed, Kitchen:N, B'fast:N, Pvt.room:N, Locker:Y, Recep:1>10p; Note: luggage room, c.c. ok, garden, not central, basic

Ostello Campidoglio, Via Corio 11, Torino; *info@ hotelcampidoglio.it/*, T:0117765808; $28bed, Kitchen:N, B'fast:Y, Pvt.room:Y, Locker:N, Recep:8a>3p; Note: wheelchair ok, resto/bar, c.c. ok, Sat TV, central

Tomato Backpackers Hotel, Via Silvio Pellico 11, Turin; T:0110209400, *Info@ tomato.to.it/*; $30Bed, Kitchen:N, B'fast:$, Pvt.room:Y, Locker:N,

Recep:8a>12m; Note: bikes, café, hot tub, lift, bag hold, parking, tea/coffee, map

23 Hostels) VENICE (Venezia) inherited much of the power and prestige that once belonged to Rome, via the post-Roman capital at Ravenna and by alliance with the Eastern Empire at Constantinople. Soon it morphed from a set of lagoons to a city-state to an independent empire of its own based on naval power in the Adriatic Sea. So it was going strong back in the Middle Ages, when most of the rest of Europe was just beginning to wake up after a long cultural snooze. Back then Venice was distribution point for the Silk Road and staging ground for the Crusades.

Famous nowadays for its canals (connecting 118 islands) and romantic atmosphere, for many Venice embodies the essence of Europe. For others— travelers and locals, too—it's a bit too much, with one of the highest tourist-to-locals ratios in the world. Tourist attractions include the Grand Canal, St. Mark's Basilica, the Molo, the Doge's Palace, the Campanile, the Old Library, and the Piazza San Marco. Hostels are expensive and the quality is fair to middling.

Holiday Center, Il Lato Azzurro, via Forti, 13, S.Erasmo Venezia; T:+39/0415230642, *info@ latoazzurro.it/*; $41bed, Kitchen:N, B'fast:Y, Pvt. room:Y, Locker:N, Recep:ltd; Note: resto/bar, bikes, bag hold, laundry, ATM, rural island

San Geremia Rooms, campo San Geremia 290, Venice; *hotelsangeremia.com*, T:041716245, *sangeremia@yahoo.it*; $33bed, Kitchen:N, B'fast:N, Pvt.room:Y, Locker:N, Recep:ltd; Note: 1a curfew, dorm age>35, cash only, lockout, no lift

Alloggi Gerotto Calderan, Campo San Geremia; T:041715562, *info@ casagerottocalderan.com/*; $30bed, Kitchen:N, B'fast:$, Pvt.room:Y, Locker:N, Recep:ltd; Note: cash only, 0100 curfew, nr train, dorm age>35, 2 bldgs

Hotel/Hostel Colombo, Viale Antonio Paolucci 5, Venice; T:041920711, *info@ venicebackpackershostel.com/*; $21bed, Kitchen:N, B'fast:$, Pvt.room:Y, Locker:N, Recep:24/7; Note: arpt trans, bar, café, lift, bag hold, parking, TV, 4th Fl no lift

Ostello de Venezia, Fondamenta delle Zitelle, 86, 133 Venice; *hostelvenice. org/*, T:0415238211, *info@ostellovenezia.it*; $32bed, Kitchen:N, B'fast:Y, Pvt.

room:N Locker:Y, Recep:24/7; Note: wh/chair ok, resto/bar, WiFi:$, island, water taxi, mkt

B&B Best Holidays, Calle delle Beccarie, San Polo 1615, Venice; *bestholidaysvenice.com/*, T:+39/415242874; $31bed, Kitchen:N, B'fast:Y, Pvt. room:Y, Locker:N, Recep:12n>12m; Note: hard find, cash only, advise ETA, bag hold

Hotel Astoria, Calle Fiubera 951, Venice; T:0415288981, *info@ hotelastoriavenezia.it/*; $21bed, Kitchen:N, B'fast:$, Pvt.Room:Y, Locker:N, Recep:24/7; Note: hard to find, bag hold, tours, c.c. ok

Youth Venice Home, Sestiere Castello, 3368, Venice; *youthvenicehome.com/*, T:3470701833, *youthvenicehome@hotmail.com*; $39bed, Kitchen:Y, B'fast:N, Pvt. room:Y, Locker:Y, Recep:>12m; Note: advise ETA, bar, tours

Casa Linger Hostel, Castello 35/41 Venice; *hotelcasalinger.com/*, T:0415285920, *hotelcasalinger@hotmail.com*; $42bed, Kitchen:N, B'fast:$, Pvt. room:Y, Locker:N, Recep:>12m; Note: luggage room, laundry, central

A Venice Fish, Sestiere Cannaregio 2205, Campo della Maddalena, Venice; *avenicefish.com/*, $35bed, *avenicefish@hotmail.com*; Kitchen:N, B'fast:N, Pvt.room:N, Locker:N, Recep:9a>11m; Note: age limit 40, bar, noon lockout, cash only, laundry

PLUS Camping Jolly, Via G. de Marchi, 7, Marghera, Venice; *plushostels. com/*, T:+39/041920312; $14Bed, Kitchen:N, B'fast:$, Pvt.room:Y, Locker:N, Recep:ltd; Note: arpt trans, pool, billiards, resto/bar, bag hold, parking

Camping Rialto, Via Orlanda, 16 Campalto, Campalto, Venice; *campingrialto. com/*, T:+39/0415420295, *rialto@camping.it*; $14Bed, Kitchen:N, B'fast:$, Pvt. room:Y, Locker:N, Recep:24/7; Note: bar, bag hold, parking, WiFi $

Generator Venice, Fondamenta Zitelle 86, Venice; T:+39/3425767349, *Info@ generatorhostels.com/*; $30Bed, Kitchen:N, B'fast:$, Pvt.room:Y, Locker:N, Recep:24/7; Note: resto/bar, wh/chair ok, lift, laundry, bag hold, tours

Camping Serenissima, Via Padana, Malcontenta, Venice; T:+39/041921850, *Info@ campingserenissima.it/*; $18Bed, Kitchen:Y, B'fast:$, Pvt.room:Y, Locker:N, Recep:ltd; Note: resto/bar, wh/chair ok, parking

Ostello Santafosca, Fondamenta Canal, Cannaregio, Venezia; *ostello@ santafosca.it*, T:+39/041715775; $29Bed, Kitchen:N, B'fast:$, Pvt.room:Y, Locker:Y, Recep: 9a/8p; Note: café, bag hold, tea/coffee, lockout, curfew, central

Backpackers Hostel Venice, Campo San Tomà 2846, Venice; *Info@ backpackershostelvenice.com/*; $37Bed, Kitchen:N, B'fast:N, Pvt.room:Y, Locker:N, Recep:24/7; Note: café, wh/chair ok, lift, luggage room

Antico Capon, Sestiere Dorsoduro 3004, Venice, *anticocapon. com/*, T:+39/0415285292, *hotelanticocapon@hotmail.com*; $33Bed, Kitchen:N, B'fast:N, Pvt.room:Y, Locker:N, Recep:2>11:30p; Note: central

Hotel Giovannina, Via Dante 113, Mestre, Venice, *hotelgiovannina.com/*, T:+39/041926396, *hotelgiovannina@libero.it/*; $23Bed, Kitchen:N, B'fast:N, Pvt. room:Y, Locker:N , Recep:24/7; Note: resto/bar, bag hold, parking, tour desk, not ctr

Venice Lagoon House, Via Tenda 11, Venice; T:+39/3881075401, *Info@ venicelagoonhouse.com/*; $30Bed, Kitchen:Y, B'fast:$, Pvt.room:Y, Locker:N, Recep:1p>1a; Note: cash only, laundry, bag hold, parking, tea/coffee, not ctr

Venice Paradise, Calle Vituri San Marco, Venice; *bbveniceparadise.com/*, T:3317805868, *veniceparadise@aruba.it*; $49Bed, Kitchen:Y, B'fast:$, Pvt.room:N, Locker:N, Recep:11a>9p; Note: laundry, luggage room, central

Backpackers House Venice, Dorsoduro 2967/A, Venice; T:+39(0)413190444, *Info@ backpackershousevenice.com/*; $28Bed, Kitchen:N, B'fast:$, Pvt.room:Y, Locker:N, Recep:8a>11p; Note: cash only, luggage room, central, basic, hard find

L'Imbarcadero, Santa Croce, 1268, Calle Zen, Venice; *Info@ hostelvenice. net/*, T:3923410861; $63Bed, Kitchen:Y, B'fast:Y, Pvt.room:Y, Locker:N, Recep:9a>10p; Note: central

Jan Palach Hostel, Isola della Giudecca, 186, Venice; T:0415221321, *info@ ostellojanpalach.it/*; $Bed, Kitchen:Y, B'fast:Y, Pvt.room:N, Locker:Y, Recep:9a//10p; Note: luggage room, tea/coffee, on island

2 Hostels) VERONA is a city of 260,000 in northern Italy, 65mi/105km west of Venice. One of the richest cities in Roman times, it was a center of painting during the Renaissance. Today it is a crossroads and handicrafts center.

Landmarks include one of Europe's oldest libraries, the Civic Museum, and many churches.

Sleep Easy Hostel, Via XX Settembre, 80, Verona; *hostelverona.org/*, T:3929155000; $35Bed, Kitchen:N, B'fast:$, Pvt.room:Y, Locker:Y, Recep:1>8p; Note: cash only, not central

Residenza Muropadri, Via Muro Padri, 8, Verona; *muropadri.it/*, *T:3473200789, muropadri@yahoo.it;* $38Bed, Kitchen:N, B'fast:Y, Pvt.room:Y, Locker:N, Recep:ltd; Note: central

VICENZA is a city of 115,000 in the Veneto region of northern Italy, and a world heritage site for its Palladian architecture.

HI Vicenza Olimpico YH, Viale Giuriolo 9, Vicenza; *hihostels.com/*, T:0444540222, *info@ostellovicenza.com;* $30Bed, Kitchen:Y, B'fast:Y, Pvt.room:Y, Locker:Y, Recep:ltd; Note: arpt trans, bikes, wh/chair ok, lift, laundry, bag hold, cntr

VOLTERRA is a town of 11,000 in Tuscany. There are Etruscan ruins and medieval architecture. There is also a museum of Etruscan art.

Ostello Volterra, Via Del Teatro 4, Loc. San Girolamo, Volterra; T:058886613, *Info@ ostellovolterra.it/*; $25Bed, Kitchen:N, B'fast:Y, Pvt.room:Y, Locker:Y, Recep:ltd; Note: resto/bar, bikes, wh/chair ok, lift, bag hold, parking, hist. bldg

6) Liechtenstein

Liechtenstein is another of those European anomalies, created out of political expedience, in this case for a seat in the Imperial government of the Holy Roman Empire. Its princes didn't set foot here for over a hundred years.

Today it is one of the wealthiest countries in the world per capita. At sixty-two square miles (160 square km), Liechtenstein is the sixth smallest independent nation in the world, home to some 35,000 people. It has more companies than people, many of them tax havens (and some specialized laundries ;-).

Liechtenstein is a beautiful landlocked country, double-landlocked in fact; i.e. it is surrounded by countries that are themselves landlocked. There is a castle at Vaduz. The town's Fürst Liechtensteinische Gemäldegalerie has some of the art collection of the princes of Liechtenstein. The State Art Collection includes works by 20th century painters, and there's also the Liechtenstein Postal Museum and the Liechtenstein National Museum. The language is German; the currency is the Swiss franc; calling code is +423.

Y. H. Schaan Vaduz FL, Untere Rüttigasse 6, Schaan; T:+423/2325022, *schaan@ youthhostel.ch/*; $40bed, Kitchen:N, B'fast:Y, Pvt room:N, Locker:Y, Recep:5p>9p; Note: bikes, billiards, wh/chair ok, bag hold, parking, hard find

7) Malta

Going to the island of Malta is like time travel, for this tiny country strategically located in the Mediterranean Sea has seen the waves of history wash across its shores for thousands of years, whether Phoenicians, Carthaginians, Greeks, Romans, Normans, Knights Hospitallers, or English. Today Malta is in the Euro-zone, speaks an Arabic dialect, is thoroughly Christian, and claims a cuisine with influences that span the Mediterranean. Sound interesting? The Megalithic Temples here are some of the oldest free-standing structures in the world. The language is Maltese, the currency is the Euro, and the phone country code is +356.

5 Hostels) SLIEMA may be contiguous to the capital Valletta in a long walk, but is distinctly different. If Valletta is the old historical Malta, Sliema is the new modern one, with many apartment blocks and new hotels. If you

want to hang around for a while, this is a good bet. VALLETTA is the capital of Malta and a UNESCO world heritage site, with architecture dating from the 16th century. They have a lively Carnival, and the food is good. Sights include the National Museum of Archeology, the National Museum of Fine Arts, the War Museum, the Manoel Theatre, and the National Library of Malta.

Hibernia House Gateway Hostel, Depiro St., Sliema; *hihostels.com/*, T:+356/25588000, *salesint@nsts.org*; $13bed, Kitchen:Y, B'fast:Y, Pvt.room:Y, Locker:Y, Recep:8a>2p; Note: café/bar, wh/chairs ok, central, lift, tours, bikes

Corner Hostel Malta, 6 St. Margaret St, Sliema; T:+356/27802780, *Info@ cornerhostelmalta.com/*; $18Bed, Kitchen:Y, B'fast:$, Pvt.room:Y, Locker:Y, Recep:2>10p; Note: arpt trans, bikes, lift, laundry, bag hold, mart, tea/cof, pkng, tours

Two Pillows, #49 Triq San Piju V, Sliema; *info@ twopillowsmalta.com/*, T:+356/21317070; $18Bed, Kitchen:Y, B'fast:$, Pvt.room:Y, Locker:Y, Recep:ltd; Note: arpt trans, bikes, laundry, bag, parking, tea/coffee, cash only

Grannys Inn Hostel, 53 Blanche Huber St, Sliema; *grannysinn. com/*, T:+356/99211751; $17Bed, Kitchen:8a>2p, B'fast:$, Pvt.room:Y, Locker:Y, Recep:8a>2p, Call; Note: arpt trans, laundry, tours, tea/coffee, bag hold

Balco Harmony Hostel, Cushcieri St, Gzira, Sliema; T:+356/21676946, *Info@ balcomalta.com/*; $30Bed, Kitchen:Y, B'fast:Y, Pvt.room:N, Locker:Y, Recep:ltd; Note: free arpt trans, laundry, bag hold, parking, nr sea

4 Hostels) ST. JULIANS is a town of almost 8000 along Malta's north coast. Originally a fishing town, it is now crucial to Maltese tourism.

Hostel Malti, 41 Birkirkara Hill, Ta Giorni, St. Julians; T:+356/27302758, *info@ hostelmalti.com/*; $17Bed, Kitchen:Y, B'fast:$, Pvt.room:Y, Locker:Y, Recep:ltd; Note: bikes, hot tub, arpt trans, laundry, bag hold, parking, tea/coffee, tours

Boho Hostel, 'Cycas' Guzeppi Xerri, St Julians; *Info@ bohohostel.com/*, T:+356/27656008; $19Bed, Kitchen:Y, B'fast:$, Pvt.room:Y, Locker:Y, Recep:ltd; Note: arpt trans, bikes, lift, wh/chair ok, tours, laundry, bag hold, parking, tea/cof

NightCap Hostel, Wilga Street, Paceville, St. Julians, *nightcapguesthouse. com/*, T:+356/27040300; $14Bed, Kitchen:Y, B'fast:N, Pvt.room:N, Locker:Y, Recep:ltd; Note: arpt trans, bikes, laundry, market, tea/coffee, tours

Highlander Guest House, Triq Elia Zammit, Paceville, St. Julians; *Info@ maltahighlander.com/*, T:+356/21376609; $25Bed, Kitchen:Y, B'fast:$, Pvt. room:Y, Locker:N, Recep:ltd; Note: laundry, a/c, luggage room

8) San Marino

Originally established as a refuge from Diocletian's persecution of Christians in 301, today San Marino is the world's smallest republic with only 30,000 people. It is totally surrounded by Italy in its remote mountain three-peak stronghold. It has the world's oldest constitution. Access is from the Italian city of Rimini. Italian is the language; Euro is the currency; calling code is +378.

Hostel San Marino, Via 28 Luglio, 224, Borgo Maggiore, San Marino; T:0549922515, *info@ hostel-sanmarino.com/*; $16bed, Kitchen:N, B'fast:$, Pvt. room:Y, Locker:Y, Recep:ltd; Note: bar, parking, a/c, c.c, tea/coffee, not central, wh/chair ok

9) Switzerland

Switzerland is much like Belgium to the west in its role as a transition state between northern and southern Europe. Here, though, the north and the

German language predominate, and the Alps provide a common identity. Switzerland is famous for its direct democracy and its historical neutrality, its banking secrecy and its watchmaking industry. It is also a high-tech economy with one of the highest incomes per capita in the world. That makes it expensive of course. The mountains are the predominant theme for recreation, with skiing in winter, hiking and biking in summer. The Swiss franc is currency; the phone code is +41; languages are German, French, Italian, and Romansch.

BADEN is a municipality of almost 20,000 some 16mi/25km northwest of Zurich, and known since antiquity for its mineral springs. There are ruins of a Roman city and castle.

YH Baden, Kanalstr. 7, Baden; *hihostels.com/*, T:+41/562216736, *baden@youthhostel.ch*; $37Bed, Kitchen:N, B'fast:Y, Pvt.room:Y, Locker:Y, Recep:7a//9:45p; Note: bag hold, closed winter, meals, c.c. ok, tours

3 Hostels) BASEL is located where Switzerland meets France and Germany (with suburbs in those countries). It sits on the Rhine and is Switzerland's only cargo port. As such it is also a rail hub and industrial center, yet still with plenty of culture and sights to see. It has a very interesting Protestant Carnival, which starts on the Monday after Ash Wednesday at 4 a.m. and lasts exactly seventy-two hours, consuming the town with festivities. Landmarks include the Protestant Münster church; the late Gothic Rathaus, or town hall; the Church of St. Martin; and the former 14th-century Franciscan church, now housing the historical museum. It is a mainly German-speaking city.

YMCA Hostel Basel, Gempenstrasse 64, Basel; *info@ ymcahostelbasel.ch/*, T:0613617309; $32bed, Kitchen:Y, B'fast:$, Pvt.room:Y, Locker:Y, Recep:7a>11p; Note: noon lockout, central, lift, wh/chair ok, parking, laundry, c.c. ok

Basel Back Pack, Dornacherstrasse 192, Basel; T:+41(0)6133300, *info@ baselbackpack.com/*; $32bed, Kitchen:Y, B'fast:$, Pvt.room:Y, Locker:Y, Recep:8a>8p; Note: café/resto/bar, bikes, noon lockout, lift, forex, c.c. ok, central

Youth Hostel Basel, St. Alban-Kirchrain 10, Basel; T:+41/612720572, *basel@ youthhostel.ch/*; $48bed, Kitchen:Y, B'fast:Y, Pvt.room:Y, Locker:N, Recep:24/7; Note: YHA chg, resto/bar, wh/chair ok, bag hold, c.c. ok, veg food

BEINWIL AM SEE is a town of 3000 in the north-center of the country. It is part of the Prehistoric Pile dwellings around the Alps UNESCO World Heritage Site.

Beinwil am See YH, Seestrasse 71, Beinwil am See; *hihostels.com/*, T:+41/627711883, *beinwil@youthhostel.ch*; $36Bed, Kitchen:Y, B'fast:Y, Pvt. room:Y, Locker:Y, Recep:8a//9:30p; Note: bikes, meals, tour desk, c.c. ok

3 Hostels) BERN's entire medieval center has been named a UNESCO world heritage site and is the most traditional in all of Switzerland. This includes the *Zytglogge* clock tower and the *Nydegbrukke* bear pit. You don't see that every day. There's also the Gothic cathedral, the City Hall, the Nydegg Church, the Federal Palace (Bundeshaus) and the Cage Tower. Einstein lived here, too.

Berne Backpackers Hotel/Hostel Glocke, Rathausgasse 75, Berne; *info@ bernbackpackers.ch/*, T:0313113771; $41bed, Kitchen:Y, B'fast:N, Pvt.room:Y, Locker:Y, Recep:8a>10p; Note: c.c. ok, laundry, club, central, few sockets, tea/cof

Bern YH, Weihergasse 4, Bern; *hihostels.com/*, T:+41/313261111, *bern@youthhostel.ch*; $39Bed, Kitchen:N, B'fast:Y, Pvt.room:Y, Locker:Y, Recep:7a/12m; Note: café, wh/chair ok, minimart, bag hold, nr train/ center

Landhaus Hotel, Altenbergstrasse 4-6, Berne; T:+41/313314166, *hotel@ landhausbern.ch/*; $42Bed, Kitchen:N, B'fast:$, Pvt.room:N, Locker:Y, Recep:>10p; Note: resto/bar, pool, bag hold, separate bunk compartments, central

BIEL-BIENNE are two names for the same city of 50,000 on the German-French language border and lake of the same name(s). The archeological site of Vingelz/Hafen is a UNESCO World heritage site. This is the heart of the Swiss watch industry. There is a beautiful and historic town center and nearby Jura mountains with funicular railway.

Lago Lodge, Uferweg 5, Nidau, Biel-Bienne; T:+41/323313732, *sleep@ lagolodge.ch*; $37Bed, Kitchen:N, B'fast:$, Pvt.room:Y, Locker:N, Recep:7a/10p; Note: resto/bar, pool, wh/chair, forex, bag hold, parking, brewery, near lake

BRAUNWALD is a village of 3000 in scenic east-central Switzerland, now part of the municipality of Glarus Sud.

Adrenalin Backpackers Hostel, Alpinaweg 3, Braunwald, T:+41/ 793472905 *Info@ adrenalin.gl/*; $32Bed, Kitchen:Y, B'fast:$, Pvt.room:Y, Locker:Y, Recep:ltd; Note: resto/bar, minimart, bikes, tour desk

BRIENZ is a town of 3000 in the center of the country, on a lake of the same name. There is a lakeside promenade, a steam train up the Brienzer Rathorn, an open-air museum of old buildings, and Europe's oldest funicular, to Glessbach Falls.

YH Brienz, Strandweg 10, Am See. Brienz; *hihostels.com/*, T:+41/339511152, *brienz@youthhostel.ch*; $34Bed, Kitchen:Y, B'fast:Y, Pvt.room:Y, Locker:Y, Recep:7:30a//10p; Note: coffee/tea, meals, bag hold, parking, bikes, lake, kids

CHATEAU-D'OEX is a town of a few thousand in the Swiss far west. There were prehistoric cave settlements and a Celtic settlement that predated the Romans. There is skiing and a balloon festival the last week of January.

YH Château-d'Oex, Route des Monnaires 67, Château-d'Oex; *hihostels. com/*, T:+41/269246404, *chateau.d.oex@youthhostel.ch*; $41Bed, Kitchen:N, B'fast:Y, Pvt.room:N, Locker:Y, Recep:7:30a>9p; Note: café/bar, bag hold, prkng, laundry

CHUR is a city of 34,000 in the Swiss east only 75mi/120km from Zurich, and considered the oldest town in Switzerland, with remains going back to the Bronze and Iron Ages. It was a Roman fort and the first Christian bishopric in the Alps. There are prehistoric and medieval archeological sites, and an active old town with many museums.

Hostel JBN, Welschdörfli 19, Chur, T:+41/812841010, *Info@ justbenice.ch/*; $43Bed, Kitchen:N, B'fast:$, Pvt.room:Y, Locker:Y, Recep:2>8p; Note: café/bar, books, coffee/tea, c.c. OK, fax, games

2 Hostels) DAVOS has a population over 11,000 at an elevation over 5000ft/1560mt, making it Europe's highest city. It is known for ice hockey and cross-country skiing, and has seven sites of Swiss historic significance. The World Economic Forum meets here.

Landgasthof Lengmatta, Lengmattastrasse 19, Frauenkirch, Davos; T:+41/814135579, *schraemlis@ lengmatta-davos.ch/*; $56Bed, Kitchen:N, B'fast:Y, Pvt.room:N, Locker:Y, Recep:ltd; Note: resto, laundry, parking, basement dorm

Davos-Youthpalace, Horlaubenstr. 27, Davos; *hihostels.com/*, T:+41/814101920, *davos@youthhostel.ch*; $25Bed, Kitchen:N, B'fast:Y, Pvt. room:Y, Locker:Y, Recep:7a>11p; Note: bikes, wh/chair, lift, café/bar, tour desk, c.c. ok, uphill, hard find

FRIBOURG is a city of 36,000 in the Swiss southeast, 17mi/28km southwest of Bern and on the border of the French and German parts of the country. It has one of the largest historic old centers in Europe, including Gothic Cathedral of Saint Nicholas and many museums. There is also a festival of religious music, an international folklore convention, a jazz parade, an international film festival and Cinéplus.

Fribourg YH, Rue de l'Hôpital 2, Fribourg; *hihostels.com/*, T:+41/263231916, *fribourg@youthhostel.ch*; $38Bed, Kitchen:N, B'fast:Y, Pvt.room:Y, Locker:Y, Recep:7:30a//10p; Note: wh/chair ok, lift, bag hold, tours, meals, maps

2 Hostels) GENEVA is a city of a half million in the far southwest French-speaking part of Switzerland, located on the lake of the same name and surrounded by mountains. It is a banking and intellectual center of Europe, with important winter sports activities. It was an early center of Calvinist Protestantism and French revolutionary political thought.

City Hostel Geneva, Rue Ferrier 2, Geneva, T:+41/229011500, *Info@ cityhostel.ch/*; $36Bed, Kitchen:Y, B'fast:$, Pvt.room:Y, Locker:Y, Recep:ltd; Note: café, lift, laundry, bag hold, parking, very near train/some noise

Geneva YH, Rue Rothschild 30 Genève; *hihostels.com/*, T:+41/227326260, *geneve@youthhostel.ch*; $36Bed, Kitchen:N, B'fast:Y, Pvt.room:Y, Locker:Y, Recep:24/7; Note: café, wh/chair ok, lift, laundry, bag hold, tours, tea/cof

GIMMELWALD is a village of 130 halfway up the mountain between Stechelburg and Murren, and connected to the rest of the world by cable car.

Mountain Hostel Gimmelwald, Nidrimatten, Chilchstatt, Lauterbrunnen; T:+41/338551704, *Info@ mountainhostel.com/*, $37Bed, Kitchen:Y, B'fast:Y, Pvt.room:N, Locker:N, Recep:11a>10p; Note: resto/bar, billiards, laundry, bag hold

3 Hostels) GRINDELWALD is an Alpine village of almost 4000 in Bern canton, south-central Switzerland. This is an all-year resort and is starting point for climbing The First.

YH Grindelwald, Geissstutzstrasse 12, Grindelwald; *hihostels.com/*, T:+41/338531009, *grindelwald@youthhostel.ch/*; $42Bed, Kitchen:N, B'fast:Y, Pvt.room:Y, Locker:Y, Recep:7:30//10p; Note: bag hold, laundry, forex, not central

Downtown Lodge, Dorfstrasse 152, Grindelwald; *downtown-lodge.ch/*, T:+41/338287730, *downtown-lodge@jungfrau.ch*; $48Bed, Kitchen:Y, B'fast:Y, Pvt.room:Y, Locker:Y, Recep:ltd; Note: bar, pool, billiards, laundry, parking, tours

Mountain Hostel, Grundstrasse 58, Grindelwald, T:+41/338543838, *Info@ mountainhostel.ch/*; $44Bed, Kitchen:N, B'fast:Y, Pvt.room:Y, Locker:Y, Recep:4>9p; Note: bar, bikes, billiards, laundry, bag hold, tours, parking, near main station

GRYON is a picturesque village of over 1000 in the French-speaking southwest.

Chalet Martin, 1882, Gryon; T:+41/797246374, *Info@ gryon.com/*; $31Bed, Kitchen:Y, B'fast:N, Pvt.room:Y, Locker:N, Recep:9:30a>10p; Note: billiards, bag hold, no shoes, cash only (no ATM), nature

10 Hostels) INTERLAKEN is located between lakes, as the name indicates, and lies in the central German-speaking part of the country. Its role as a

foundation stone of the Swiss tourism industry goes back to its origins in the early 1800's, when good transportation links could shuttle passengers in to view the fabled landscapes already well known in the artworld. Today they still come for the mountain air and outdoor activities.

Backpackers Villa Sonnenhof, Alpenstrasse 16, Interlaken; T:0338267171, *mail@ villa.ch/*; $32bed, Kitchen:Y, B'fast:Y, Pvt.room:Y, Locker:Y, Recep:ltd; Note: bag hold, laundry, parking, forex, c.c. ok, mountain views

Balmer's Herberge, Hauptstrasse 23, Matten b. Interlaken; T:0338221961, *mail@ balmers.com/*; $34bed, Kitchen:Y, B'fast:Y, Pvt.room:Y, Locker:Y, Recep:24/7; Note: resto/bar, club, forex, laundry, bag hold, c.c. ok, noon lockout

Funny Farm Backpackers, Hauptstrasse 36, Interlaken; T:0338281281, *info@ funny-farm.ch/*; $22bed, Kitchen:N, B'fast:$, Pvt. room:Y, Locker:N, Recep:24/7; Note: bar, restaurant, club, forex, parking, laundry, tours, c.c. ok

Lazy Falken Backpacker, Spielmatte 8, Unterseen; T:0338223043, *info@ lazyfalken.ch/*; $34bed, Kitchen:Y, B'fast:Y, Pvt.room:Y, Locker:Y, Recep:ltd; Note: bar, café, parking, laundry, bag hold, forex, c.c. ok

Happy Inn Lodge, Rosenstrasse 17, Interlaken; T:0338223225, *brasserie17. ch/ws/br/en/happyinn/hostel/*; $27bed, Kitchen:Y, B'fast:$, Pvt.room:Y, Locker:Y, Recep:6a>1a; Note: bar, parking, bag hold, c.c. ok

AlpLodge/BackPackers Interlaken, Marktgasse 59 Interlaken, T:+41/338224748, *Info@ alplodge.com/*; $28Bed, Kitchen:Y, B'fast:Y, Pvt.room:Y, Locker:Y, Recep:2p>12m; Note: bar, bikes, lift, laundry, bag hold, tours, prkng

YH Interlaken, Am Bahnhof Ost, Untere Bönigstrasse 3, Interlaken; *hihostels.com/,* T:+41/338261090, *interlaken@youthhostel.ch*; $40Bed, Kitchen:N, B'fast:Y, Pvt.room:Y, Locker:Y, Recep:7a>11p; Note: resto, bikes, billiards, lift, parking

Hua Villa, Waldeggstrasse 41, Interlaken, *huavilla.ch/*, T:+41/338211628, $33Bed, Kitchen:Y, B'fast:$, Pvt.room:Y, Locker:N, Recep:ltd; Note: arpt trans, bikes, tour desk, parking, forex, luggage room, maps

Lake Lodge, Feld 17, Iseltwald, *lakelodge.ch/*, T:+41/338451120; $33Bed, Kitchen:Y, B'fast:Y, Pvt.room:Y, Locker:N, Recep:4:30p>10p; Note: bikes, laundry, tour desk, parking, kayak, nr market, not central

River Lodge, Brienzstrasse 24, Interlaken Ost, T:+41(0)338224424, *welcome@ riverlodge.ch/*; $33Bed, Kitchen:Y, B'fast:$, Pvt.room:Y, Locker:N, Recep:ltd; Note: bikes, wh/chair ok, bag hold, tours, minimart, parking, laundry, café, campsite

LA TZOUMAZ is a family-oriented resort in the Swiss canton of Valais. In the non-ski summer season, there are paragliding, fishing and climbing. Lake Geneva and the medieval town of Sion are near. There are over 250mi/400km of ski runs.

La Tzoum'Hostel & Chalet, Les Crus, La Tzoumaz; T:+41(0)796841034, *tzoumhostel.ch/*; $42Bed, Kitchen:Y, B'fast:$, Pvt.room:Y, Locker:N, Recep:ltd; Note: resto, bikes, parking, laundry, coffee/tea, bag hold

LAAX is a resort town in the eastern part of Switzerland, with around 1300 full-time residents. In addition to winter sports, there is also a lake.

Backpacker Deluxe Hotel Capricorn, Via Cons 405, Laax; T:+41/819212120, *Info@ caprilounge.ch/*; $32Bed, Kitchen:Y, B'fast:$, Pvt.room:Y, Locker:N, Recep:5>8p; Note: resto/bar, bikes, luggage room, parking

LANGNAU IM EMMENTAL is a town of 9000 in the central part of the country. It is important for its markets and dairy farming. Better stock up on cheese. The oldest house in Langnau, now housing the Regional Museum, was built before 1600. Cultural events include Langnau Jazz Nights and the International Cartoon Festival.

Emme Lodge, Mooseggstrasse 32, Langnau im Emmental; *emmelodge. ch/*, T:+41/344024526; $24Bed, Kitchen:Y, B'fast:$, Pvt.room:Y, Locker:N, Recep:5p>; Note: luggage room, tour desk, parking

2 Hostels) LAUSANNE is a city of 100,000 in an urban area of 300,000 in far western Switzerland, on the northern shore of Lake Geneva. Historic buildings include the early Gothic Cathedral of Notre-Dame; the Saint-François Church; and the city hall. The castle, now the Historical Museum of the Ancient

Bishopric, is a vestige of the 13th Century residences of the bishops. Château Saint-Maire is now the seat of cantonal government.

Lausanne Guesthouse, Chemin des Epinettes 4, Lausanne; T:+41/ 216018000, *lausanne-guesthouse.ch/*; $40Bed, Kitchen:Y, B'fast:$, Pvt.room:N, Locker:Y, Recep:ltd; Note: wh/chair ok, laundry, bag hold, parking

YH Lausanne – Jeunotel, Ch. du Bois-de-Vaux 36, Lausanne; *hihostels.com/*, T:+41/216260222, *lausanne@youthhostel.ch*; $44Bed, Kitchen:N, B'fast:Y, Pvt. room:Y, Locker:N, Recep:24/7; Note: resto/bar, wh/chair, bag hold, parking

3 Hostels) LAUTERBRUNNEN is a municipality of 2500 in the valley of the same name, which contains numerous other towns. With possible roots in the Roman era, it is clearly attested from the medieval. The cable car between Stechelberg and Schilthorn and the Trachsellauenen silver mine are listed as Swiss heritage sites of significance.

Valley Hostel, Fuhren, Lauterbrunnen, T:+41/338552008, *Info@ valleyhostel. ch/*; $35Bed, Kitchen:Y, B'fast:$, Pvt.room:Y, Locker:N, Recep:8a//10p; Note: pool, bag hold, tours, parking, forex, near train station

Hotel Jungfrau, Lauterbrunnen; T:+41/338566464, *mail@ hoteljungfrau. ch/*; $34Bed, Kitchen:N, B'fast:$, Pvt.room:Y, Locker:N, Recep:ltd; Note: cafe, bikes, pool, luggage room, parking, coffee/tea, c.c. ok, central

Camping Jungfrau, Weid 406, Lauterbrunnen; T:+41/338562010, *Info@ camping-jungfrau.ch*; $33Bed, Kitchen:Y, B'fast:$, Pvt.room:Y, Locker:N, Recep:>8p; Note: pool, resto/bar, minimart, bike, laundry, bag hold, coffee/ tea, parking, tours

LOCARNO is a town of 15,000 in the southern Italian-speaking part of the country. That means it's warm. Landmarks include 14th Century castle of the dukes of Milan; the Pretorio, or law court, in which the Pact of Locarno, was initiated in 1925; and several old churches, including the pilgrimage church of Madonna del Sasso.

YH Locarno, Via Varenna 18, Palagiovani, Locarno; *hihostels.com/*, T:+41/917561500, *locarno@youthhostel.ch*; $35Bed, Kitchen:N, B'fast:Y, Pvt.room:Y, Locker:Y, Recep:3>10p; Note: café, bikes, wh/chair ok, lift, laundry, bag hold, TV

4 Hostels) LUCERNE is a small city in the German-speaking central part of Switzerland, and a mainstay of the local tourist destinations. It is on a lake and within sight of Switzerland's highest mountains. Traditional and alternative cultures coexist and many festivals are held in the warm season. The Spreuerbrücke, Lucerne's oldest bridge, is roofed and decorated with some fifty-six paintings, scenes from the Dance of Death, something of a Middle Age precursor to 1970's Grateful Dead imagery, I guess.

The old town contains the old town hall and historical museum, Am Rhyn House, St. Peter's Chapel, the Hofkirche and the Mariahilf Church, Bertel Thorvaldsen's Lion of Lucerne" monument, and the Glacier Garden. There are steamer services on the lake and cableways to ski resorts.

Backpackers Lucerne, Alpenquai 42, Lucerne; T:0413600420, *info@ backpackerslucerne.ch*; $35bed, Kitchen:Y, B'fast:N, Pvt.room:N, Locker:Y, Recep:ltd; Note: laundry, fore, c.c. ok, bag hold, on lake not central

Lion Lodge Lucerne, Zürichstrasse 57, Lucerne; T:0414100144, *info@ lionlodge.ch/*; $35bed, Kitchen:Y, B'fast:N, Pvt.room:Y, Locker:Y, Recep:8a>10p; Note: restaurant, parking, laundry, no lift

Youth Hostel Luzern, Sedelstrasse 12, Lucerne; T:0414208800, *luzern@ youthhostel.ch/*; $40bed, Kitchen:N, B'fast:Y, Pvt.room:N, Locker:Y, Recep:7a>12m; Note: parking, c.c. ok, not central, skyhlights

Twins Minbak Hostel, Eisfeldstrasse 2a, Lucerne; *twinsminbak.com/*, T:+41/794403821, *ka31666@naver.com*; $34Bed, Kitchen:Y, B'fast:$, Pvt.room:N, Locker:N, Recep:ltd; Note: laundry, parking, nr lake, train p-u, cash, Korean comic books

MONTREUX is a town of 23,000 comprising three resorts in French-speaking western Switzerland along Lake Geneva. It is famous for its healthy climate, its 13th Century Chateau de Chillon, and especially its annual Jazz Festival.

YH Montreux, Passage de l'Auberge 8, Montreux-Territet; *hihostels.com/*, T:+41/219634934, *montreux@youthhostel.ch*; $40Bed, Kitchen:N, B'fast:Y, Pvt. room:Y, Locker:Y, Recep:7:30//10p; Note:bikes, lake/not central, prkng, meals, tours, nr train

PONTRESINA is a town of a couple thou in the far eastern former Romansch-speaking part of the country. Landmarks include the *Church of Santa Maria, Grand Hotel Kronenhof* and the *Spaniola tower.* It lies on an old wine route across the mountains. There are glaciers and skiing.

Pontresina YH, Via da la Staziun 46, Pontresina; *hihostels.com/,* T:+41/818427223, *pontresina@youthhostel.ch*; $60Bed, Kitchen:N, B'fast:Y, Pvt. room:Y, Locker:Y, Recep:7:30a//9p; Note: resto, pool, bikes, bag hold, parking

RAPPERSWIL-JONA is a combined municipality of over 25,000. It has always been an important crossroads and is today an important rail junction. Rapperswil is known for roses, its castle, the wooden bridge to Hurden with chapel, and a Capuchin monastery.

Rapperswil-Jona, Hessenhofweg 10, Busskirch, Jona; *hihostels.com/,* T:+41/552109927, *jona@youthhostel.ch*, $42Bed, Kitchen:N, B'fast:Y, Pvt.room:Y, Locker:?, Recep:7:30//10p; Note: lake, bikes, laundry, tours, café, parking

SCHAFFHAUSEN is a city of over 33,000 in the canton of the same name, and known for its nearby Rhine River and spectacular Rhine Falls. Besides the Protestant Munster (monastery), landmarks include Munot Fort, the parish church, the old and new town halls, and the Haus zum Ritter, or the Knight's House, with frescoes by Tobias Stimmer.

Schaffhausen YH, Randenstr. 65, 'Belair', Schaffhausen, T:+41526258800, *schaffhausen@youthhostel.ch*; $33Bed, Kitchen:N, B'fast:Y, Pvt.room:N, Locker:Y, Recep:8a//9p; Note: bikes, café/bar, tour desk, meals, c.c. ok

SCHWYZ is a town of almost 15,000 in the center of the country and from which the name of the country comes. The entire town is considered part of the Swiss national heritage. It dates from at least the 8th Century and the first Alemanni settlements.

Hirschen Backpackers Hotel/Pub, Hinterdorfstrasse 14, Schwyz; *Info@ hirschen-schwyz.ch/,* T:+41/418111276, $32Bed, Kitchen:Y, B'fast:$, Pvt.

room:Y, Locker:Y, Recep:10a//11p; Note: resto/bar, laundry, bag hold, tours, prkng, maps

SOLOTHURN is a town off 16,500 in the northern mostly-German-speaking part of the country. It may have been a Roman way-station, but definitely dates back to st least the medieval era. There are eighteen sites listed as being of significance for Swiss heritage. The number eleven has special significance here.

Solothurn, Lanhausquai 23, 'Am Land', Solothurn; *hihostels.com/*, T:+41/326231706, *solothurn@youthhostel.ch*; $34Bed, Kitchen:N, B'fast:Y, Pvt. room:N, Locker:Y, Recep:7:30a//9:30p; Note: bikes, wh/chair ok, lift, laundry

2 Hostels) ST. MORITZ is a town of 5000 and one of the most exclusive and expensive ski resorts in the world. Alpine tourism was born here in 1861 and it has hosted the Winter Olympics twice. Summertime is nice, too, great for hiking. Train stops here.

Randolins Backpackers, via Curtins 2, St Moritz, T:+41/818308383, *willkommen@ randolins.ch/*; $72Bed, Kitchen:N, B'fast:Y, Pvt.room:Y, Locker:N, Recep:ltd; Note: resto, gym, hot tub, bikes, tours, parking, laundry, bag hold, skiing

St. Moritz Bad, Via Surpunt 60, St. Moritz; *hihostels.com/*, T:+41/818366111, *st.moritz@youthhostel.ch*; $40Bed, Kitchen:N, B'fast:Y, Pvt.room:Y, Locker:Y, Recep:8a>10p; Note: resto/bar, bikes, billiards, bag hold, parking, tours, laundry

STEIN AM RHEIN is a town of 3000 on Switzerland's northern border with Germany, which contains a well-preserved historic center and fresco-painted medieval buildings. Many buildings are registered on the list of those with historical significance.

Stein am Rhein, Hemishoferstr. 87, Stein am Rhein; T:+41/527411255, *stein@youthhostel.ch*; $33Bed, Kitchen:N, B'fast:Y, Pvt.room:Y, Locker:Y, Recep:8a//10p; Note: closed winters, bag hold, tours, parking

VEZEY is a town of over 18,000 in the western French-speaking part of Switzerland, and famous as the birthplace of Nestle and its headquarters. Landmarks include Jean Jacques Rousseau's favorite restaurant, St. Martin's Church, and Nestle's Alimentarium Museum.

Vevey Hotel, Grande Place 5, Vevey; *reservation@ veveyhotel. com/*, T:+41/219223532; $39Bed, Kitchen:Y, B'fast:$, Pvt.room:Y, Locker:Y, Recep:8a//8p; Note: lift, laundry, parking, maps, tea/coffee, central

WINTERTHUR is a city of over 100,000 only 19mi/30km from Zurich, and well-connected by train to neighboring countries, also. *Albanifest* in late June is a multi-day festival in honor of one of the patron saints. Both Swiss folk metal and punkabilly music have roots here, yep. Architecture is nice. This is a good alternative to pricey Zurich.

Depot 195 - Hostel Winterthur, Lagerplatz 4, Winterthur; T:+41/ 522031363, *Info@ depot195.ch/*; $39Bed, Kitchen:Y, B'fast:$, Pvt.room:N, Locker:Y, Recep:7a//10p; Note: café/bar, wh/chair ok, lift, laundry, bag hold, tea/coffee

2 Hostels) ZERMATT is where you go to climb the Matterhorn. It's also a car-free zone, internal combustion, that is; electric or nothing, way cool. Tourism is the only business.

Zermatt YH, "Winkelmatten" Staldenweg 5, Zermatt; T:+41/279672320, *zermatt@ youthhostel.ch/*; $39bed, Kitchen:N, B'fast:Y, Pvt.room:Y, Locker:Y, Recep:>10p; Note: dinner inc, resto/bar, tours, laundry, c.c. ok, kiosk, terrace, view

Matterhorn Hostel, Schluhmattstrasse 32, Zermatt, T:0279681919, *info@ matterhornhostel.com/*; $33bed, Kitchen:Y, B'fast:$, Pvt. room:Y, Locker:Y, Recep:8a>9p; Note: resto/bar, TV/DVD, central, bag hold, c.c. ok

3 Hostels) ZURICH was once an outpost of the Celtic Helvetii and Romans before falling under the influence of the Franks and Alemanni, and before joining the Swiss Confederation, a group united in opposition to the Austrian Habsburgs. Its location at the crossroads of trade routes put it at the center of political and economic events on the cutting-edge of history. Soon it became

a manufacturing powerhouse, and a bastion of Protestantism, democratic reform, AND finance. Culture followed, and Zurich became the center of the Dada art movement. But it was not all inspired. Its banks' role in laundering Hitler's money became known in the 1990's and it repaid millions to Jewish families plundered.

Today it is the largest and wealthiest city in Switzerland. It's beautiful, too, but expensive. It has major film, art, and music festivals, including the dance-and-techno-oriented "Street Parade," which attracts a million people. Raemistrasse, just east of the city centre, is known as the city's "art mile." Notable museums include the Swiss National Museum, and the Museum of Fine Arts. Historic architecture is centered in the old town, including the 8th C. Grossmunster, 13th C. St. Peter's Church, and the Fraumunster, with windows by Marc Chagall. With its increasing ethnic diversity, it is one of Europe's liveliest of modern cities.

Youth Hostel Zurich, Mutschellenstrasse 114, Zurich; T:0433997800, *zuerich@ youthhostel.ch/*; $44bed, Kitchen:Y, B'fast:Y, Pvt.room:Y, Locker:Y, Recep:24/7; Note: non-members $6 extra, luggage, laundry, bar, parking, distant, large

Langstars, Langstrasse 120, Zurich; *langstars.ch/*, T:0433179655, *fo@langstars.com;* $48Bed, Kitchen:N, B'fast:Y, Pvt.room:N, Locker:Y, Recep:8a>12m; Note: resto/bar/club, tours, bag hold, red-light dist

City Backpacker-Hostel Biber, Niederdorfstrasse 5, Zurich; T:+41/ 442519015, *sleep@ city-backpacker.ch/*; $41Bed, Kitchen:Y, B'fast:$, Pvt.room:Y, Locker:Y, Recep:8a//10p; Note: minimart, laundry, bag hold, coffee/tea, books, stairs

Part III: Greece & The Balkan Peninsula

10) Albania

Albania is truly the oddball nation of the Balkans. Likely descendants of the ancient Illyrians who shared the European outback with the Celts prior to the arrival of Germanic tribes, still they fared little better until united under the Ottoman banner. By adopting Islam as their religion, they were given a privileged position in the empire, and also consolidated something of a homeland for themselves, theretofore poorly defined. Annexed by the Italian fascists then the Nazis during WWII, they became Communist afterwards, with one of the most closed paranoid states to have ever existed (compare to North Korea in 2012). Much of the Islamic culture was destroyed.

Communism ended in 1991, and Albania quickly got a rude brush with capitalism in massive Ponzi schemes that made international news in 1997. The Kosovo war (Kosovans are ethnic Albanians) also brought many refugees and ensuing problems. Things are better now and Alabania is open for business and tourism. Albanian is the language, but if you can't find someone to speak English, then try Italian. Lek (ALL) is the currency; phone code is +355.

BERAT, like Tirana, is somewhat centrally located, and small at less than 80,000 people. Following the Greeks, Romans, Byzantines and Bulgarians, the Ottomans made Berat an important city and ultimately a center of Albanian national revival. Crafts guilds were many and varied. Today it is known for the architecture of its historic center, earning it a world heritage designation.

Berat Backpackers, 295 Gorica, Berat; *info@ beratbackpackers.com/*, T:693064429; $13bed, Kitchen:Y, B'fast:Y, Pvt.room:N, Locker:N, Recep:24/7; Note: wh/chairs ok, bar, lounge, parking, bag hold, TV

2 Hostels) SARANDA is on the Albanian "Riviera," directly across from the Greek Island of Corfu. There is a ferry. The ancient city of Butrint, world heritage site, is near.

Backpackers SR-The Bunker, Rruga Mithat Hoxha #10, Lagja 4 Saranda; *backpackerssr.hostel.com/*, T:+355/694345426; $13bed, Kitchen:Y, B'fast:Y, Pvt.room:N, Locker:N, Recep:24/7; Note: nr Corfu ferry, tours, bag hold, laundry, forex

Hairy Lemon, Coastal Rd, Saranda; *saranda@ hairylemonhostel.com*, T:+355/693559317; $14bed, Kitchen:Y, B'fast:Y, Pvt.room:Y, Locker:Y, Recep:24/7; Note: lift, bag hold, laundry, free tour, forex, prkng, not central, view

3 Hostels) TIRANA, and Albania in general, is nothing if not chaotic and prone to extremes. Upon becoming Communist, the previous Turkish and Italian architecture was demolished or abandoned in favor of gray Bolshevik modern Stalinist style—yuk. After that, capitalism brought disorder and irregularity to an ill-prepared city. This ultimately led to great population migrations toward the countryside such that it's hard to tell where the city ends and pasture begins. It's nothing to see a five-storey building sitting out in the middle of a field, and I bet you could find cows grazing in the city if you looked hard enough. Still Tirana has its pleasures, and the cafes and bars are active. There are castles, a historic bridge, mosques, mosaics and museums. Skanderberg Square lies more or less at the center of it all. It's a mess, but really not a bad one.

Hostel-Albania, rr. Beqir Luga 56, Tirana; *Lira@ Hostel-Albania.com*, T:0672783798; $14bed, Kitchen:Y, B'fast:Y, Pvt.room:N, Locker:Y, Recep:ltd; Note: prkng, forex, laundry, bag hold, tours, garden, kittens! cats?

Freddy's Hostel, Ground Floor, 75 Bardhok Biba St, Tirana; *freddyshostel. com/*, T:(0)682035261; $16bed, Kitchen:N, B'fast:Y, Pvt.room:Y, Locker:N, Recep:24/7; Note: luggage room, a/c, central, hard to find

Oresti Hostel, 32 Bardhok Biba St, Tirana; *orestihostel.com/*, T:(0)682022313; $19bed, Kitchen:N, B'fast:N, Pvt.room:Y, Locker:N, Recep:24/7; Note: parking, forex, luggage room, a/c, non-party, ext. of Freddy's

11) Bosnia & Hercegovina

If the Balkans (mostly ex-Yugoslavia) consists primarily of a single ethnic group and language family, i.e. southern Slavic, it certainly consists of at least three culturally different "constituent peoples," all of them present in modern Bosnia—Serbs with their orthodox Christian church and Cyrillic script, Croats with their Catholic church and Roman script, and lastly Bosniaks, with their Islam (Arabic script would be too perfect).

In an area previously settled by Illyrians and Celts, Slavs came to settle in the last half of the first millennium AD, and eventually established a political entity which became the Kingdom of Bosnia. It was long-lasting, but not stable, however, and the Ottoman Turks finally annexed it in 1463 and ruled for more than four centuries. These Slavs were last to convert to Christianity, which may have made them more convertible to Islam by the Ottoman Turks. Whatever, it worked, of course, and Bosnia to this day has almost more vestiges of Turkish culture, including *kilims* and cuisine, than does much of Turkey itself.

By the 19th century Ottoman Turkey was in serious decline, and Austria-Hungary assumed control in 1879. Germany and Russia signed off on it, but not Serbia, and all bets were off when a Serb nationalist in the Bosnian capital of Sarajevo killed the Austrian archduke and started WWI. After the war Bosnia joined the nascent Yugoslavia, though Bosnian Muslims were not well-represented in the political mix, and internal boundaries were redrawn to minimize their influence. WWII was horrific, with Serbian-nationalist Chetniks no better than the Nazis, but Bosnia remained as one of six constituent republics in the post-war Communist government and it prospered as a center of the defense industry. Post-Communist independence finally came in 1991.

Unfortunately it is politically divided between Serb-dominated *Republika Srpski* on one hand, and a union of Croats and Bosniaks on the other, and that's the good news. The bad news is that the Muslims endured a Serb-sponsored genocide/ethnic cleansing from 1992-95 in the process. The rest is silence. None of Bosnia's horror is a reason to avoid tourism here, quite the contrary in fact. The famous city of Sarajevo is here and so is the historic city of Mostar. The countryside is beautiful and underpopulated. The food is good. The currency is the convertible Mark (BAM); the language is Bosnian (Serbo-Croatian); the calling code is +387.

BANJALUKA is the main city of the Republika Srpska region of Bosnia and site of many uprisings against the Ottoman overlords in the 19th century. In 1993 Bosnian Serbs destroyed two large historic mosques in the city dating from the Ottoman period, the Ferhadija and the Arnaudija mosques. This is the center from which Croats and Bosnians were raped and massacred in the name of "ethnic cleansing" during the Bosnian War of 1992-95. There is a concentration camp. I just report the facts. You do what you want.

City Smile Hostel, Skendera Kulenovića 16, Banjaluka, Rep. Serbski; *hostel-banjaluka.com*, T:+387/51214187; $15bed, Kitchen:Y, B'fast:N, Pvt.room:Y, Locker:Y, Recep:24/7; Note: coffee & tea, parking, luggage room

5 Hostels) MOSTAR is the main city in the Hercegovina part of B & H. It was named after the keepers of its most famous landmark, the old bridge (*stari most*), built by the Ottomans and spanning the Neretva River. Halfway between Sarajevo and the sea, this has been a trade route and river crossing since antiquity. The city as we know it was constructed by the Turks in their fashion, and, after recent years as part of Austria-Hungary, Yugoslavia, and then the Serbian siege, it has been reconstructed in that fashion. If you want to see how Ottoman Turkey used to be, then go to Mostar. There are Greek and Roman ruins, too. The bridge is a World Heritage site. Islam is the religion here, so be prepared to take your shoes off when going inside (and please don't bitch about it; it's impolite).

Guest House Taso, M.Tita 187, Mostar; *guesthousetaso.com*, T:061523149, *guesthousetaso@gmail.com*; $14bed, Kitchen:Y, B'fast:N, Pvt.room:Y, Locker:N, Recep:24/7; Note:free pick-up, club, parking, tours, age limit 45

Hostel Miturno, Brace Fejica 67, Mostar; T:+387/36552408, *bookings@ miturno.ba*; $14bed, Kitchen:Y, B'fast:$, Pvt.room:Y, Locker:N, Recep:24/7; Note: bar, laundry, luggage room, a/c, c.c. ok, forex, central

Rooms Denino, Trg Ivana Krndelja 11F, Mostar; *sobe-denino.com*, T:+387/36550372, *maida_begic@yahoo.com*; $14bed, Kitchen:N, B'fast:$, Pvt. room:Y, Locker:Y, Recep:24/7; Note: resto/bar, pick-up, bag hold, laundry, forex, central

Hostel Miran, Pere Lažetića 13 (Carina), Mostar; *hostelmiran-mostar.com*, T:061823555, *meskic_mo@hotmail.com*; $13bed, Kitchen:Y, B'fast:$, Pvt.room:Y, Locker:N, Recep:24/7; Note: laundry, bag hold, forex, tours, family-run

Hostel Dino, Mladena Balorde 1 (Musala Sq), Mostar; *hostel-dino.hostel.com/*, T:061968119, *dino.hostel@gmail.com*; $13bed, Kitchen:N, B'fast:$, Pvt.room:Y, Locker:Y, Recep:24/7; Note: pick-up, prkng, laundry, bag hold, cntr, nr bus

7 Hostels) SARAJEVO is the capital of B & H, high up in the Dinaric Alps, and is a world city in every sense, until recently having adherents of four major religions within its environs, and having once hosted the Winter Olympics. During the Ottoman era it was constructed largely in Turkish style and had many times the population of any other Balkan city. Eventually it was annexed by Austria-Hungary and WWI started right here when Archduke Franz Ferdinand (no, not the R&R group) was assassinated by a Serb nationalist. In the War of Independence following the breakup of Yugoslavia, Sarajevo was besieged and blockaded by Serb forces from 1992-5, resulting in tens of thousands of casualties and much physical damage.

Today Sarajevo prospers again and is one of the fastest-growing cities in the region. It has film and jazz festivals, a music subculture, and was one of the highlights of my "Hypertravel" project. Principal mosques and Islamic structures are the Gazi Husreff-Bey's Mosque, the Mosque of Ali Pasha, the *medrese* (madrasah), the Imaret (a free kitchen for the poor), the *hamam* (public baths), and a late 16th-century clock tower. Museums include the Mlada Bosna, the Museum of the Revolution, and a Jewish museum. Did I mention that it's a travel bargain? Hostel quality is good. Many buildings are still riddled, by bullets, not mysteries. But wait...

Travellers' Home, Ćumurija 4, Sarajevo; T:(0)70242400, *info@ myhostel. ba*; $16bed, Kitchen:Y, B'fast:Y, Pvt.room:Y, Locker:Y, Recep:24/7; Note: café, parking, tours, laundry, bag hold

Residence Rooms, s.h.Muvekita 1, Sarajevo; *residencerooms.com.ba/,* T:066801727, *residencerooms@gmail.com*; $20bed, Kitchen:Y, B'fast:Y, Pvt. room:Y, Locker:Y, Recep:24/7; Note: café, laundry, bag hold, central, tours

Haris Youth Hostel, Vratnik Mejdan 29, Sarajevo; T:(0)61518825, *info@ hyh.ba/*; $20bed, Kitchen:Y, B'fast:N, Pvt.room:Y, Locker:Y, Recep:8a>4p; Note: bar, hubbly-bubbly, views, laundry, bag hold, c.c. ok, uphill

Hostel City Center Sarajevo, Saliha Hadzihuseinovica, Muvekita 2/3; T:(0)62993330, *hcc.sarajevo@hcc.ba*; $20bed, Kitchen:Y, B'fast:Y, Pvt.room:N, Locker:Y, Recep:24/7; Note: laundry, bag hold, tours, a/c, c.c. ok, stairs

B & B Divan, Mula Mustafe Baseskija 54, Sarajevo; T:(0)33238677, *info@ pansiondivan.ba/*; $20bed, Kitchen:N, B'fast:$, Pvt. room:Y, Locker:Y, Recep: 24/7; Note: laundry, tours, a/c, c.c. ok, central, dorm room in hotel

Hostel Tito 46, Marsala tita 46, Sarajevo; T:+387/63693275, *info@ hostel-tito46.com/*; $14bed, Kitchen:Y, B'fast:$, Pvt.room:Y, Locker:Y, Recep:ltd; Note: laundry, travel desk, forex, ATM, TV, bike rent, central

Hostel Ljubcica, Mula Mustafe Baeskije 65, Bascarsija, Sarajevo; *hostelljubicica.net/,* T:033535829, *taljubic@bih.net.ba*; $9bed, Kitchen:N, B'fast:$, Pvt. room:N, Locker:Y, Recep:24/7; Note: bar, laundry, bag hold, parking, cntr, pick-up

12) Croatia

Croatia is the most western of the three Serbo-Bosnian-Croatian countries and forms something of a pincers formation around a wedge-like Bosnia, which more-or-less represents the leading edge of Ottoman domination in the region.

These southern Slavs have been in the region at least since the seventh century, gradually edging Roman settlements back toward the sea, an area under Croat control today and which until recently still spoke the Romance Dalmatian language.

For the first two centuries of their existence in the area, Croats were an independent kingdom before entering a personal union with Hungary in 1102. As Venice assumed control over the Dalmatian coast and the Ottomans threatened the whole peninsula, Croatia joined the House of Habsburg as a defensive strategy in 1526, and a military frontier was created and enforced. As a result Croatia was able to stay out of Ottoman influence, while Bosnia remained within.

In the 20th century the political landscape changed: Austria-Hungary fell, and the union of Serbs, Croats and Slovenes eventually became the nascent Yugoslavia. They became Communist after WWII, of course, and independent of Russia, but not Serbia. The Croatian War of Independence in the early 1990's was brutal, but Croatia prevailed and today life is good. That Dalmatian coast is Croatia's tourist gold these days, too, with cities like Dubrovnik and Split leading the way. Hostel quality is not bad, either, though they're not very good with formalities like websites. I prefer those with them (hint hint). *Kuna* (HRK) is the currency; Croat is the language; the calling code is +385.

3 Hostels) DUBROVNIK is one of Europe's top tourist destinations for over a hundred years, its walled medieval city the main draw. As Ragusa, this was a maritime city that goes back to the Roman era, was later ruled by the Byzantines, and rivaled Venice in the Middle Ages, before becoming a colony of it. Though it later paid tribute to the Turkish Ottomans, Ragusa was a free city until the Austrian Habsburgs took over in 1815.

At that point Dubrovnik was Europe in microcosm, with German, Latin, and Slavic languages all spoken within its domain. Then came Yugoslavia and Communism. After Croatia's declaration of independence in 1991, Dubrovnik was besieged by the rump Yugoslavia for seven months, Montenegro claiming that Dubrovnik belonged to it. The siege was finally lifted and damage to the old city repaired. There are 2km of walls.

The old city is a UNESCO World Heritage site. Landmarks include two 14th C. convents at the ends of the city, the Rector's Palace, numerous fortresses, a 16-sided fountain and bell tower, and a 15th C. Jewish synagogue. The island of Lokrum has gardens and orange groves, in addition to a fortress and monastery. Museums include the Museum of Dubrovnik, the Franciscan monastery, the Maritime Museum, and the Dubrovnik State Archives. There is a 45-day long summer festival. There are many cheap accommodations, but few have dorms. Here are some that do.

Fresh Sheets Hostel Dubrovnik Old Town, Svetog Šimuna 15; T:0917992086, *freshsheetshostel.com/*, $28bed, *beds@igotfresh.com*; Kitchen:Y, B'fast:Y, Pvt.room:Y, Locker:Y, Recep:ltd; Note: tours, stairs, forex, maps

Vila Micika, Mata Vodopica 10, Lapad, Dubrovnik; T:020437332, *info@ vilamicika.hr/*; $28bed, Kitchen:N, B'fast:N, Pvt.room:Y, Locker:Y, Recep:24/7; Note: free bus/ferry pickup, resto/bar, supermkt, laundry, prkng, a/c

HI Dubrovnik YH, Vinka Sagrestana 3, Dubrovnik; *hihostels.com*, T:+385/20423241, *dubrovnik@hfhs.hr*; $26bed, Kitchen:Y, B'fast:Y, Pvt.room:N, Locker:N, Recep:ltd; Note: by old city, resto, bag hold, c.c. ok, uphill

HVAR is a city and island off the Croatian coast, and over forty miles long. The old city originally founded by the Greeks is one of Europe's oldest. The city was a medieval naval base. The divided fields of Stari Grad Plain are a UNESCO world heritage site, evidence of the agricultural style of the ancient Greeks.

Dink's Place, Ive Roića 5, Vrisak, Hvar; T:0917866923, *info@ dinksplace. com/*; $16bed, Kitchen:Y, B'fast:N, Pvt.room:Y, Locker:Y, Recep:ltd; Note: luggage room, laundry, parking, forex, min. stay 2 nights

2 Hostels) PULA lies at the tip of the Istrian peninsula and is the largest city in the county of the same name. It entered the pages of history with the Greeks a millennium before the Common Era and then as the *Histri* during the Roman Era. The history of rulers here is like a rollcall of Western history — Ostrogoths, Byzantines, and Charlemagne, Venice, Genoa, and Pisa. Slavs eventually outnumbered Italians and the Istrian peninsula joined Croatia and Yugoslavia in 1947. Winemaking, fishing and tourism are the major industries. Roman ruins, including an amphitheatre, and beaches top the list of tourist destinations.

Pula Art Hostel, Maruliceva 41, Pula; T:+385/98874078, *booking@ pulaarthostel.com/*; $19bed, Kitchen:Y, B'fast:N, Pvt.room:N, Locker:Y, Recep:ltd; Note: luggage room, laundry, forex, a/c, central

HI Pula YH, Zaljev Valsaline 4, Pula; *hihostels.com/*, T:+385/52391133, *pula@hflls.hr*; $18bed, Kitchen:N, B'fast:Y, Pvt.room:N, Locker:N, Recep:ltd; Note: resto/bar, laundry, luggage ok, c.c. ok, town far near beach

12 Hostels) SPLIT is Croatia's second city and the Dalmatian Coast's largest. As such it is the transportation hub for the region, with connections over land and sea. Its origins involve the construction of Roman Emperor Diocletian's retirement palace here, and after the fall of the Empire in 476, governance was handled variously by the Byzantines, Venetians, and Hungary, the Dalmatian coast an entity effectively separate from the Slavic Croatian hinterlands. The number of Croats continued increasing, though, so by the fall of Venice in 1797, they were a clear majority and upon the dissolution of Austria-Hungary after WWII, the area came under the rule of Croatia and Yugoslavia.

During WWII Split was fiercely anti-Fascist and pro-Tito, the emerging Communist strongman of Yugoslavia. Post-WWII Split fared better than most of Yugoslavia, with its prosperous shipyards. Croatia declared independence from Yugoslavia in 1991. Tourism is the main industry now. The historic center, part of the palace and a world heritage site, is the main attraction. Museums include the Meštrović Gallery, the Archaeological Museum, the Museum of Croatian Archaeological Monuments, the City Museum, the Art Gallery, and the Ethnographic Museum, housed in the Venetian Gothic town hall. By European standards the weather is sublime and the prices low.

Tchaikovsky Hostel Split, Petra Ilica Cajkovskog 4, Split; T:021317124, *info@ tchaikovskyhostel.com/*; $17bed, Kitchen:N, B'fast:N, Pvt.room:N, Locker:Y, Recep:>10p; Note: art trans, bag hold, mart, parking, tours, central, coffee/tea

CroParadise Green Hostel, Culica Dvori 31, Split

CroParadise Blue Hostel, Rijecka 3, Split; T:0914444194, *blue@ croparadise. com/*; $19bed, Kitchen:Y, B'fast:N, Pvt.room:Y, Locker:Y, Recep:>11p; Note: arpt trans, café, laundry, parking, tea/coffee, TV, a/c, hard to find

Kamena Lodge, Don Petra Perosa 20, Mravince, Split; T:021269910, *info@ kamenalodge.com/*; $26bed, Kitchen:Y, B'fast:$, Pvt.room:Y, Locker:Y, Recep:24/7;Note: bar, pool, bag hold, laundry, tours, out of town

Silver Central Hostel, Kralja Tomislava 1, Split; *silvercentralhostel.com/*, T:0989955878, *silvercentralhostel@gmail.com*; $21bed, Kitchen:N, B'fast:N, Pvt. room:Y, Locker:Y, Recep:>11p; Note: cash, bag hold, laundry, a/c, tours, central

Hostel Adria, Poljicka Cesta, 58 Bajnice, Split; T:0911930722, *info@hostel-adria.com*; $16bed, Kitchen:Y, B'fast:Y, Pvt.room:Y, Locker:Y, Recep:ltd; Note: coffee/tea, parking, TV, bag hold, laundry, far from Split, on sea

Al's Place Hostel, Petra Kružića 10, Split; T:0989182923, *info@ hostelsplit. com/*; $23bed, Kitchen:Y, B'fast:N, Pvt.room:N, Locker:N, Recep: 9:30a/9:30p; Note: forex, laundry, bag hold, a/c, very small, close winter

Design Hostel Goli & Bosi, Morpurgova poljana 2, Split; T:38521510999, *info@ golibosi.com/*; $27bed, Kitchen:N, B'fast:$, Pvt.room:Y, Locker:Y, Recep:24/7; Note: resto/bar, bag hold, lift, wh/chair ok, a/c, c.c. ok, central

Silvergate Hostel, Hrvojeva 6, Split; *silvergatehostel.com/*, T:0989955878, *silvergatehostel@gmail.com*; $20bed, Kitchen:N, B'fast:N, Pvt. room:Y, Locker:Y, Recep:24/7; Note: parking, bag hold, laundry, a/c, no bunks

Split Hostel Booze & Snooze, Narodni trg 8, Split; T:021342787, *info@ splithostel.com/*; $19bed, Kitchen:N, B'fast:N, Pvt.room:N, Locker:Y, Recep:8a>10p; Note: arpt trans, bag hold, tea/coffee, a/c, tours, central, pub crawl

Diocletian's Palace Hostel, Dioklecijanova 5, Split; T: 098858141, *hostel@ diocletianpalace.com/*; $15bed, Kitchen:N, B'fast:$, Pvt.room:Y, Locker:Y, Recep:24/7; Note: age>45, resto/bar/café, lounge, TV, bag hold, laundry, bikes

Hostel Split Backpackers, Kralja Zvonimira 17, Split; *splitbackpackers. com/*, T:021782483, *splitbackpackers@gmail.com*; $27bed, Kitchen:Y, B'fast:N, Pvt. room:Y, Locker:Y, Recep:8a>11p; Note: near ferry/bus/train, bag hold, tours, a/c, c.c. ok

2 Hostels) ZADAR was originally populated by pre-Indo-European speakers and became a city in Roman times. It thrived during the Byzantine era. Venice later fortified the city during the Renaissance era, but still the Ottomans attacked, and then the Austrians remodeled. Roman ruins survive to this day,

including the forum. Other attractions are St. Donat's 9th C. circular church, St. Mary's Church and the Romanesque Church of St. Krševan, consecrated in 1175. There are also the 13th C. Cathedral of St. Stošija (Anastasia), and the Franciscan church and monastery. Zadar has an archaeological museum, the state archives, a theatre, and a small branch of the University of Zagreb. Tourism and maritime industries dominate the economy.

Hostel Elena, ćirila Ivekovića 4, Zadar; *hostel-elena-zadar.hr/*, T:0915723439, *zlucic6@gmail.com*; $23bed, Kitchen:Y, B'fast:N, Pvt room:N, Locker:Y, Recep:ltd; Note: luggage room, a/c, in old city

Drunken Monkey Hostel, Jure Kastriotića Skenderbega 21, Zadar; *drunkenmonkeyhostel.com/*, T:023314406; $19bed, Kitchen:Y, B'fast:N, Pvt. room:Y, Locker:Y, Recep:ltd; Note: bar, pool, tours, parties, not central, @beach

11 Hostels) ZAGREB is the capital and largest city of Croatia. It has been a city since at least the start of the last millennium, though a Roman city preceded it going back another thousand years at least. It was originally two cities—Gradec the fortress and Kaptol the church settlement—which gradually grew together. Gradec has the Gothic-style Church of St. Marcus, the Baroque Church of St. Catherine, the palaces of Zrinski and Oršić, and the Neoclassical Drasković Palace. Kaptol has the Gothic Cathedral of St. Stephen and the Baroque palace of the archbishops of Zagreb, with a chapel of St. Stephen. For culture there are the Academy of Sciences and Arts, the University of Zagreb, various museums and the Croatian National Theatre. It is well-connected to the rest of Europe, and while there is not the fun 'n sun of the coast, it is well worth a day or two or three.

Chillout Hostel Zagreb, Fra Andrije Kačića Miošića 3, Zagreb; T:014849605, *info@ chillout-hostelzagreb.com/*; $16bed, Kitchen:Y, B'fast:N, Pvt. room:N, Locker:Y, Recep:24/7; Note: café/bar, bag hold, forex. a/c, c.c. ok, new, central

Buzz Hostel, Babukićeva 1b, Zagreb; T:012320267, *reception@*

Old Town Zagreb/Buzz BP, đorđićeva 24, Zagreb, T:014816748, *oldtownzagreb@ buzzbackpackers.com/*; $23bed, Kitchen:Y, B'fast:N, Pvt.room:Y, Locker:Y, Recep:>11p; Note: coffee/tea, laundry, bag hold, forex, tours, non-party

Funk Hostel & Club, Poljička 13, Zagreb; T:016314530

Funk Lounge, Ivana Rendića 28, Zagreb, T:015552707, *recepcija@ funklounge. hr/*; $24bed, Kitchen:Y, B'fast:N, Pvt.room:Y, Locker:Y, Recep:24/7; Note: arpt trans, resto/bar, bikes, laundry, bag hold, parking, tours, cash, central

Hostel Nocturno, Skalinska 2a, Zagreb; *nokturno.hr/*; $19bed, Kitchen:Y, B'fast:N, Pvt.room:Y, Locker:Y, Recep:24/7; Note: resto/bar, coffee & tea, bike rent, laundry, tours, luggage room

Fulir Hostel, Radićeva 3a, Zagreb;T:014830882, *fulir@ fulir-hostel.com/*; $17bed, Kitchen:Y, B'fast:N, Pvt.room:Y, Locker:Y, Recep:>10p; Note: laundry, luggage room, central, arpt trans, tea/coffee

Ravnice Y.H., Ravnice 1 38, Zagreb, *ravnice-youth-hostel.hr/*, T:012332325, *ravnice-youth-hostel@zg.t-com.hr*; $23bed, Kitchen:Y, B'fast:Y, Pvt.room:Y, Locker:Y, Recep:>10p; Note: bag hold, laundry, parking, TV, wh/chair ok, lift, not central

Hostel Mali Mrak Zagreb, Dubicka 8, Zagreb; *hostel-zagreb.com/*, T:+385/ 16389109; $19bed, Kitchen:N, B'fast:N, Pvt. room:Y, Locker:Y, Recep:24/7; Note: bag hold, laundry, forex, a/c, c.c. ok, not central, parking, tea/coffee

Youth Hostel Zagreb, Petrinjska St #77, Zagreb; *hihostels.com/*, T:+385(0)14841261, *zagreb@hfhs.hr*; $22bed, Kitchen:N, B'fast:N, Pvt. room:N, Locker:Y, Recep:24/7; Note: HI, wh/chair ok, lift, bag hold, parking

Hostel Lika, Pašmanska 17, Zagreb; *hostel-lika.com/*, T:098561041, *hostel-lika@yahoo.com*; $15bed, Kitchen:N, B'fast:$, Pvt.room:Y, Locker:Y, Recep:>10p; Note: laundry, parking, a/c, bar, café, luggage room

13) Greece

Greece is where Europe began, specifically Western Europe, west of Egypt and Babylon and Jerusalem, at least, its most illustrious contemporaries. The Greece of classical antiquity emerged in Athens and culminated in the

"Greater Greece" of Alexander the Great that stretched from Greece to Central Asia, and left Greek-speakers and Greek culture all over the world. It now lies far to the east of the major modern Western Europe population centers of London, Paris, and Rome.

Still western it is, with traditions of language, philosophy, science, and government that were tried, tested, and transmitted directly to Rome and elsewhere over two thousand years ago. After then being dominated by Rome it eventually entered into a sort of partnership, with the "new Rome" of the Eastern (Byzantine) Roman Empire established at Constantinople, Greek of speech, culture and religion. For over 1000 years it was one of history's greatest empires.

Constantinople fell to the Ottoman Turks in 1453 and the rest of Greece fell soon thereafter, only regaining independence in 1830, minus Constantinople (Istanbul). Politics since then have been a roller-coaster of leftists and rightists battling for the hearts and minds of the people in a never-ending struggle. Only in religion and alphabet is Greece perhaps closer to the Slavic Eastern Europe of which it is a contiguous part, and which barely existed in the classical age, within the region at least. Greece has little to do with former master and eastern neighbor Turkey, and largely defines itself that way.

Still Greece is connected to them all by road, boat and plane. Tourism is a mainstay of the economy, and Greece has no less than seventeen UNESCO World Heritage Sites. Aside from the classical sites, Greece is best known for its islands, many of which are party central for gap-year kids with the means to get there. They along with Thessaloniki and Athens constitute the touristic Athens. Greek is the language. The phone code is +30. The currency is Euro; wait a minute...

10 Hostels) ATHENS is where Western civilization began, with accomplishments in philosophy, politics, art, and literature that are unsurpassed to this day. Athens is also one of the world's oldest cities, documented from 1400 BC, when it played a role in the preclassical Mycenaean culture, and today it's the largest city and capital of Greece. After centuries of neglect as a part of the Ottoman Empire, Athens today has returned to much of its previous vitality and importance. It has also overcome much of its horrendous smog problem of a few decades ago, and today is fairly pleasant, especially in the tourist areas under the Parthenon.

Piraeus is the major port and is only a short train ride away. It resembles nothing so much as a modern airport with ferries coming and going constantly. As always the main problem in Athens is the economy. The main tourist sights center on the ancient Acropolis and its crown jewel Parthenon. Then there is the National Archeological Museum. Those expecting an eastern Rome-like "museum city" full of medieval art and architecture will be disappointed. During the long civil war Athens was mostly depopulated and destroyed.

Only the Plaka below the Acropolis maintains some of that original ambience, with streets devoted to certain crafts and other vestiges of that era. Still the Acropolis is not the only classical site of interest. There is also the Roman-built Odeum theatre built in 161 AD and now used in the summer festival of music and drama, and the Theatre of Dionysius to which it is attached. Others are found in the Agora, including the Theseum, a 5th Century BC temple. Then there are the 42-foot-high Horologium water clock and the Byzantine church Aylos Eleftherios.

Athens Intl YH, Viktoros Ougko 16, Metaxourgio; T:2105232540, *info@ athens-international.com/*; $13bed, Kitchen:N, B'fast:$, Pvt.room:Y, Locker:Y, Recep:24/7; Note: max. stay 7N, laundry, lift, a/c, bag hold, colorful 'hood

Student & Travelers Inn, 16 Kydathineon, Plaka, Athens; T:2103248802, *info@ studenttravellersinn.com/*; $24bed, Kitchen:N, B'fast:$, Pvt.room:Y, Locker:N, Recep:24/7; Note: bar, café, laundry, bag hold, cold, few outlets

Athens Backpackers, 12 Makri St, Makryanni, Athens; T:+30/2109224044; *info@ backpackers.gr/*; $29bed, Kitchen:Y, B'fast:Y, Pvt.room:Y, Locker:Y, Recep:24/7; Note: bar, café, a/c, c.c. ok, laundry, bag hold, parking, tours

Athens Studios, 12 Makri St, Makrigianni, Athens; T:+30/2109235811, *info@ athensstudios.gr/*; $33bed, Kitchen:Y, B'fast:Y, Pvt.room:Y, Locker:N, Recep:8a>12m; Note: bar, bag hold, laundry, lift, a/c, c.c. ok, good location, roof view

AthenStyle, Agias Theklas, No 10, Athens; T:+30/2103225010, *info@ athenstyle.com/*; $26bed, Kitchen:Y, B'fast:Y, Pvt.room:Y, Locker:Y, Recep:24/7; Note: bar, laundry, a/c, c.c. ok, location, rooftop bar

Hotel Fivos, 23 Athinas St, Monastiraki, Athens, Greece; *hotelfivos.gr/ en/*, T:+30/2103226657; $13bed, Kitchen:N, B'fast:Y, Pvt.room:Y, Locker:N, Recep:24/7; Note: bar, travel desk, a/c, c.c. ok, central, outside noise

Hostel Zorba's, 10 Gkyilfordou St., Victoria Square, Athens; T:2108224927, *info@ zorbashotel.com/*; $14bed, Kitchen:N, B'fast:$, Pvt.room:Y, Locker:Y, Recep:24/7; Note: c.c.+5%, bar, laundry, bag hold, a/c, colorful area

Neo Olympos Hotel, 38 Theodorou Diligianni St, Athens; T:2106223433, *info@ hotelneosolympos.com/*; $13bed, Kitchen:N, B'fast:Y, Pvt.room:Y, Locker:Y, Recep: 24/7; Note: bag hold, a/c, c.c. ok, close to metro but not sights

Pagration Hostel, 75 Damareos St, Athens; *athens-yhostel.com/*, T:2107519530, *y-hostels@otenet.gr*; $16bed, Kitchen:Y, B'fast:N, Pvt.room:Y, Locker:N, Recep:24/7; Note: laundry, non-tourist area, pay for shower

Athens Easy Access, Satovriandou 26, Athens; *athenseasyaccess.com/*, T:+30/2105243211; $22bed, Kitchen:N, B'fast:Y, Pvt.room:Y, Locker:N, Recep:24/7; Note: bar, laundry, lift, a/c, c.c. ok, free tour, interesting 'hood

3 Hostels) CORFU is one of Greece's best-known islands. Lying off the northwest coast, it is as close to Albania as it is to Greece, and centuries of domination by Italy and Britain make it culturally more European than most of Greece. Its location on the ferry run from Italy to Greece, back during Communism when that was the only international surface route, also has made it a staple on Western tourist circuits.

Many of the hostels are self-contained compounds, I suppose so that you can get shit-faced and not have to worry how to get home. Of course if you only do that, then you'll miss much of the rich history of Corfu, which was part of the Venetian republic for many years and still carries vestiges of that era. That makes it different from the rest of Greece and highly worth a look around. The Royal Palace, once the residence of British governors and now a museum, survived the destruction of WWII.

Pink Palace, Agios Gordios Beach, Sinarades, Corfu I; T:2661053025, *info@ thepinkpalace.com/*; $30bed, Kitchen:N, B'fast:Y, Pvt.room:Y, Locker:Y, Recep:24/7; Note: bar, club, a/c, c.c. ok, activities, parties, compound

Sunrock Backpackers', Sunrock (Vrachos), Pelekas Beach, Sinarades; *sunrockcorfu.com/*, T:2661094637, *sunrock77@gmail.com*; $24bed, Kitchen:N, B'fast:Y, Pvt. room:Y, Locker:N, Recep:24/7; Note: arpt. p-u, isolated, family-run, beach, WiFi $

Corfu Backpackers' Inn, Agios Gordios Beach, Corfu Island; T:6945230727, *info@ corfubackpackers.com/*; $22bed, Kitchen:N, B'fast:Y, Pvt.room:Y, Locker:N, Recep:24/7; Note: free dinner & arpt.pickup, resto-bar, club, pool, activities

2 Hostels) CRETE is the largest and most populous of the Greek Islands and is in fact a center of Greek culture more ancient than Athens itself. The Minoan culture here flourished at more or less the same time as that of ancient Egypt, and to this day Crete still has a culture distinctively its own. Minoan sites are found at Knossos, Phaestus, and elsewhere on the island. There is an Archeological Museum in Heraclion, the capital.

Rethymno Youth Hostel, 41 Tobazi St, Rethymno, Crete Island; T:2831022848, *info@ yhrethymno.com/*; $14bed, Kitchen:Y, B'fast:$, Pvt.room:N, Locker:N, Recep:8a>11p; Note: few sockets, close to everything, bar

Youth Hostel Plakias, Mirthios, Rethymno, Crete Island; *yhplakias.com/*, T:+30/2832032118; $13bed, Kitchen:N, B'fast:$, Pvt. room:N, Locker:N, Recep:ltd; Note: min. stay 2N Apr-Oct, bar, parking, bag hold, far from town/beach

3 Hostels) IOS ISLAND is part of the Cyclades Group in the Aegean. It has developed a bit since its hippie days of a few decades ago. Today Chora is a picturesque town of boutiques and bars, and the beaches are open for business. The archeological site of Skarkos dates back to the Cyclades culture which was the first high culture of Greece.

Far Out Beach Club, Mylopotas Beach, Ios Island; T:30/2286092305, *village@ faroutclub.com/*; $13bed, Kitchen:N, B'fast:$, Pvt.room:Y, Locker:N, Recep:24/7; Note: bar, restaurant, pool, laundry, forex, close to beach, bus to town

Markos Village, Chora, Ios Island; T:+30/2286091059, *george@ markosvillage.com/*; $14bed, Kitchen:N, B'fast:$, Pvt.room:Y, Locker:Y, Recep:24/7; Note: resto-bar, club, a/c, c.c. ok, parking, balconies, walk to town

Purple Pig Stars, Mylopotas Beach, Ios Island; T:2286091302, *info@ purplepigstars.com/*; $13bed, Kitchen:Y, B'fast:N, Pvt.room:Y, Locker:N, Recep:ltd; Note: resto-bar, laundry, pool, a/c, c.c. ok, parking, tours, on beach

MYKONOS ISLAND is a major tourist destination. Attractions include 16th C. windmills, the medieval Church of Paraportiani, the Square of Three Wells, and, of course, lots of water. It is the point of departure for the sacred island of Delos. There is air service to Athens and boat connections to elsewhere in the Cyclades Group of islands.

Paraga Beach Hostel, Mykonos Camping, Paraga Beach; *paragabeachhostel. com/*; $13bed, Kitchen:Y, B'fast:$, Pvt.room:Y, Locker:Y, Recep:24/7; Note: free arpt. p-u, bar, resto, pool, laundry, forex, c.c. ok, basic

PAROS ISLAND has abandoned marble quarries and mines and is well-connected to Piraeus with several ferries per day. There are many villages, but Parikia is the main town, with an archeological museum and an ancient Christian church. The Parian Chronicle, which recounts artistic milestones in ancient t Greece, was found here in 1627.

Ampeli Studios Apts, Parikia, Paros Is; *ampeli-studios-paros.a1hostels. com/*, T:6939089289, *info@ampelistudios.com*; $17bed, Kitchen:Y, B'fast:N, Pvt. room:Y, Locker:Y, Recep:ltd; Note: bag hold, laundry, central, a/c, on beach, port pick-up

2 Hostels) SANTORINI ISLAND is also in the Cyclades group, the remains of a huge volcano that erupted and whose caldera then sunk below the water, leaving an island ring around a large lagoon. The beaches have much black sand, the color dependent on the geologic layer exposed. Wear sandals. The climate is a desert one.

Anny Studios, Perissa Beach, Santorini Island; *annystudios.com/*, T:2286031626, *hotelanny@sanforthnet.gr*; $20bed, Kitchen:Y, B'fast:$, Pvt. room:Y, Locker:N, Recep:ltd; Note: bar, pool, forex, laundry, tours, a/c, beach near, town far

Katerina & John Hotel, Perissa, Santorini Island; *matrix-santorini.com/*, T:2286082833, *cheaphotelperissa@gmail.com*; $9bed, Kitchen:N, B'fast:N, Pvt. room:Y, Locker:N, Recep: 24/7; Note: ferry shuttle, parking, pool, a/c, bag hold, scooter rent

5 Hostels) THESSALONIKI is Greece's second city, as it was long ago in the Byzantine Era as "co-capital" with Constantinople. If Athens was the cultural capital of ancient Greece, then Thessaloniki is the cultural capital of the modern one. Equal parts Greek, Balkan, Anatolian and Mediterranean, it has always stood along the border of cultures mixing and mingling as circumstances demanded, be it ancient Macedonians, Illyrians, Thracians, and Slavs, or modern Turks, Jews, Muslims, Slavs, and...oh yeah, Greeks.

There are transport links in all directions. Thessaloniki was also an important early Christian center. Paul wrote First Thessalonians here. In the 9th century Greek missionaries Cyril and brother what's-his-name methodically standardized the Old Church Slavonic language, the first literary language for Slavs. There are many Byzantine churches still standing, including the Ayia Sofia, the church of Ayia Dimitrios, the Panaghia Chalkeon, and the church of Osios David. Today it's a party town.

RentRooms, Konstantinou Melenikou 9, Thessaloniki; T:2310204080, *info@ rentrooms-thessaloniki.com/*; $24bed, Kitchen:N, B'fast:Y, Pvt.room:Y, Locker:Y, Recep:ltd; Note: resto/bar, café, bike rent, a/c, luggage room

Little Big House, Andokidou 24, Thessaloniki; T:2313014323, *contact@ littlebighouse.gr/*; $22bed, Kitchen:Y, B'fast:$, Pvt.room:Y, Locker:Y, Recep:ltd; Note: free coffee/tea, bag hold, tours, c.c. ok, near old city

Studios Arabas, Sachtouri 28, Ano Poli, Thessaloniki; *hostelthessaloniki. com/*, T:30/6973817188, *pappas3kala@gmail.com*; $16bed, Kitchen:Y, B'fast:N, Pvt.room:Y, Locker:N, Recep:ltd; Note: a/c, laundry, tours, tea/coffee, hard to find, steep climb

Pension Tzitzifies, Agiou Dimitriou-Oikon-Agia Triada-Dimos Thermaikou; *pension-tzitzifies.gr/*, T:+30/6932336127, *linaras@otenet.gr*; $18bed, Kitchen:Y, B'fast:N, Pvt.room:Y, Locker:N, Recep:ltd; Note: min. 3N, advise ETA, parking, beach

Hotel Rex, 39 Monastiriou St., Thessaloniki; T:+30/2310517051, *info@ rexhotelthessaloniki.gr/*; $25bed, Kitchen:N, B'fast:Y, Pvt.room:Y, Locker:N, Recep:24/7; Note: gay friendly, bag hold, laundry, forex, tours, near train

14) Kosovo

Kosovo is a mess. Once the Roman province of Dardania, it became part of the medieval Serbian Empire, which withdrew after losing the Battle of Kosovo to the Ottoman Turks in 1389. Still they never forgot, and always claimed it as their cradle of the culture. Albanians claim their ancestors were here even before all that, and regardless, they greatly outnumbered the Serbs at the time of the fall of Ottoman Turkey, precise reconstructions of the past being tricky business, what with the fog of memory and all.

So when Slobodan Milosevic moved to limit Kosovo's autonomy, tempers flared. Following the Bosnian War in the 1990's, the Kosovo question was left unaddressed, so they duked it out. By this time, of course, NATO was in no mood for Serb atrocities, so they bombed Belgrade and proceeded to administer Kosovo. It declared independence in 2008. And that's the way it stands. Euro is the best currency to have. Serbo-Croatian and Albanian (and English) are the best languages to know. Calling code? Yeah, right…

PRISTINA is the capital and largest city of the mess called Kosovo. It is rapidly rebuilding after much destruction in the Kosovo war, mostly in the modern style. Fortunately not all of the old style was obliterated. These are the best English-speakers between the UK and the UAE (thank you, NATO), the food is good, and it's cheap. Serbs think it's still theirs. Say hey to the Professor for me. "Show me a former war zone and I'll show you a travel bargain." — H. Karges

Velania Guest House, Velania 4/34, Pristina; T:038531742, *info@ guesthouse-ks.net/*; $13bed, Kitchen:Y, B'fast:N, Pvt.room:Y, Locker:N, Recep:24/7; Note: laundry, bag hold, parking, coffee/tea, in the 'burbs, hard to find

15) Macedonia

Better known as the ancient kingdom of Phillip II and Alexander the Great, the modern independent republic of Macedonia is the "other" component of the ex-Yugoslavia, the one that is landlocked, besides Kosovo, and somewhat different from all the rest. For one thing, it has historic connections with Greece, resulting in a naming problem for the modern country, FYROM the country like the artist formerly known as TAFKAP.

For another thing, its language is more closely related to Bulgaria, with which it is mutually intelligible. Add to that a large Albanian Muslim minority, and there is potential for problems. After many years of being known as "southern Serbs," Macedonia is only now coming to grips with its own identity, which is a work in progress. It has never been independent before, and is by definition multi-ethnic, generally Slavic, mostly ethnically Bulgarian. This is the backwash of the former Yugoslavia, but that's not bad.

What with disruptions in trade in the first decade of its existence, independence has not been easy, but political resolutions have made life better the last decade and Macedonia is rapidly incorporating into Europe. Its natural beauty, cultural offerings and warm climate also make it a popular tourist destination, almost one million per year at last count. There are art, poetry and music festivals, especially in summer. It is connected by road to all its neighbors. Macedonian is the language, *denar* (MKD) is dinero, and +389 is the phone code.

4 Hostels) SKOPJE is home to about a third of Macedonia's two million people. Following on the efforts of Neolithic tribes (mostly Illyrian), Romans, Byzantines, Bulgarians, and Serbs, the Ottoman Turks ruled here for over five hundred years, giving Skopje a distinct appearance for which it was famous. Since then it has industrialized and been hit with an earthquake, which left some 1,070 persons dead and more than 120,000 homeless. It also altered the city's appearance drastically and introduced modern architecture.

Landmarks include a Byzantine fortress, an Oriental bazaar, a stone bridge and the Millennium Cross on Mt. Vodno. Then there are the Medieval monastery of Nerezi, a medieval Turkish inn, the Kuršumli Han, and several mosques. There is a healthy nightlife and festivals in the summer. Mother Teresa is the favorite daughter.

Urban Hostel, Mother Teresa 22, Skopje; T:+389/26142785, *contact@ urbanhostel.com.mk/*; $18bed, Kitchen:Y, B'fast:Y, Pvt.room:Y, Locker:Y, Recep:24/7; Note: hot tub, bar, café, laundry, bag hold, arpt trans, parking, central, coffee/tea

Shanti Hostel 2, St. Prespanska 18, Madjir Maalo, Skopje

Shanti Hostel, Rade Jovcevski Korcagin 11, Madjir Maalo, Skopje; *shantihostel.com/,* T:+389/26090807, *hostelshanti@gmail.com;* $14bed, Kitchen:Y, B'fast:Y, Pvt.room:Y, Locker:Y, Recep:24/7; Note: bag hold, laundry, prkng, @ bus, cntr

City Hostel, Str. Tome Arsovski nu.6, Skopje; *info@ hostel-skopje. com/* ; T:+38/971447369; $10bed, Kitchen:Y, B'fast:Y, Pvt.room:Y, Locker:Y, Recep:ltd; Note: arpt trans, cafe, parking, bag hold, tours, parking, bikes, laundry, tea/cof

16) Montenegro (Crna Gora)

Though it sounds more like a casino than a country, Montenegro ("Black Mountain" in any language) is in fact that small country that lies north of Albania, south of Bosnia, and west of Serbia, the last two to which it was long attached as part of Yugoslavia. Variously ruled by Romans, Byzantines, Serbs, Bulgarians, and Ottomans, before finally establishing a Montenegrin identity and polity, in the past century Montenegro was first a Kingdom, before becoming a constituent state in Yugoslavia.

In fact it has an even longer history with Serbia, only having separated culturally after the fall of the Serbian Empire in the wars of the Kosovo region in the 14th century, and the changes that then there occurred under Ottoman rule. Montenegro was also the last to leave Yugoslavia, some fifteen years after most of the rest (so don't be surprised if you can't find it on older maps; it's that part of Serbia that bordered the sea).

After participating in the Croatian War of the early 1990's with Serbia, to gain Dubrovnik and the land around it, while handing Bosnian refugees over to the Serbs, Montenegro finally voted for independence in 2006. The economy has shown steady growth since then, and the coast is rapidly developing for tourism. Development so far seems to have a distinct Russian flavor to it, though, so it may be too late for the kind of Italian-flavored coast of Croatia. Selling passports to fugitive tycoons is a dubious career move, also. Montenegrin (Serbo-Croat) is speech; Euro is currency; phone code is +382.

3 Hostels) BUDVA is one of the oldest settlements on the Adriatic coast, with roots going back past the Roman to the Greek era. It was ruled by the Venetians during the years of the Renaissance. That is the era of the original architecture in Old Town, Budva's main tourist attraction. Unfortunately it was destroyed in the 1979 earthquake, but has since been rebuilt. The infrastructure has yet to keep up with the tourist boom, though, and millionaires are snapping up real estate and squeezing the locals out, or at least out of their fishing jobs and into jobs servicing the rich. On the other hand, there was only one hostel when I visited only three years ago, so things are progressing.

MOJO Budva, 3 Vojvodanska, Budva; *MOJOBudva@gmail.com*, T:+382(0)69711986, *facebook.com/MOJO.Budva/*; $11bed, Kitchen:Y, B'fast:Y, Pvt. room:Y, Locker:N, Recep:ltd; Note: arpt trans, bikes, laundry, bag hold, hard find

Montenegro Hostel Budva, Vuka Karadzica12, Budva; *montenegrohostel. com/*, T:069039751, *montenegrohostel@gmail.com*; $14bed, Kitchen:Y, B'fast:N, Pvt.room:Y, Locker:Y, Recep:>12m; Note: pool, resto, tours, laundry, old town, nr beach

Saki-Hostel, IV proleterska BB, Budva; *saki-apartmani.com,* T:067368065, *sakiadrovic@yahoo.com;* $13bed, Kitchen:N, B'fast:$, Pvt.room:Y, Locker:N, Recep:24/7; Note: arpt trans, hot tub, resto/bar, billiards, cash only, laundry

KOTOR is a world heritage site for its old town architecture, and the dramatic landscape only enhances its tourist appeal. There are the Romanesque cathedral of St. Tryphon and the Baroque church of Our Lady of the Rocks on an islet in the Bay of Kotor. Situated on the coast to the north of Budva, this is a nice alternative to the more established tourist towns, both in Montenegro and Croatia.

Montenegro Hostel Kotor, Pjaca od Mlijeka b.b., Kotor; *montenegrohostel. com,* T:069039751, *montenegrohostel@gmail.com;* $17bed, Kitchen:Y, B'fast:$, Pvt. room:Y, Locker:Y, Recep:>12m; Note: resto, tours, a/c, old town, laundry, views

PODGORICA is Montenegro's capital and largest city, though at only 150,000 people it's not overwhelming. Centrally located, it is on a historic trade route through the region. If you have any official business — onward visas, etc. — this is where you come.

Montenegro Hostel Podgorica, Djecevica 25, Podgorica; T:069039751, *montenegrohostel.com/,* $20bed, *montenegrohostel@gmail.com;* Kitchen:Y, B'fast:N, Pvt.room:Y, Locker:Y, Recep:>12m; Note: parking, central, smoking inside

TIVAT is yet another coastal option, lying halfway between Budva and Kotor. The big attraction here is nautical tourism — marinas and yachting clubs. There are good beaches and an ex-Club Med.

Hostel Anton, Mazina bb, Tivat; *hostelanton.com/,* T:+382/69261182, *hostel.anton09@gmail.com;* $14bed, Kitchen:N, B'fast:Y, Pvt.room:Y, Locker:N, Recep:24/7; Note: bar, laundry, parking, a/c, sea views

17) Serbia

Of the three Serbo-Croatian-Bosnian-speaking countries, Serbia is the most Eastern of the group, with Cyrillic alphabet and Orthodox religion and a close political ally in Russia. It used to be a Roman colony (Emperor Constantine was born here) and then was ruled by the Byzantine Empire, its own empire, then the Ottoman, before asserting its independence again in the late 1800's. It scored major territorial gains against Bulgaria. It even started WWI, and won.

Thus emboldened Serbia continued its rise by forming the Kingdom of Serbs, Croats, and Slovenes (later to become Yugoslavia) with the other Balkan states, of which it was the most prominent and longest-lasting member. After decimation in WWII, communist "partisans" rose to power in the aftermath and ruled without opposition until 1989 when Slobodan Milosevic's rise to power and attempts to limit regional autonomy induced the breakup of the federation and the start of war. Crimes against humanity ensued, and Serbia has been an international pariah until recently. *Dinar* (RSD) is the currency; Serbian (Coatian, Bosnian) is the language; the calling code is +381.

17 Hostels) BELGRADE is the capital and largest city of Serbia, located at the confluence of the Danube and Sava rivers. This is a good example of a city belonging to a place, not a people. It was successively Thraco-Dacian, Celt, Roman, Slav, Bulgarian, Ottoman, and Habsburg, before becoming the capital of Serbia again in 1841. It was the capital of Yugoslavia from inception to dissolution 1918-2006. All of which says nothing about Constantine the Great or Attila the Hun or Frederick Barbarossa or Suleyman the Magnificent or Prince Maximilian, but they were all here.

Belgrade was at the heart of WWI, and emerged stronger in the aftermath. It tried to remain neutral in WWII, but didn't succeed. The Axis Powers invaded and occupied, until liberated by Tito's partisans. Though communist, Belgrade was prominent in the nonaligned movement. Yugoslavia's breakup and Serbia's unwillingness to accept it finally hit home when NATO bombed Belgrade in the Kosovo War in 1999. Mass demonstrations removed Slobodan Milosevic from office the next year.

By virtue of its size, Belgrade is the center of almost everything in Serbia: industry, fashion, media, etc. It took some hits from NATO bombing in the Kosovo war, but it wasn't really known for its architecture anyway. What it IS known for is nightlife. Hostel quality is generally good and there is some diversity and creativity, too, like free beer. Unfortunately there is also a lot of smoking inside, and kitchens are not a given. There are a LOT of them, too, maybe the most in the world, which seems a bit disproportionate, so percentage-wise, they're very under-represented here, just a sampling. Have fun. Despite all the wars, Serbians really can be very nice people.

Sun Hostel, Novopazarska 25, Belgrade; *sun.hostel.com/*, T:(0)641121040, *hostel.sun@gmail.com*; $10bed, Kitchen:Y, B'fast:N, Pvt.room:Y, Locker:Y, Recep:24/7; Note: pool, bikes, party, tea/coffee, not central, laundry, tours, bag hold

Star Hostel, Cara Urosa 37, Belgrade, *starhostelbelgrade.com/*, T:0112184104, *hostel_star@yahoo.com*; $13bed, Kitchen:Y, B'fast:Y, Pvt.room:Y, Locker:Y, Recep:24/7; Note: arpt trans, bikes, laundry, tea/coffee, bar, tours, bag hold

Montmartre Hostel Belgrade, Nušićeva 17/5, Belgrade; *montmartre-hostel. com/*, T:0113224157, *montmartrehostel@gmail.com*; $18bed, Kitchen:Y, B'fast:Y, Pvt.room:Y, Locker:Y, Recep:24/7; Note:arpt trans, bag hold, laundry, cash

Hedonist Hostel, Simina 7, Belgrade; *office@ hedonisthostelbelgrade. com/*, T:0113284798; $14bed, Kitchen:Y, B'fast:N, Pvt.room:N, Locker:Y, Recep:8a>11p; Note: bag hold, laundry, tours, a/c, bikes, tea/coffee

Time Hostel, Cara Lazara St #9, Apt #3, Belgrade; *time-hostels.com/*, T:+381(0)113285160; $20bed, Kitchen:Y, B'fast:N, Pvt.room:Y, Locker:Y, Recep:24/7; Note: laundry, bag hold, parking, tours, central, supermkt

Chillton Hostel, Kataniceva 7; T:0113441826, *chilltonhostel@gmail.com*

Chillton 2, Vase Carapica (Vasina) 15, Belgrade; *chilltonhostel.com/*, T:0113283333, *chillton2@gmail.com*; $17bed, Kitchen:N, B'fast:Y, Pvt.room:Y, Locker:Y, Recep:24/7; Note: arpt trans, bar, lift, 2N min, bag hold, laundry, tours

Manga Hostel, Resavska 7, Belgrade; T:+381/113243877, *fun@ mangahostel. com/*; $17bed, Kitchen:Y, B'fast:N, Pvt.room:Y, Locker:Y, Recep:24/7; Note: bag hold, laundry, a/c, tricky to find, coffee & tea

Spirit Hostel, Brace Baruh 20b, Belgrade; T:+381/112920055, *office@ spirithostel.com/*; $17bed, Kitchen:Y, B'fast:Y, Pvt.room:Y, Locker:Y, Recep:>12m; Note: arpt trans, lift, bag hold, laundry, coffee/tea, welcome drink, parking

Green Studio Hostel & Lounge, Karadordeva 61, Belgrade

Green Studio Hostel, Karadordeva 69, Apt 42, Belgrade, T:0637562357, *greenstudiohostel.com/*, $10bed, *greenstudiohostel@gmail.com*; Kitchen:Y, B'fast:N, Pvt.room:Y, Locker:Y, Recep: 24/7; Note: bar, café, bikes, bag hold, laundry, @ train

1001 Nights Hostel, Bulevar Kralja Aleksandra 40, Belgrade; T:0113247658, *1001nightshostel.com/*, $12bed, *1001nightshostel@gmail.com*; Kitchen:N, B'fast:N, Pvt. room:Y, Locker:Y, Recep:24/7; Note: tea/cof, bag hold, prkng, free tour, central

Hostel 360, 21 Knez Mihailova St, Belgrade; *hostel360.com/*, T:+38/1112634957, *skile@sbb.rs*; $18bed, Kitchen:Y, B'fast:N, Pvt.room:Y, Locker:Y, Recep:24/7; Note: luggage room, laundry, lift, a/c, c.c. ok, 5th Fl, center

Hostel Zetska, Zetska 5, Belgrade; T:+38/1621648892, *info@ hostelzetska5. rs/*; $17bed, Kitchen:N, B'fast:N, Pvt.room:Y, Locker:Y, Recep:24/7; Note: luggage room, tour desk, laundry, a/c, central

Hostel Kris, Kneza Milosa 54, Belgrade; *hostelkris.weebly.com/*, T:+38/1665010206, *hostelkris@yahoo.com*; $13bed, Kitchen:Y, B'fast:N, Pvt. room:N, Locker:N, Recep:ltd; Note: cozy, laundry, luggage room, parking, a/c

Arka Barka Floating Hostel, Bulevar Nikole Tesle bb, Park Usce; *arkabarka. net/*, T:0649253507, *arkabarkahostel@gmail.com*; $20bed, Kitchen:N, B'fast:Y, Pvt. room:Y, Locker:Y, Recep:24/7; Note: bar, bag hold, prkng, on river not ctr

Good Morning Hostel, Takovska 36-38, Belgrade; T:0113295031, *info@ goodmorninghostels.com/*; $8bed, Kitchen:N, B'fast:N, Pvt.room:Y, Locker:Y, Recep:ltd; Note: luggage rm $, laundry, tours, parking, a/c

3 Hostels) NIS is Serbia's number three city and the largest in southern Serbia. While that may seem rather mundane, Constantine the Great was also born here, as was Justin I who founded the Byzantine Justinian Dynasty, and Attila the Hun once destroyed the town. When the Serbs in Nis attempted to achieve

their freedom from the Ottoman Turks in 1809, the local commander ordered an array of skulls to be displayed as a deterrent. That today is one of the tourist attractions. There is also an Ottoman fortress, a 5th C. Byzantine crypt and a Nazi concentration camp.

The Garden Hostel, Vojislava Ilica 12, Nis; *thegarden.rs/,* T:+381/18236165, *thegarden@live.com*; $14bed, Kitchen:N, B'fast:N, Pvt. room:Y, Locker:N, Recep:24/7; Note: bag hold, laundry, prkng, wh/chair ok, walk>cntr, family-run

Hostel Kosmopolit, Anastasa Jovanovica 15, Nis; *hostelkosmopolit.com/,* T:063472705, *hostelkosmopolit@hotmail.com*; $14bed, Kitchen:Y, B'fast:$, Pvt. room:Y, Locker:Y, Recep:24/7; Note: bar, café, pool, bikes, tours, bag hold, laundry

Hostel Nis, Dobricka 3A, Nis; *hostelnis.rs/,* T:+381/18513703, *hostelnis@ sezampro.rs*; $16bed, Kitchen:Y, B'fast:$, Pvt.room:Y, Locker:Y, Recep:24/7; Note: bar, tours, bag hold, c.c. ok, parking, central, @Univ

2 Hostels) NOVI SAD is the "Athens of Serbia," or so it has the reputation. It is also Serbia's second city, and capital of the province of Vojvodina. Located in the northernmost corner of the country the province and city have always been culturally mixed between Germans, Hungarians, and Serbs. Petrovaradin Fortress reflects Novi Sad's status as a military frontier against the Ottomans. Tourism is on the rise, and the July EXIT festival is a big deal, now one of Europe's major summer events.

Hostel Sova, Ilije Ognjanovica 26, Novi Sad, T:+381/216615230, *kontakt@ hostelsova.com/;* $13bed, Kitchen:Y, B'fast:N, Pvt.room:Y, Locker:Y, Recep:24/7; Note: arpt trans, laundry, luggage room, parking, smoking

Downtown NoviSad Hostel, Njegoseva 2, 2nd Fl, Novi Sad; *hostelnovisad. com/,* T:0641920342, *downtownnovisad@yahoo.com*; $18bed, Kitchen:Y, B'fast:N, Pvt. room:Y, Locker:N, Recep:ltd; Note: arpt trans, laundry, bag hold, tours

SUBOTICA is the other city, besides Novi Sad, of the Vojvodina region of Serbia, far up in the northern corner of the country. And like Novi Sad, it is multi-ethnic, Hungarians forming the majority. Unlike much of Serbia, there is some interesting architecture, including Art Nouveau style. This wouldn't be a bad place to cross a border.

Incognito Hostel, Huga Badaliceva 3ʳᵈ St, Subotica; *info@ hostel-subotica. com/*, T:062666674; $13bed, Kitchen:Y, B'fast:$, Pvt.room:Y, Locker:Y, Recep:>6p; Note: cash only, resto/bar, parking, luggage room, a/c, central

18) Slovenia

Bounded by Italy and Austria to the west and north, with Hungary and Croatia to the east and south, Slovenia has always been the most western of the Slavic Balkan countries. It is also one of the most diverse, with a Slavic language mutually unintelligible to its neighboring South Slavs, and significant dialectical differences within the country. That's because it was one of the first on the scene, and so was oriented toward Catholicism and the Western Slavs, before the Magyars separated them.

Slovenes were conquered by Rome, Huns, Lombards, Charlemagne, and Magyars, before finally establishing their own Slovene identity. The Habsburgs and Austria-Hungary still dominated, though, until Slovenia's joining with South Slav states to form Yugoslavia after WWI. There they were first out the door, too, drawing up plans for independence in 1987, long before the Berlin Wall fell. They were fully independent by 1991. The country has coast, mountains, forests and plains, with weather to match. Nature figures prominently in tourist activities, and casinos, too. Euro is currency, Slovene is the language; the calling code is +386.

2) BLED is best known for the glacial lake of the same name, summer home to princes, kings, and dictators. There is a castle and and an island in the middle of the lake which contains a church. Before that there was a shrine

to the Slavic goddess of love and fertility. Hmmm… Try the *kremma rezina*, a local pastry.

Bled Backpackers Hostel, Grajska cesta 21, Bled; *bled-hostel.com/*, T:(0)40332706, $21bed, Kitchen:N, B'fast:$, Pvt.room:N, Locker:Y, Recep:ltd; Note: arpt trans, resto/bar, bikes, wh/chair ok, bag hold, tours, parking, castle & lake

Castle Hostel 1004, Grajska cesta 22, Bled; *hostel1004.com/*, T:(0)31523056, *castle.1004@gmail.com*; $14bed, Kitchen:N, B'fast:$, Pvt.room:N, Locker:Y, Recep:24/7; Note: arpt trans, café, bar, tours, bag hold, laundry, central

BOVEC is a town up in the Julian Alps on the northwest border with Italy, though historically it was most influenced by Germans. There is a national park nearby.

Adrenaline-Check Open Air Hostel, Soca 38, Bovec; T:+386/41383662, *info@ adrenaline-check.com/*, $12bed, Kitchen:Y, B'fast:$, Pvt.room:N, Locker:N, Recep:ltd; Note: bar, parking, tours, nature, pitch tent ok

CELJE is the third-largest town in Slovenia. With distant roots in the proto-European Halstatt culture, Celje has been ruled by Celts, Greeks, and especially Romans (it was founded by Emperor Claudius as Claudia Celeia) before becoming the small Slavic city that it is today. More recently it has been a bone of contention between Germans and Slavs, with extreme atrocities in WWII. Things are calmer now, and sights include a 13th century monastery and 16th century palace.

MCC Hostel, Mariborska Cesta 2, Celje, Slovenia; T:+386(0)34908742, *mcc.hostel@ mc-celje.si/*; $24bed, Kitchen:N, B'fast:N, Pvt. room:Y, Locker:Y, Recep:ltd; Note: bar, bag hold, laundry, central, free bike

IZOLA ("island") is on the small bit of coast that Slovenia can call its own (since Italy apparently hogged most of it in the area). It's no longer an island, but it's a tourist destination because of its hot springs. Summers are lively, with concerts and festivals.

Hostel Stara Sola, Korte 74, Izola; *info@ hostel-starasola.si,* T:(0)56421114; $22bed, Kitchen:Y, B'fast:$, Pvt.room:Y, Locker:Y, Recep:>8p; Note: parking, a/c, c.c. ok, remote location 5mi/8km to town

5 Hostels) LJUBLJANA is the capital and largest city of Slovenia. This is where Eastern Europe meets Western, and Northern Europe meets Southern. It is documented from the 12th century and was part of the Habsburg Empire by 1335, where it would remain until 1797. It was briefly a Napoleonic city before returning to Austria, all of which crumbled down in WWI. After that it joined the Yugoslavian confederation until independence in 1991. But that's politics, not culture(s). Located at the transit point between Romance, Germanic and Slavic cultures, it has always been something of a crossroads. There have always been multiple languages, German and Italian in addition to the Slavic.

There is a castle in both Germanic and Roman styles, from both classic and Renaissance periods. The Town Hall, Cathedral, and others are also noted for their architecture, though after an earthquake in 1895 much of Ljubljana has a modern, yet tasteful, appearance. Museums include the National Museum of Slovenia, the Slovenian Museum of Natural History, the National Gallery, and the Gallery of Modern Art. The city has a thriving scene for arts and culture, including a subculture. Sidewalk cafes line the river. It's a little peach of a city, almost reminds me of Tallinn.

Zeppelin Hostel, Slovenska cesta 47, Ljubljana; T:059191427, *info@ zeppelinhostel.com/;* $27bed, Kitchen:Y, B'fast:Y, Pvt.room:N, Locker:Y, Recep:>10p; Note: laundry, bag hold, tea/coffee, tours, TV, push-button showers, central

Fluxux Hostel, Tomšičeva 4, Ljubljana; T:+386/12515760, *info@ fluxus-hostel.com/;* $25bed, Kitchen:Y, B'fast:N, Pvt.room:Y, Locker:N, Recep: advise ETA; Note: bag hold, laundry, parking, tea/coffee, tours, c.c. ok, central

H2OSTEL, Petkovškovo nabrežje 47, Ljubljana; T:+386/41662266, *info@ h2ohostel.com/;* $21bed, Kitchen:Y, B'fast:N, Pvt.room:Y, Locker:Y, Recep:>11p; Note: advise ETA, laundry, bikes, tours, luggage room, on river

Alibi M14 Hostel, Miklošičeva cesta 14, Ljubljana; T:+386/12511244, *info@ alibi.si/;* $16bed, Kitchen:Y, B'fast:N, Pvt.room:Y, Locker:Y, Recep:9a>10p; Note: laundry, luggage room, TV, city tour, c.c. ok, central, no lift

Aladin Hostel, Tugomerjeva 56, Ljubljana; *bookings@aladin-hostel.com*, T:(0)41666477; $14bed, Kitchen:Y, B'fast:N, Pvt.room:Y, Locker:N, Recep:ltd; Note: arpt trans, bikes, bar, café, billiards, market, bag hold, laundry, tours, tea/cof, far

2 Hostels) MARIBOR is Slovenia's second-largest city with almost 100,000 inhaitants. Historically Austrian German, and with a famous Jewish quarter, the last century saw major disputes over ownership of the territory between Germans and Slavs. After Slovene independence in 1991 and incorporation into the EU, Maribor concentrated on small businesses and tourism. There is a castle, winter sports, and medieval architecture. The scenic Old Town lines the Drava River. RUSE is a small town nearby. There is a historical church, once destroyed by Ottomans, and then rebuilt. This is rural Slovenia.

Hostel Vetrnica/Pinwheel, Mariborska cesta 31, Ruse; *info@ hotel-veter.si*, T:+386(0)266900; $26bed, Kitchen:N, B'fast:$, Pvt.room:Y, Locker:N, Recep:24/7; Note: hotel w/dorms, resto/bar, prkng, wh/chair ok, forex, a/c, c.c. ok

Hostel Pekarna, Ob železnici 16, Maribor; *mkc-hostelpekarna.si*, T:059180880, *hostelpekarna@mkc.si*; $22bed, Kitchen:N, B'fast:$, Pvt.room:N, Locker:Y, Recep:ltd; Note: bar, parking, laundry, a/c, c.c. ok, bikes, central

Part IV: Southeast Europe

19) Bulgaria

The Thracians, Greeks and Romans each once colonized the area now known as Bulgaria, before Slavs swarmed in to populate it in the 6th century. But the Bulgars ruled, they an eastern steppes tribe who adopted the Slavic language, the Bulgarian form of which is now considered one of the most "original." Such are the zigzags of history. The First Bulgarian Empire lasted for several centuries before being defeated by the Byzantines in 1018. After re-establishing their empire, five centuries of Ottoman rule came in 1393. It was not pretty, and with the help of Russia, independence finally came in 1878. A period of militarism followed, including losses in WWI & II, before the period of one-party Communist rule and rapid industrialization.

Free elections in 1990 brought a ten-year rough patch, but things are better now and Bulgaria is now a member of NATO and the EU. Tourist attractions include the ancient cities of Plovdiv and Nesebar, national parks, and the rock-hewn churches of Ivanovo. Nestinarstvo is a ritual fire dance. Bulgarian folk music is renowned. They dance; they sing; they rock; sounds good to me. The food is good, too. Bulgarian is the language; the currency is *lev* (BGN); the calling code is +359.

NESSEBAR is a culture-rich city on the Black Sea coast, beginning with the Greek colony of Mesembria in the 6th century BC. Much of the world's ancient history left its mark here at one time or other. The entire town is a world heritage site. Remains include the 6th C. Old Metropolitan Church and the 12th C. New Metropolitan Church.

Guest House Edelweiss, ul.Edelweiss 5, Nessebar; *hostelnesebar.com/*; $12bed, Kitchen:Y, B'fast:N, Pvt.room:Y, Locker:N, Recep:ltd; Note: laundry, forex, a/c, TV, in apt. block

2 Hostels) PLOVDIV is Bulgaria's second city and is centrally located within the country. It is historically a rich agricultural region, only to become industrialized in the Communist era. In the old Trimontium quarter of the city, parts of the Roman walls remain. The medieval ruins of Tsar Ivan Asen II's fortress and Bachkovo monastery are nearby. Cultural institutions include a museum.

Plovdiv Guesthouse, 20 Saborna St., Plovdiv; *info@ plovdivguest.com*, T:032622432; $12bed, Kitchen:Y, B'fast:Y, Pvt.room:Y, Locker:N, Recep:24/7; Note: laundry, a/c, c.c. ok, central, WiFi $, parking

Hikers' Hostel, 53 Saborna St, Plovdiv; *plovdiv@ hikers-hostel.org/*; T:+359/885194553; $13bed, Kitchen:N, B'fast:$, Pvt.room:Y, Locker:N, Recep:24/7; Note: free airport pick-up, a/c, bar, laundry, multiple locations

RUSE began its history as a Roman fortified harbor and reached the peak of its importance as a base for the Ottoman Turks. Located on the far northern border of the country, on the right bank of the Danube, it is known for its Neo-Baroque-Rococo architecture. There are also festivals, museums, and other places of cultural interest.

Villa Slanchevo, 14 Stara Planina St, Pisanets, Ruse; *villaslanchevo.hostel. com/*, T:+359/885447452; $13bed, Kitchen:Y, B'fast:Y, Pvt.room:N, Locker:Y, Recep:24/7; Note: 25 kms>Ruse, wh/chair ok, parking, laundry

8 Hostels) SOFIA is the capital and largest city of Bulgaria, and is located in the western part of the country. Its role as Bulgaria's main city only arose after liberation from the Ottoman Empire not even a hundred-and-fifty years ago, when the population was little over 10,000 people. After suffering huge losses

during the era of the WW's, Sofia is doing better in the era of the www's. Travelers have flocked to Sofia *en masse,* it being something of a convenient crossroads between Athens, Istanbul, and Belgrade.

This is the main overland backpacker route east from Budapest. Prices are good, the food is good, and the beer is cold. There are world heritage sites, green areas, and museums. Besides the restored St. George, Boyana, and St. Sofia churches, historical monuments include two mosques and the Alexander Nevsky Cathedral. There are many museums, and the city is attractive and well-proportioned. The entertainment is lively.

Canape Connection, 12A William Gladstone St, Sofia; T:24416373, *hostel@ canapeconnection.net/*; $14bed, Kitchen:Y, B'fast:Y, Pvt.room:Y, Locker:N, Recep:24/7; Note: bag hold, tours, nr cafes/bars

Hostel Mostel, Makedonia Blvd 2, Sofia; *info@ hostelmostel.com/*, T:0889223296; $13bed, Kitchen:Y, B'fast:Y, Pvt.room:Y, Locker:Y, Recep:24/7; Note: bag hold, parking, travel info, central, free dinner, coffee/tea

Internet Hostel Sofia, 50A Alabin St, 2nd Fl, 6 Apt, Sofia; T:0889138298, *interhostel@yahoo.co.uk*, $13bed, *internethostelsofia.hostel.com/*; Kitchen:Y, B'fast:N, Pvt. room:Y, Locker:Y, Recep:24/7; Note: resto/bar, bag hold, laundry, central

Hostel Lavele, 14 Lavele St, Sofia; *lavelehostel.com/*, T:0884080283, *lavelehostel@gmail.com*; $12bed, Kitchen:N, B'fast:Y, Pvt.room:Y, Locker:Y, Recep:ltd; Note: bag hold, laundry, tour info, c.c. ok, central, no bunks

Hostel Gulliver, Dondukov Blvd. 48, 2nd Fl, Sofia; *hostelgulliver.com/*, T:029875210, *info@gulliver1947-bg.com*; $12bed, Kitchen:N, B'fast:Y, Pvt.room:Y, Locker:N, Recep:24/7; Note: laundry, travel info, central, coffee/tea

Elysia Hostel, Pop Bogomil St. 8, Sofia; *elysiahotel.com/*, T:0897085791, *elysiahotel@gmail.com*; $15bed, Kitchen:Y, B'fast:Y, Pvt.room:Y, Locker:N, Recep:24/7; Note: parking, bag hold, wh/chair ok, central

Art Hostel, 21/A, Angel Kanchev St, Sofia; *art-hostel@ art-hostel. com/*, T:+359/29870545; $16bed, Kitchen:Y, B'fast:Y, Pvt.room:Y, Locker:N, Recep:24/7; Note: bar, laundry, luggage room, c.c. ok, garden

Orient Express Hostel, 8A Christo Belchev St, 3rd Fl, Sofia; T:0888384828, *orientexpresshostel.com/*; $12bed, *orientexpresshostel@yahoo.com*; Kitchen:Y,

B'fast:Y, Pvt.room:Y, Locker:Y, Recep:24/7; Note: bar/club, laundry, bag hold, cntr

VARNA is Bulgaria's third city and its seaside resort. The area it occupies has been occupied since pre-history: Varna culture, then Thracians, Greeks, Romans, and Ottomans that read like a TOC to Western civilization in addition to the Slavs who live here now. These ruins are now tourist sites, too, especially ancient Roman Odessus, and the beach. The Crusades ended here, also, contemporaneous with the Ottoman Conquest. There are the 4th C. Aladzha Monastery, overlooking the city from the north and a 5th/6th C. basilica remaining from an ancient Genoese colony. Varna was once named Stalin.

Yo-Ho-Hostel, bul Russestr 23, Varna; *hostel@   yohohostel.com/*, T:(+359)886382905; $9bed, Kitchen:Y, B'fast:Y, Pvt.room:Y, Locker:N, Recep:24/7; Note: bar, forex, parking, travel info, Ziggy the dog, central

3 Hostels) VELIKO TARNOVO means "old" Tarnovo, and that defines the place, medieval and walled and the most important city in the Second Bulgarian Empire of the 12th-14th centuries. It even called itself the "Third Rome" at the time. The Ottomans crushed all that. Tarnovo gets the last laugh, though, with today almost as many tourist sites as Istanbul itself, if not Rome. Did I mention that the houses, built in terraces, appear to be stacked one atop the other? There are also the Church of the Forty Martyrs and the 14th C. Church of St. Peter and St. Paul. There are eleven monasteries, including Sveta Troitsa ("Holy Trinity"), and the town has an archaeological museum.

Hostel Mostel, 10 Yordan Indjeto St, Veliko Tarnovo; T:0897859359, *getinfo@   hostelmostel.com;* $13bed, Kitchen:Y, B'fast:Y, Pvt.room:Y, Locker:Y, Recep:24/7; Note: bar, parking. laundry, luggage room, dinner

Nomads Hostel, 27 Gurko St, Veliko Tarnovo; T:+359/62603092, *info@   nomadshostel.com/*; $12bed, Kitchen:Y, B'fast:Y, Pvt.room:N, Locker:Y, Recep:24/7; Note: bar/club, laundry, luggage, a/c, c.c. ok, central, views

Guest House Stambolov, Ulitsa Stefan Stambolov 27, V. Tarnovo; *hotelstambolov.com/*, T:0888835048, *stambolov27@abv.bg;* $13bed, Kitchen:N, B'fast:$, Pvt.room:Y, Locker:Y, Recep:24/7; Note: resto/bar, laundry, bag hold

20) Hungary

The area that is now Hungary was up for grabs for years after the Huns destroyed the Pax Romana that had prevailed there for the first several hundred years of the Common Era. The Goths, Lombards, Avars, and others all made a play for the territory that the Huns left behind. The Magyars until then were a tribe from the remote northern woods who then built an empire that effectively lasted from 895AD until 1526, enduring a Mongol assault once, and repelling it definitively the second time. They weren't so lucky against the Ottoman Turks, who held sway from 1525 until 1699. That's when the Austrian Habsburgs took over, then the dual monarchy, then the Communists, and now, a free democratic Hungary? We all hope so.

But are the people still ethnically Hungarian? Good question. Sometimes a language that once was synonymous with a race of people becomes attached to a place regardless of the ultimate disposition of the original people. It's no stranger than a Latin language next door in Romania in a sea of Slavs where Rome once ruled only a couple hundred years. Hungary has long been in the European mainstream, contributing Bartok and Liszt, tokay and goulash, and much more to the general culture. Oh yeah, and there are also some 1500 thermal springs and 450 public baths in Hungary. Now we know why the northerners settled here. The language is Hungarian (Magyar), the currency is Forint (HUF) and the calling code is +36.

18 Hostels) BUDAPEST is the capital and largest city of Hungary and is the union of Buda and Pest on opposite sides of the Danube. Always something of an ethnic, uh... goulash, Hungary suffered heavily during WWII with its large Jewish population. Communism wasn't much better, but at least Budapest was on the front lines of resistance. The Hungarian Revolution of 1956 even brought the big bear in growling.

And when the writing was on the wall, even before the Berlin Wall came down, Hungary was right there, opening the border to Austria to let East Germans push their Ladas toward West Germany. These are happier days and

Budapest just may have the most hostels of any city in the world. That's good for you, of course, since quantity usually implies quality in a free market. This is just a sampling.

Tourist destinations include the Chain Bridge that connects Buda with Pest across the Danube River; Buda Castle that overlooks the city from atop Buda Hill; the Parliament Building; St. Stephen's Basilica; Heroes' Square; and Central Market Hall. Then there's Pest, with its Belváros (Inner Town), containing the Town Hall (Fővárosi Tanács), the Inner Town Parish Church (Belvárosi plébániatemplom) and the Hungarian National Museum, located just outside the Belváros, the Neo-Renaissance State Opera House, the National Theatre, and the Museum of fine Arts. Hostel quality is good.

Hostel Relax, Láncszem u.10, Budapest; T:0036/203216883, *info@ hostelrelax.hu/*; $10bed, Kitchen:Y, B'fast:N, Pvt.room:Y, Locker:N, Recep:ltd; Note: bag hold, laundry, parking, tours, near airport, not central

Corvin Point Hostel 1082 Nap utca 4, 1st Fl, VIII Dist, Budapest; *info@ corvinpoint.com/*, T:+36/705440224; $11bed, Kitchen:Y, B'fast:N, Pvt.room:Y, Locker:Y, Recep:24/7; Note: arpt trans, prkng, bikes, tours, bag hold, laundry, tea/cof

Homemade Hostel, Budapest, Teréz krt 22; *info@ homemadehostel.com/*, T:0613022103; $16bed, Kitchen:Y, B'fast:N, Pvt.room:Y, Locker:Y, Recep:24/7; Note: arpt trans, lift, laundry, tea/cof, non-party, bag hold, tours, nr metro, no bunks, cash

Budapest Centrum Hostel, Nádor St 26, Budapest; T:+36/302969069, *budapestcentrumhostel.com/*; $20bed, Kitchen:Y, B'fast:Y, Pvt.room:Y, Locker:Y, Recep:ltd; Note: hot tub, arpt trans, laundry, bag hold, tea/cof, cash, café, bikes, tours

Homeplus Hostel, Budapest, Balassi Bálint St 27; T:0619502494, *info@ homeplushostel.hu/*; $10bed, Kitchen:Y, B'fast:N, Pvt.room:Y, Locker:Y, Recep:24/7; Note: arpt trans, café, lift, parking, tours, cash, bag hold, tea/cof, laundry

Tigar Tim's Place, Budapest, Teréz körút 58, *tigertimsplace.com/*, T:06202928320, *tigertimsplace@hotmail.co.uk*; $19bed, Kitchen:Y, B'fast:N, Pvt. room:Y, Locker:Y, Recep:24/7; Note: tours, bag hold, laundry, tea/coffee, lift

Astoria City Hostel, 7th Dist. Rakoczi ut 4, 3rd Fl, Doorbell 27, Budapest; T:+36/12661327, *staff@ astoriacityhostel.com/*; $16bed, Kitchen:Y, B'fast:Y, Pvt. room:Y, Locker:Y, Recep:24/7; Note: tours, bag hold, laundry, cash, cntr, bikes, lift

Black Sheep Hostel, Budapest, Akácfa St 7; *blacksheepbudapest.com/*, T:06303718544, *info@blacksheephostel.hu*; $16bed, Kitchen:Y, B'fast:N, Pvt. room:Y, Locker:Y, Recep:24/7; Note: cash, bar, tours, bag hold, laundry, cntr, pub crawls

Hostel Good Mo , Budapest, Bajcsy-Zsilinszky Way 49; *hostelgoodmo.com/*; T:06304869897; $16bed, Kitchen:Y, B'fast:N, Pvt.room:N, Locker:Y, Recep:ltd; Note: arpt trans, café, bar, tours, laundry, bag hold, lift, tea/cof

Carpe Noctem (original), 1067 Budapest, Szobi St. 5; T:06203658749

Carpe Noctem Vitae, Erzsebet korut 50, Budapest; T:+36/706700382, *info@ carpenoctemvitae.com/*; $14bed, Kitchen:Y, B'fast:N, Pvt. room:N, Locker:Y, Recep:24/7; Note: arpt trans, lift, tours, laundry, bag hold, parties, tea/cof, cash, partyy

LowCostel Hostel, Budapest, Hungária körút 190; T:06304571490, *info@ lowcostelhostels.com/*; $10bed, Kitchen:Y, B'fast:$, Pvt. room:N, Locker:Y Recep:ltd; Note: café, bikes, tour desk, prkng, laundry, forex, not central, hard to find

MetroMM Budapest, 1072 Budapest, Nagy Diófa St 19; T:0617899325, *info@ metrommbudapest.hu/*; $16bed, Kitchen:Y, B'fast:N, Pvt.room:Y, Locker:Y, Recep:24/7; Note: tour desk, luggage room, laundry

11th Hour Cinema Hostel, 1053 Budapest, Magyar St. 11; T:0612662153, *11thhourcinemahostel.com/*; $12bed, Kitchen:Y, B'fast:N, Pvt.room:Y, Locker:Y, Recep:24/7; Note: 2N min, bar/lounge, laundry, bag hold, central, tea/coffee

Bazar Hostel, 1074 Budapest, Dohány St 22; T:06209207205, *info@ bazarhostel.com/*; $11bed, Kitchen:Y, B'fast:N, Pvt.room:Y, Locker:Y, Recep:24/7; Note: bar, tour desk, luggage ok, laundry, Jewish area of Pest

The Groove Hostel, 1137 Budapest, Szent István körút 16; T:0617868038, *stay@ groovehostel.hu/*; $11bed, Kitchen:Y, B'fast:N, Pvt. room:Y, Locker:Y, Recep:24/7; Note: parking, luggage room, TV, balcony, central

Aventura Boutique Hostel, Visegrádi utca 12, Dist. 13, Budapest; T:0612390782, *info@ aventurahostel.com/;* $16bed, Kitchen:Y, B'fast:$, Pvt.room:Y, Locker:Y, Recep:24-7; Note: no c.c., tours, laundry, bag hold, safety dep

Bridge Hostel Budapest, 1053 Budapest, Kossuth Lajos St 14; *bridgehostel. eu/,* T:+36/703892141; $20bed, Kitchen:Y, B'fast:$, Pvt.room:Y, Locker:Y, Recep:24/7; Note: cash only, free tour, lift, TV, central, non-party

2 Hostels) PECS is located close to the border with Croatia, and has always been a religious center as well as a trade and crafts center, and more recently a center of coal mining. The city was founded by the Romans in the 2nd century and, after long being referred to as *Quinque Basilicae* ("Five Churches"), the episcopate was founded in 1009.

The Ottomans conquered Pecs in 1526; the name Pecs is Turkish for "five." For over a hundred years Pecs was an Ottoman city in classic style — mosques, baths and minarets, etc. — remnants of which still survive today and are prime tourist destinations. The mosque is now a Roman Catholic church. Other sights include the world heritage 4th C. Christian necropolis of Sopianae. The mines have closed.

Nap Hostel Pecs, Pécs, Király utca 23-25; T:+36/72950684, *info@ naphostel. com/;* $13bed, Kitchen:Y, B'fast:N, Pvt. room:Y, Locker:N, Recep:24/7; Note: café/bar, travel desk, bag hold, laundry, coffee & tea, central

Ecohun, Petofi Sándor út 71, Kiskassa, near Pécs; *ecohun.org/,* T:+36/72377063, *durant.eva@gmail.com;* $13bed, Kitchen:Y, B'fast:Y, Pvt. room:Y, Locker:N, Recep:24/7; Note: parking, bag hold, laundry, organic farm, no bunks

REVFULOP is a town on the northern shore of Lake Balaton and the starting point for an annual swimming race across the lake. Tourism and viticulture are the big industries. The historical downtown and port are major attractions.

Hullam Hostel, Hungary, Révfülöp-Balaton, Füredi út 6; T:0687463089, *info@ balatonhostel.hu/;* $16bed, Kitchen:Y, B'fast:N, Pvt.room:Y, Locker:N, Recep:24/7; Note: bar, parking, bag hold, laundry, tour desk, goulash!

21) Moldova

The history of Moldova, also previously known as Moldavia and/or Bessarabia, is intricately intertwined with that of Romania, as there's nothing but a river separating them. They speak the same language, but Moldova used to be a part of the USSR. In fact throughout history the borders between them were fluid and shifting. As with Romania it enters history in the early centuries of the Common Era. It suffered repeated invasions and in 1538 became tributary to the Ottomans. It was ceded to the Russians in the 19th century, and the process of Russification began. Moldova alternately protested and requested help from Romania, but to no avail, and it became a Soviet Republic.

The USSR even tried to wedge the two apart, insisting that the Moldovan language be written in Cyrillic instead of the Roman alphabet. Moldova indeed was one of the first countries to break with the USSR, in spite of the fact that Big Bro Romania wasn't really any better. On the other border exists the proto-state of Transnistria consisting of majority Ukrainians and Russians with no sympathy at all toward the government of the land they continue to occupy. The Moldovans failed to thrive immediately, too, instead re-electing the same Communists in 2001 that once ruled with an iron hand.

Still they inch their way toward a new future with a market economy. The wines are reportedly good. Moldovan/Romanian and Russian are the languages, currency is the *leu* (MDL) and the calling code is +373.

2 Hostels) CHISINAU is the principal city of Moldova and is centrally located. Originally a monastery village, most of its growth has come in the last two centuries. Thus there is little ancient architecture to enjoy viewing, but still the atmosphere is pleasant enough. There are easy road connections to Romania and Ukraine.

Retro Moldova Hostel, St. Cosbuc 3, Ap. 24, Chisinau; T:+37322227091, *retromoldovahostel.webs.com/*; $15bed, Kitchen:N, B'fast:Y, Pvt.room:N, Locker:Y, Recep:24/7; Note: arpt trans, parking, tours, laundry, bag hold, new, hard find

Central Youth Hostel, Pruncul 6, Apt. 1, Chisinau; *luxlana.net/*, T:(0)69165529, *c_sveta@mail.ru*; $14bed, Kitchen:N, B'fast:N, Pvt.room:N, Locker:N, Recep:24/7; Note: arpt trans, laundry, bag hold, tours, share flat, hard find, central

22) Romania

What do you get when you take a province 2000 years ago extending from the Black Sea and beyond the Carpathians; populate them with ancient East European tribes; colonize with ancient Romans for a couple hundred years; import other tribes to work the gold and silver mines; impose Latin as the *lingua franca*; beat lightly to mix; allow to settle; penetrate with Goths, Huns, Avars, Bulgars, Pechenegs, and others; then include as side-dishes in successive Ottoman, Habsburg, and Austria-Hungarian Empires; fight a World War; allow a couple decades of independence; fight another war; become Communist in a paranoid egomaniacal police state; before finally emerging toward the end of the second millennium as a modern European country (and garnish to taste)?

It might look a lot like Romania, successor to a remote Roman colony almost two thousand years ago, and still speaking a form of the language, far removed from its cultural kin far to the west. The persistence of a vast East European peasantry who considered themselves citizens of Rome, and spoke a variety of Latin, with little or no contact with the great highly civilized Latin countries of the West is one of the great anomalies of history. It is also a great lesson to anthropolinguists, especially considering that their language is probably closer to the original Latin than is French, and was colonized only a relatively brief two hundred years. The Romanian language is not even attested before the 1500's and no literature was written in it before the 1800's.

Feudalism lasted until the 1700's. Romania first became a country in 1862 with the union of Wallachia and Moldavia. History is not always written by the powerful. Even the tourist sites in Romania tend to be focused on nature — rural-based and folk-oriented. Few of the names would you recognize, but your knowledge of Europe would be incomplete without a visit to Romania. Romanian is the language; *leu* is currency; calling code is +40.

2 Hostels) BRASOV is a city in the Transylvania region of Romania west of the Carpathians. Saxons were invited in during the 12th century to settle Transylvania and Teutonic knights to protect that region of then-Hungary. They built the "crown city" of Brasov, and the descendants of many of those settlers stayed on. Then the 19th century saw an influx of Hungarians. Romanians have had to struggle hard for equal rights throughout their history in Brasov. Most Germans were deported at the end of WWII and Romania became Communist. Now it is an all-season tourist center with winter sports and "Dracula's Castle." The old town contains many historic buildings, including the town hall, the watchtower (also called Trumpeter's Tower), the Orthodox St. Nicholas' Church, the Gothic Protestant Church and St. Bartholomew's Church, which dates from the 13th century, the oldest building in Braşov.

Jugendstube Hostel, 13 Michael Weiss St Apt 5, Brasov; T:+40/742136660, *office@ jugendstube.ro/*; $14bed, Kitchen:Y, B'fast:Y, Pvt.room:Y, Locker:Y, Recep:24/7; Note: arpt trans, bag hold, laundry, tours, coffee/tea, eggs, central

Rolling Stone Hostel, Strada Piatra Mare 2A, Braşov; T:0268513965, *office@ rollingstone.ro/*; $12bed, Kitchen:Y, B'fast:Y, Pvt.room:Y, Locker:Y, Recep:24/7; Note: arpt trans, bar, bikes, bag hold, laundry, tours, forex, parking

6 Hostels) BUCHAREST is the capital and largest city of Romania, and a fairly modern one at that, documented from only around 1500. It became capital of Walachia in 1659, under Ottoman suzerainty, after which it grew rapidly. In 1862 it became capital of Romania, and even got some press as the "Little Paris (*Micul Paris*)" around that time, but I wouldn't go that far. It takes more than an *Arcul de Triumf* to call yourself Paris.

Nevertheless the city is pleasant enough. Landmarks include the House of the People (Casa Poporului), Creţulescu Church, evolution Square (formerly Palace Square), the Romanian Athenaeum, the former royal palace (now the National Art Museum), Curtea Veche (Old Court) church, the church of the former Antim Monastery (1715) and Stavropoleos church (1724). There are the Museum of the History of the City of Bucharest, the Art Museum of Romania, and the Village Museum, made up of peasant houses brought from various parts of the country.

Hostel Tina, Odobesti 2b, Bloc N3B, 9 Fl, Ap. 38, Dist 3 i/com 38C; *hosteltina.com,* T:0314015964, *cparpala@yahoo.com*; $16bed, Kitchen:N, B'fast:Y, Pvt.room:Y, Locker:Y, Recep:advise ETA; Note: lift, laundry, printer, tea/coffee

Doors Hostel, Olimpului St #13, Bucharest; T:+40/213362127, *office@ doorshostel.com/*; $12bed, Kitchen:Y, B'fast:Y, Pvt.room:Y, Locker:Y, Recep:24/7; Note: bar, parking, tours, laundry, bag hold, hard find, tea/coffee

Hostel Byzanthin, Dr. Caracas Constantin, #22 St, Bucharest; *hostel-byzanthin.ro/,* T:+40/786606097, *byzanthin@yahoo.com*; $11bed, Kitchen:N, B'fast:Y, Pvt. room:Y, Locker:N, Recep:ltd; Note: homestay, central, laundry, parking

HI Vila Gabriela YH, Str.Margaritarului 18, Vila A 104, Otopeni, Judet Ilfov; *vilagabriela.com/,* T:0213522053, *pensiuneagabriela@yahoo.com*; $21bed, Kitchen:Y, B'fast:Y, Pvt.room:Y, Locker:N, Recep:24/7; Note: bag hold, laundry, tours, nr arpt.

Funky Chicken Hostel, St. Gen. Berthelot 63, Bucuresti; T:0213121425, *funkychickenhostel.com/,* $11bed, *funkychickenhostel@hotmail.com*; Kitchen:Y, B'fast:N, Pvt.room:Y, Locker:N, Recep:24/7; Note: wh/chair ok, central, laundry

Wonderland Hostel, Strada Coltei 48, Bucuresti, T:+40/727076020, *wonderlandhostel.blogspot.com/,* $13bed, *hostelwonderland@yahoo.com*; Kitchen:N, B'fast:N, Pvt.room:Y, Locker:N, Recep:>4a; Note: bar/club, bag hold, laundry, cntr

2 Hostels) CLUJ NAPOCA is Romania's second city and the unofficial capital of Transylvania. It was first documented in 1213 in Latin and shortly after in various other languages. The early village was Hungarian and Saxons were invited to settle. With them came crafts, guilds and increased prosperity. When Ottoman Turks occupied Hungary, Cluj (Klausenberg) assumed a prominent place in independent Transylvania and Europe, too. Not until the end of WWI was Transylvania united with Romania and the process of Romanization begun. Until then, Romanians had been third-class citizens, after Hungarians and Saxons. Hungarians in fact were the majority ethnicity

here until fifty years ago. The Germans occupied Cluj in WWII and 16,000 Jews were sent to Auschwitz. After the war came years of Communism until the revolution of 1989.

Today the economy is active after a shaky capitalist start. It may not be as romantic as some of the Carpathian towns, but it is poised for greatness. Right now that means leadership in the high-tech field. And then there's tourism, with abundant sights and sounds for a traveler's enjoyment, such as: the house in which Matthias I Corvinus (king of Hungary, 1458–90) was born; the Roman Catholic cathedral of St. Michael; the Bánffy Palace, now a fine arts museum; botanical gardens; a 14th C. Gothic church; an Orthodox cathedral; an ethnographic museum; castles in the countryside; music and nightlife; festivals, too.

Hostel Transylvania, Luliu Maniu 26, 1st Fl, Cluj-Napoca; *hostelcluj.com/*, T:+40/264443266, *transylvaniahostel@yahoo.com*; $15bed, Kitchen:Y, B'fast:N, Pvt. room:Y, Locker:Y, Recep:24/7; Note: billiards, laundry, bag hold, tours, central

Retro Hostel, Potaissa St.11-13, Cluj-Napoca; T:+40/264450452, *retro@ retro.ro/*; $14bed, Kitchen:Y, B'fast:$, Pvt.room:Y, Locker:Y, Recep:24/7; Note: bar, café, bikes, bag hold, laundry, tour desk, tea/coffee, minimart

CONSTANTA, located on the Black Sea, is one of Romania's largest cities and the oldest, being documented from 600BC. At that time it was a Greek city, before passing to the Romans. After that it belonged to the Bulgarians, Wallachians, and Ottomans. Today it is a major port and center of tourism, beaches and archeology the main draw.

Eol777, Str. Aviator Vasile Craiu nr 3, Jud Constanta; *hosteleol777.ro/*, T:0727555556, *razvan_jianu@yahoo.com*; $13bed, Kitchen:Y, B'fast:N, Pvt. room:Y, Locker:N, Recep:ltd; Note: bag hold, laundry, parking, free airport pickup!

4 Hostels) SIBIU is a Transylvanian fortified city and historically the most important of the seven Saxon cities of the region. Ottomans and Austro-Hungarians came and went, and after WWI the region became part of Romania. Many Germans left after WWII and the advent of Communism,

but not all. One became mayor. The historical center is the main attraction for tourism. There are three squares and remains of the city walls, the Brukenthal Museum, a massive Lutheran cathedral, an Orthodox cathedral, and an 18th-century Roman Catholic Church.

Felinarul Hostel, Strada Felinarului, Sibiu, Romania; T:0269235260, *info@ felinarulhostelsibiu.ro*; $17bed, Kitchen:Y, B'fast:Y, Pvt.room:N, Locker:Y, Recep:ltd; Note: café-bar, parking, bag hold, laundry, tours, bikes, central

Sibiu Travelers/Villa Teilor, St. Teilor 4, Sibiu; *sibiutravelershostel.com,* T:0765816544, *info@villateilor.com*; $17bed, Kitchen:Y, B'fast:Y, Pvt.room:N, Locker:Y, Recep:24/7; Note: bag hold, laundry, parking, forex, near train/bus

Old Town Hostel, Piața Mică 26, Sibiu; T:0269216445, *contact@ hostelsibiu. ro/*; $16bed, Kitchen:Y, B'fast:N, Pvt.room:Y, Locker:N, Recep:24/7; Note: bikes, café/club, central, bag hold, laundry, tours, tea/cof, "nice old bldg"

PanGeea Hostel, Avram Iancu, nr. 4, Sibiu; *sibiuhostel.ro/en/*, T:0747294806, *Pangeeahostel@gmail.com*; $16bed, Kitchen:Y, B'fast:$, Pvt. room:Y, Locker:Y, Recep:24/7; Note: bar/café, hot tub, laundry, bag hold, mart, parking, tea/cof

2 Hostels) SIGHISOARA is another Saxon town in Transylvania and is an exemplary medieval town. The town surrounds a hill. On top stands a citadel with a ring of walls, nine standing towers, and a number of medieval churches. It was a center of arts, crafts and associated trades. It was also the home of Vlad Dracul, Vlad the Impaler's father.

HI Burg YH, Strada Bastionului 4-6, Sighisoara; *burghostel.ro,* T:0265778489, *burghostel@ibz.ro*; $13bed, Kitchen:N, B'fast:$, Pvt. room:Y, Locker:N, Recep:24/7; Note: resto/bar, tour desk, bag hold, TV, central

Gia Hostel, Str. Libertatii 41, jud Mures; *hotelgia.ro/*, T:0265772486, *office@ cazareinsighisoara.ro*; $16bed, Kitchen:Y, B'fast:N, Pvt.room:Y, Locker:N, Recep:24/7; Note: laundry, bag hold, tours, parking, nr train, old hotel=hostel

2 Hostels) SUCEAVA is located in the far north of the country, near the border with Ukraine. It is the former capital of Moldavia, and from 1775 until 1918 it was part of the Austrian Habsburg Empire, after which it was incorporated into Romania. It was heavily industrialized during the Communist Era,

but since then has developed some tourism. There are numerous historical churches, museums, and citadel, including the 14th C. Mirăuți Church, the 16th C. Church of St. George, and the Church of St. Demetrius.

Irene's Hostel, Strada Armenească 4, Suceava; *ireneshostel.ro/*, T:0744292588, *ireneshostel@gmail.com;* $15bed, Kitchen:Y, B'fast:N, Pvt.room:Y, Locker:N, Recep:24/7; Note: laundry, tours, prkng, bag hold, @bus terminal, central

Lary Hostel, Str. Vlaicu Aurel, 195, Suceava; *hostelsuceava.ro/*, T:0747086329, *laryhostel@yahoo.com,* $15bed, Kitchen:N, B'fast:$, Pvt.room:Y, Locker:Y, Recep:24/7; Note: bar/club, parking, laundry, tours, not central

2 Hostels) TIMISOARA is Romania's third largest city, and is located in the western region of Banat, only a stone's throw from Serbia. It is documented from the 13th century as a part of Hungary. In 1552 it was conquered by the Ottoman Turks and became capital of a new province created by them. That was the status until 1716 when it came under Austrian rule. As a part of Europe it became industrialized and modernized, opening the region's first beer factory in 1717, and becoming the first city in Europe with electric lights, in fact. After WWI it became part of Romania, Communist until the 1989 revolution. Landmarks include the Roman Catholic cathedral, the Serbian cathedral, and the regional museum, housed in a restored 14th C. palace.

Hostel Costel, Str. Petru Sfetca Nr.1 (ex-Vidra), Timisoara; T:0726240223, *office@ hostel-costel.ro/*, $12bed, Kitchen:Y, B'fast:N, Pvt.room:Y, Locker:Y, Recep:24/7; Note: bike rent, parking, bag hold, laundry, TV, pets ok

Freeborn Hostel, Str Patriarh Miron Cristea 3, Timisoara; *freebornhostel. com/*, T:0743438534, *freebornhostel@gmail.com;* $12bed, Kitchen:Y, B'fast:N, Pvt. room:Y, Locker:Y, Recep:24/7; Note: wh/chair ok, parking, tours, forex, bag hold, laundry

ABOUT THE AUTHOR

American ex-pat Hardie Karges took his first extended international trip at the age of twenty-one in 1975 and traveled to his first ten countries within two years, all for less than two thousand dollars. Thus began a way of life that has taken him to some 150 countries (and counting), living and working in a dozen of them, learning several languages and trading in folk art and cottage industry products. He has also published poetry and created videos, before finally deciding to write about what he knows best—travel. His first book, "Hypertravel: 100 Countries in 2 Years," was published in 2012. The full set of "Backpackers & Flashpackers" is projected to include eight to ten volumes and be completed in 2014.

If you would like more information, or to make an inquiry or just leave a comment, please visit our blog at *backpackers-flashpackers.net/* or our *BackpackersFlashpackers* page on FaceBook.

Printed in Great Britain
by Amazon

80885389R00119